# Multifaith Views in Spiritual Care

# Multifaith Views in Spiritual Care

**Daniel S. Schipani, editor**

Published by Pandora Press
Kitchener, Ontario

In collaboration with the SIPCC
Society for Intercultural Pastoral Care and Counseling
Gesellschaft für interkulturelle Seelsorge und Beratung
Düsseldorf, Germany

## Multifaith Views in Spiritual Care

Copyright © 2013 Daniel S. Schipani
Published by Pandora Press
www.pandorapress.com

All rights reserved.

Book and cover design by Rachel A. Denlinger.

Cover photograph, "Double rainbow reflected on Highway 550, New Mexico," © Mary Hockenbery, photographer (used by permision of Collection:Flickr).

ISBN-13: 978-1926599304

Library and Archives Canada Cataloguing in Publication

   Multifaith views in spiritual care /
Daniel S. Schipani, editor.

"In collaboration with the SIPCC."

ISBN 978-1-926599-30-4

   1. Spiritual direction.  2. Counseling—Religious aspects.
3. Religious life.  I. Schipani, Daniel S., II. Society for Intercultural Pastoral Care and Counseling

BL624.M85 2013           204'.4           C2013-900516-1

# Contents

**Gratitudes** vii

**Contributors** ix

1 | **A rainbow of blessing** 1
Spiritual care in multifaith settings
Daniel S. Schipani

2 | **Journey toward Creator and the realm of peace** 15
Two voices on Aboriginal spiritual caregiving
Melody A. McKellar and Roger Armitte

3 | **The world is one family** 31
Principles of Hindu spiritual care
Dinesh C. Sharma

4 | **Three *yanas* for wise caring** 45
A Buddhist perspective on spiritual care
Danny Fisher

5 | **Vulnerability as a path to the Divine** 65
Jewish spiritual care
Mychal B. Springer

6 | **Do justice, love kindness, walk humbly** 85
A Christian perspective on spiritual care
Kathleen J. Greider

7 | **The Crescent of compassionate engagement**     109
Theory and practice of Islamic spiritual care
*Nazila Isgandarova*

8 | ***Worldviewing* competence for narrative interreligious dialogue**     131
A Humanist contribution to spiritual care
*Hans Alma and Christa Anbeek*

9 | **The heart of the matter**     149
Engaging the *spirit* in spiritual care
*Daniel S. Schipani*

**Epilogue**
Competencies for wise interfaith spiritual care     167

# Gratitudes

Many people contributed creative energy, time, and other resources to make this book possible. I am especially grateful to the nine colleagues who chose to join me in this project—Hans Alma, Christa Anbeek, Roger Armitte, Danny Fisher, Kathleen J. Greider, Nazila Isgandarova, Melody A. McKellar, Dinesh C. Sharma, and Mychal B. Springer. They contributed a rainbow of complementary views in spiritual care. In the course of our numerous exchanges, they became not only my partners but also my teachers. I am also thankful for the inspiration and wisdom I have received the last few years from Leah Dawn Bueckert and Gayle Gerber Koontz regarding the intersecting arenas of spiritual care and theology; their gifts were particularly meaningful for this project.

Many thanks go to those who collaborated as research assistants—Alicia Buhler, Jamie Lynn Ross, and Karla Minter. A number of North American, Latin American, and European colleagues, too many to name, have continued to provide timely encouragement and support, and to make available necessary accountability. Special recognition is due to the Society for Intercultural Pastoral Care and Counseling whose president, Helmut Weiss, enthusiastically endorsed the research and publication project.

During the final stages of the writing and editing process, Rosalie Grove and David Schipani provided opportune help as critical readers, and Heidi King served efficiently and generously as copy editor. Rachel Denlinger designed the cover and the book layout, preparing it for publication. Christian Snyder, Pandora Press publisher, made sure that the book would be ready in a timely manner.

Last but not least, I acknowledge the support and encouragement of my colleagues and the staff at the Anabaptist Mennonite Biblical

Seminary and, especially, Dean Rebecca Slough and President Sara Wenger Shenk. The Association of Theological Schools in the United States and Canada endorsed the project and gave us a grant and a forum for collaborative reflection under its project, "Christian Hospitality Practices in a Multifaith Society."

Daniel S. Schipani

# Contributors

**Hans A. Alma** was born in Nijmegen, the Netherlands, and grew up in Apeldoorn, a large village in the eastern part of the Netherlands. She studied andragogy at Leiden University and psychology at the Radboud University Nijmegen. She received her PhD from VU University Amsterdam with a study on the way people appropriate the Christian tradition through processes of identification (*Identiteit door verbondenheid: Een godsdienstpsychologisch onderzoek naar identificatie en christelijk geloof*). She was Assistant Professor of Psychology of Religion at VU University Amsterdam (1997–2000), Utrecht University (1997–2000), and Leiden University (2000–2006), and was appointed Professor of Psychology and Meaning of Life at the University of Humanistic Studies (Utrecht) in 2003 where she became vice-chancellor in 2007.

Professor Alma's research and teaching are in the fields of religious development, imagination and the search for meaning, aesthetic and religious experiences, and psychological conditions for interreligious dialogue. Some of her publications in English are: "Self-Development as a Spiritual Process: The Role of Empathy and Imagination in Finding Spiritual Orientation," *Pastoral Psychology* (2008); "Religious and Aesthetic Experiences: A Psychological Approach," in *At the Crossroads of Art and Religion: Imagination, Commitment, Transcendence* (2008), edited by T. H. Zock; "Imagination and Transcendence: The Transcendental Dimension in Art from a Psychological Point of View," in *Visual Arts and Religion* (2009), edited by H. Alma, M. Barnard & V. Kuester.

**Christa Anbeek** was born in Barneveld, a small village in the Netherlands' central region. She studied theology at VU University Amsterdam where she earned a PhD in Buddhist-Christian studies. She also was educated and ordained as a minister of the Remonstrant Church in the Netherlands. Dr. Anbeek was Lecturer in Religious Studies at the Faculty of Theology, Tilburg University (1998–2010), specializing in Buddhism and Christianity while also engaged in clinical practice as a spiritual counselor at Meerkanten Mental Hospital (now called GGZ Centraal). Currently she is Associate Professor of Existential Philosophy at the University of Humanistic Studies at Utrecht.

The main focus of Dr. Anbeek's research is on the relation between religion, worldviews, and meaning of life, especially with regard to the end of life. Her publications include: *Denken over de dood: De boeddhist Nishitani en de christen W. Pannenberg vergeleke* (Thinking about death: The Buddhist Nishitani and the Christian Pannenberg compared) (1994); *Zin in zen: De aantrekkingskracht van het zenboeddhisme in Nederland en België* (Meaning through Zen Buddhism in the Netherlands and Belgium) (2003); and *Overlevingskunst: Hoe televen met de dood van eendierbare* (The art of surviving: How to live with the death of a beloved one) (2010). Some of her publications in English are: "Self-Development as a Spiritual Process: The Role of Empathy and Imagination in Finding Spiritual Orientation," *Pastoral Psychology* (2008); "Religious and Aesthetic Experiences: A Psychological Approach," in *At the Crossroads of Art and Religion: Imagination, Commitment, Transcendence* (2008), edited by T. H. Zock; "The Beauty of Ten Thousand Blooming Flowers," *Journal of the European Society of Women in Theological Research* (2009); and "Women and the Art of Living: Three Women Writers on Death and Finitude," in *Essays in the Philosophy of Humanism* (2010).

**Roger Armitte** was born in Sainte Rose du Lac, Manitoba, Canada, and raised near Riding Mountain National Park. His grandparents were from the nearby Ebb-and-Flow Ojibway (or Chippewa) Reserve, and his grandmother was a Medewiwin Healer who began teaching him traditional customs when he was around four years old.

Since Roger was recognized as Elder in 1990, he has served in a variety of roles throughout and beyond Manitoba. Until recently, he was Elder-in-Residence at the Aboriginal Students Centre, University of Manitoba, where he conducted pipe ceremonies and counseled both native and non-native students and staff. Elder Armitte is a certified counselor with expertise in the fields of suicide prevention, life skills, domestic violence, and substance abuse. He has lectured in several departments at the University of Manitoba, especially on topics of holistic medicine in healing. He has made numerous appearances in the media and in documentaries on spiritual life and human relationship with the environment. He currently serves as a Spiritual Health Specialist in the

Spiritual Health Services department of the Health Sciences Centre in Winnipeg, Manitoba.

**Danny Fisher** is a professor and Coordinator of the Buddhist Chaplaincy Program at University of the West (UWest) in Rosemead, California. Prior to his appointment at UWest, he served on the adjunct faculty for Antioch Education Abroad's Buddhist Studies in India program. Born and raised in Crawfordsville, Indiana, he earned a BD in religion from Denison University (Granville, OH), an MDiv from Naropa University (Boulder, CO), and a PhD in Buddhist studies at UWest. Rev. Fisher was ordained as a lay Buddhist minister by the Buddhist Sangha Council of Southern California in 2008. In addition, he is certified as a mindfulness meditation instructor by Naropa University in association with Shambhala International. He also serves on the advisory council for the Upaya Buddhist Chaplaincy Program, and in 2009 became the first-ever Buddhist member of the National Association of College and University Chaplains.

Rev. Fisher is a blogger for *Shambhala Sun, Buddhadharma: The Practitioner's Quarterly*, elephantjournal.com, and Patheos. He has also written for *Tricycle: The Buddhist Review, Inquiring Mind, Religion Dispatches, The Journal of Buddhist Ethics, The Journal of Global Buddhism, The Journal of Religion & Film, Eastern Horizon, New York Spirit*, Alternet's *Wiretap Magazine*, and other publications. In addition, he has commented on Buddhism in America and other religious issues for CNN, the Religion News Service, Buddhist Geeks, E! Entertainment Television, and *The Washington Post's On Faith*.

**Kathleen J. Greider** is the Edna and Lowell Craig Professor of Practical Theology, Spiritual Care and Counseling at Claremont School of Theology, in the Claremont (CA) Lincoln University consortium. She also serves as pastoral psychotherapist and clinical supervisor at The Clinebell Institute for Pastoral Counseling and Psychotherapy. Her research and teaching interests include spiritual care, practical and pastoral theology, interculturality, the interplay of social and personal change, and depth psychology. She has authored numerous articles and books, including *Reckoning with Aggression: Theology, Violence, and Vitality* (1997) and *Much Madness is Divinest Sense: Spiritual Wisdom in Memoirs of Soul Suffering* (2007); and co-edited *Healing Wisdom: Depth Psychology and the Pastoral Ministry* (2010). Ordained by the United Methodist Church and a Fellow in the American Association of Pastoral Counselors, she has experience in clinical pastoral work in general hospital and in-patient psychiatric settings, pastoral counseling and psychotherapy, spiritual direction, and parish ministry.

Professor Greider holds an MDiv from Harvard Divinity School (Cambridge, MA) and a PhD from Union Theological Seminary in New York City. She has lectured in France, Germany, Ghana, Great Britain, Israel, South Africa, South Korea, and Poland. She grew up on a farm in Pennsylvania, the daughter of tenant farmers.

**Nazila Isgandarova** was born and raised in Azerbaijan, a country located in the Caucasus region of Eurasia. She views her roles as caregiver, administrator, and instructor as opportunities to make a positive contribution to the research and practice of Islamic spirituality in society and to Muslim identity in particular. As a Muslim woman chaplain, she provides religious and spiritual care not only to Muslims but also to patients from different ethnic, spiritual, and religious backgrounds.

Dr. Isgandarova is an internationally published researcher focusing on Islamic spiritual and religious care in health care settings, pastoral counseling in multifaith contexts, and Muslim identity in the West. She has led many research projects on religious and spiritual issues in a clinical setting and presented lectures and workshops in national and international conferences. Some of that work has been published and is used by spiritual caregivers and pastoral counselors in Canada. Dr. Isgandarova currently works as a Spiritual and Religious Care Coordinator with the Ontario Multifaith Centre and the Cummer Lodge Long Term Care Home. She also serves as an adjunct faculty member of Emmanuel College of Victoria University in the University of Toronto, Ontario. She holds a DMin in pastoral counseling, marriage and family studies from Wilfrid Laurier University, Waterloo, Ontario.

**Melody A. McKellar's** maternal Aboriginal roots are Mohawk from the province of Quebec, Canada, with a smidgeon of Cree mixed in on her paternal side. The European cultural side of the family is French. This makes her a Métis woman, one of three distinct Aboriginal groups in Canada. Her birth community is The Pas in northern Manitoba. Elder McKellar was adopted and raised in southern Manitoba by a non-Aboriginal family in the small village of Clearwater. Her birth family was Roman Catholic, having long ago given up the practice of traditional spiritual ceremonies due to colonization by the dominant culture. Her adoptive family are members of the United Church of Canada, the (Protestant) spiritual tradition in which she was raised. Since her early teens, Elder McKellar was called to a spiritual life. She studied at an Aboriginal theological college of The United Church of Canada—Dr. Jessie Saulteaux Resource Centre (Toronto, ON)—which honors both the Christian and the traditional Aboriginal beliefs and practices.

Elder McKellar has practiced her traditional spiritual way for thirty years and is also a minister with The United Church of Canada. Upon graduation from seminary, she was program staff at The Dr. Jessie Saulteaux Resource Centre and then principal. Elder McKellar was a member of the teaching faculty and pipe carrier for the college, offering cultural and cross-cultural teachings and ceremonies. She is completing a Sacred Theology Master at The University of Winnipeg in Manitoba and is currently a member of the Spiritual Care Department of Selkirk (MB) Mental Health Centre, where she serves as an Aboriginal Elder.

**Daniel S. Schipani** was born and raised in Pehuajó, a city in the Province of Buenos Aires, Argentina. He holds a PsyD from Universidad Católica Argentina (Buenos Aires) and a PhD in practical theology from Princeton Theological Seminary. He is currently Professor of Pastoral Care and Counseling at the Anabaptist Mennonite Biblical Seminary in Elkhart, Indiana. Before accepting that position, he was Professor of Pastoral Counseling at the Evangelical Seminary of Puerto Rico (San Juan, PR). An ordained minister in Mennonite Church USA, he also serves as a psychotherapist and pastoral counselor (volunteer) at a local community health center for economically vulnerable care receivers, especially immigrants from Latin America. His academic work includes clinical supervision of students in chaplaincy and pastoral and spiritual counseling.

Professor Schipani's research and teaching interests include formation and transformation processes and intercultural and interfaith pastoral care and counseling. He is the author or editor of over twenty-five books on pastoral counseling, education, and practical and pastoral theology. His texts include *The Way of Wisdom in Pastoral Counseling* (2003); with Leah Dawn Bueckert, *Spiritual Caregiving in the Hospital: Windows to Chaplaincy Ministry* (2006, 2011), and *Interfaith Spiritual Care: Understandings and Practices* (2009); and *Nuevos caminos en psicología pastoral* (2011). He is also a visiting professor in various academic institutions and lectures widely in North America, Latin America, and Europe. He is a member of several professional and academic organizations, including the Society for Intercultural Pastoral Care & Counseling, and the International Academy of Practical Theology.

**Dinesh C. Sharma** was born in the town of Ajmer (Rajasthan), India, into a very pious family where the day began with worshipping Mother Goddess and Lord Hanuman. Since childhood, he witnessed his parents' devotion and dedication toward the Almighty Lord. Pandit Sharma completed a BS degree at Doaba College in Jalandhar, India. His law degree was granted by the Law Faculty of Delhi University, and he was called to the bar the same year of graduation. In 1990 he moved to Canada together with his family. He has been an active member in the religious activities sponsored by the Hindu Society of Manitoba and for the last ten years has served as chairperson of the society's Religion Committee.

Pandit Sharma completed courses in the Spiritual Diversity: Hope & Healing program at the University of Winnipeg and in clinical pastoral education at Selkirk Mental Hospital, in addition to Reiki training. In recognition of his services, the Management of Hindu Society of Manitoba appointed him as one of the priests in the Temple. In this capacity, he is able to help people in need of spiritual care and their families on a volunteer basis, and especially those who have lost loved ones. He is also a Marriage Commissioner appointed by the Government of Manitoba, and a member of Manitoba Multifaith Council, serving on its Education Committee. As a spiritual caregiver, Pandit Sharma feels especially indebted to the care and guidance of his spiritual guru under whom he has deepened Vedic knowledge and practice.

**Mychal B. Springer** was born and raised in Brookline, Massachusetts. She received a BA degree from Yale College (New Haven, CT) in 1987. In 1992 she was ordained a Conservative rabbi and received an MA in Judaic studies at The Jewish Theological Seminary (JTS) in New York City. She is currently Director of the Center of Pastoral Education at the JTS, where she holds the Helen Fried Kirshblum Goldstein Chair in Professional and Pastoral Skills. She established the center in 2009. Before that she was Associate Dean of the Rabbinical School at JTS for seven years during which time she directed a Wabash Center grant on integrative teaching and learning in the rabbinical school. As Associate Dean, she served as the rabbinical school's Director of Field Education.

Rabbi Springer is a certified supervisor in the Association for Clinical Pastoral Education and a certified Jewish chaplain in the National Association of Jewish Chaplains. She completed a clinical pastoral education residency and supervisory training at the HealthCare Chaplaincy in Manhattan, and worked in New York City as a chaplain and supervisor at Memorial-Sloan Kettering Cancer Center, Lenox Hill Hospital, and

Beth Israel Medical Center. She went on to become Director of Pastoral Care and Education at Beth Israel. Immediately prior to going to JTS, Rabbi Springer was the Associate Director of the Jewish Institute for Pastoral Care at the HealthCare Chaplaincy. In the summer of 2007, she conducted a training course in pastoral care and pastoral care supervision at B'Ruah, a spiritual care program at Sha'arei Tzedek Medical Center in Jerusalem.

# A rainbow of blessing
## Spiritual care in multifaith settings
*Daniel S. Schipani*

Spiritual caregivers serve today within challenging realities of spiritual and religious plurality, diversity, and particularity. Connected with that complex phenomenon, a significant shift has been taking place in the field, away from a monoculture approach and also from what many consider a "monopoly" of Christian pastoral care; the shift is in part reflected in the change of terminology, from *pastoral* to *spiritual* care. The latter is becoming the preferred term in reference to caregiving settings other than a Christian (or another) faith community.[1] Further, in recent years representatives of different faith traditions such as Jewish, Muslim, Buddhist, and others have made important contributions to theory and practice, and to interfaith spiritual care in particular, while focusing on the specific nature and resources of their traditions.[2] Others have also proposed a more inclusive, "multifaith" approach with equality of professional status and complementary participation in public health care settings among

---

[1] For a persuasive argument against the *pastoral* label in health care institutions, see Patricia (Pam) Morrison Driedger, "Different Lyrics but the Same Tune: Multifaith Spiritual Care in a Canadian Context," in *Interfaith Spiritual Care: Understandings and Practices*, ed. Daniel S. Schipani and Leah Dawn Bueckert (Kitchener: Pandora Press, 2009), 138–41.

[2] See, for example, Rabbi Dayle A. Friedman, ed., *Jewish Pastoral Care: A Practical Handbook from Traditional & Contemporary Sources*, 2nd ed. (Woodstock, VT: Jewish Light Publishing, 2005); Nazila Isgandarova, "Islamic Spiritual Care in a Health Care Setting," in *Spirituality and Health: Multidisciplinary Explorations*, ed. Augustine Meier, Thomas St. James O'Connor, and Peter L VanKatwik (Waterloo, ON: Waterloo University Press, 2005), 85–104; Bilal Ansari, "Seeing with Bifocals: The Evolution of a Muslim Chaplain," *Reflective Practice: Formation and Supervision in Ministry* 29 (2009): 170–77; and Mikel Monnett, "Developing a Buddhist Approach to Pastoral care: A Peacemaker's View," in *Injustice and the Cure of Souls: Taking Oppression Seriously in Pastoral Care*, ed. Sheryl A. Kujawa-Holbrook and Karen B. Montagno (Minneapolis: Fortress Press, 2009), 125–30.

spiritual caregivers from various religious and nonreligious (such as the Humanist) traditions and perspectives.[3] Therefore, the challenge before us offers the opportunity to further critical and constructive reflection and to engage in dialogue and cooperation around shared spiritual care concerns in multifaith settings.

The project leading to this book builds on the fruits of recent and ongoing work in interfaith spiritual care.[4] The project was designed with a twofold purpose: to foster appreciation for the uniqueness and special gifts of seven faith traditions together with a deeper understanding of commonalities and differences among them; and to encourage collaboration among spiritual care practitioners and scholars. This book is intended for chaplains;[5] pastors and other religious caregivers; Clinical Pastoral Education students and supervisors; counselors and psychotherapists, both in training and already in practice; and others interested in the expanding field of spiritual care in our multifaith world.

Most professional spiritual caregivers have been clinically trained according to well-established patterns and practices such as those of the Clinical Pastoral Education programs. In other words, many of us have much in common regarding specialized "professional" or "ministerial" formation, narrowly speaking. At the same time, all of us hold the assumption that the normative frameworks of our work, whether primarily philosophical or theological, play a major role in both formation and practice. So, key questions addressed in this book include: what is the nature of the role of one's tradition or "faith," broadly viewed, in one's caregiving practice and theory?; what difference, if any, does such particular tradition or faith make in multifaith settings and, especially, in interfaith situations?

Representatives of seven traditions—Aboriginal, Hindu, Buddhist, Jewish, Christian, Islamic, and Humanist—were invited to participate

---

[3] Michael Pergola, "Nurturing Inter-spiritual Hearts and Interfaith Minds," in *Reflective Practice: Formation and Supervision in Ministry* (2009), 119–27; Tabitha Walther, "Interfaith Formation for Religious Leaders in a Multifaith Society: Between Meta-spiritualities and Strong Religious Profiles," ibid., 128–34.

[4] Schipani & Bueckert, eds., *Interfaith Spiritual Care: Understandings and Practices*. Much of the content of this text deals primarily, although not exclusively, with how Christian caregivers practice and reflect on caring well for people of other faiths. The other major published work in the field of interfaith spiritual care is, *Handbuch Interreligiöse Seelsorge*, edited by Helmut Weiß, Karl Federschmidt, Klaus Temme, and K. Federschmidt (Neukirchen-Vluyn: Neukirchener Verlag, 2010).

[5] Even though the word "chaplain" is still widely used in the English-speaking world, in some settings in Canada, the United States and elsewhere it is being replaced by "spiritual care (or health) professional (or specialist)."

in this project. Each one was asked to reflect and write a three-part essay focusing on the following themes: (1) Sources or "foundations" of the tradition such as scriptures, philosophies, and teachings, and how they inform, illumine, and orient spiritual care in general, and caregiving specifically, in multifaith social contexts and institutional settings (e.g., hospital or other health care center). (2) How the spiritual care tradition actually "works" in practice, including whether or to what extent it makes possible offering *interfaith* spiritual care in the sense of caring for people of other faiths. Description and analysis of caregiving situations or case studies illustrating caregiving approaches and practices were encouraged, including verbatim material as much as possible. (3) A profile of wisdom in spiritual care by identifying core competencies such as attitudes, knowledge, and skills that define professional excellence.

Recent and ongoing research in our field focuses on the foundations and the dynamics of interfaith spiritual care as a work of practical and pastoral theology.[6] In the course of our practice of spiritual care and in collaboration and conversation with others, we have identified reliable guidelines for competent and duly-contextualized caregiving practice as provided primarily but not exclusively in health care institutions. The remainder of this chapter presents a sevenfold view of the present situation in the field together with challenges and opportunities for the years ahead. Readers will see, first, a number of findings related to current understandings of interfaith care and the way forward for further research in the field. Then they will be introduced to the contributions of spiritual care professionals and theoreticians writing explicitly from the unique perspectives of their particular traditions.

## Mapping the field

First of all, we must note that there is no general agreement in the field concerning semantics. Many of us continue to prefer the term "interfaith" while others employ the concept "interreligious," which tends to be more widely accepted in Western Europe.[7] In other contexts such as Latin America, "inter-confessional" and "inter-spiritual" are sometimes

---

[6] Daniel S. Schipani, "Interfaith Pastoral Care in the Hospital: A Project in Pastoral and Practical Theology," in *Secularization Theories, Religious Identity and Practical Theology: Developing International Practical Theology for the 21st Century*, International Practical Theology Volume 7, ed. Wilhelm Grab and Lars Charbonnier (Berlin: LIT Verlag, 2009), 407–14.

[7] See for instance, Helmut Weiss, "Interreligious and Intercultural Pastoral Care and Counseling: Notes from a German Perspective," in *Interfaith Spiritual Care: Understandings and Practices*, ed. Schipani & Bueckert, 235–58.

used but not yet in a systematic way.

Second, the proposed way of integrating the three constructs—spirituality, faith, and religion—is as follows. We adopt the understanding of faith as a human universal, as helpfully articulated by James Fowler.[8] Thus understood, faith may or may not find expression in terms of specific religious traditions and content. Spirituality in this light is the overarching construct connoting a fundamental human potential as well as a need or longing for meaning, communion, existential orientation, and a disposition for relationship with a transcendent power. These words by Scott Richards and Allen Bergin reflect a widely used way to refer to religion and spirituality: "We view religious as a subset of the spiritual… [r]eligious expressions tend to be denominational, external, cognitive, behavioral, ritualistic, and public. Spiritual experiences tend to be universal, ecumenical, internal, affective, spontaneous, and private."[9] The category "faith" is employed to connote, as in Fowler, developmentally patterned kinds of construals: patterned knowing (beliefs), patterned valuing (commitment, devotion), and patterned constructions of meaning (usually in the form of an underlying narrative).[10] Both faith and religion are considered subsets of "spiritual," thus implying that humans are, fundamentally, spiritual beings.

Third, intentionality in addressing the social realities of spiritual and religious diversity and particularity is crucial yet long overdue in the field of pastoral care and counseling and in the discipline of pastoral theology in particular. Recent developments regarding reflection on spiritual care in health care institutions[11] and, especially, on chaplaincy[12] and on

---

[8] James H. Fowler, *Stages of Faith: The Psychology of Human Development and the Quest for Meaning* (San Francisco: Harper and Row, 1981).

[9] Scott P. Richards and Allen E. Bergin, *Handbook of Psychotherapy and Religious Diversity* (Washington, DC: American Psychological Association, 2000), 5.

[10] James H. Fowler, *Faith Development and Pastoral Care* (Philadelphia: Fortress Press, 1987), 54–57.

[11] See, for example, Harold G. Koenig, *Spirituality in Patient Care: Why, How, When, and What*, 2nd ed. (Philadephia and London: Templeton Foundation Press, 2007); Elizabeth Johnston Taylor, *What Do I Say? Talking with Patients about Spirituality* (Philadelphia and London: Templeton Foundation Press, 2007); and Christina M. Puchalski and Betty Ferrell, *Making Health Care Whole: Integrating Spirituality into Patient Care* (West Conshohoken, PA: Templeton Press, 2010).

[12] See Robert G. Anderson and Mary A. Fukuyama, eds., *Ministry in the Spiritual and Cultural Diversity of Health Care: Increasing the Competency of Chaplains* (New York: The Haworth Pastoral Press, 2004); Leah Dawn Bueckert and Daniel Schipani, eds., *Spiritual Caregiving in the Hospital: Windows to Chaplaincy Ministry*, rev. ed. (Kitchener, ON: Pandora Press, 2011).

mental health[13] can enrich the larger field of pastoral and spiritual care and the discipline of pastoral theology. New resources are available in the area of psychotherapy which may also be critically considered and creatively appropriated as well. For instance, the American Psychological Association (APA) has recently embraced a sustained, focused concern on spirituality and religious diversity. In fact, in recent years the APA has published a number of valuable works on psychotherapy and spirituality.[14] Furthermore, contributions explicitly linking spiritual direction and pastoral care are also pertinent for interfaith care situations.[15]

Fourth, it is very helpful, indeed necessary, for both practitioners and theoreticians in the field to pay attention to existing research and reflection on *intercultural* care and counseling because, in principle, interfaith spiritual care can be viewed and approached as a special form of intercultural care. This can be documented, for example, concerning *core competencies* identified as essential for effective practice, as articulated in the pioneering work of David Augsburger and Emmanuel Lartey regarding pastoral counseling,[16] and Derald Wing Sue and David Sue in

---

[13] See Phil Barker and Poppy Buchanan Barker, eds., *Spirituality and Mental Health: Breakthrough* (Hoboken: John Wiley and Sons, 2004); Mary Ellen Coyle, Peter Gilbert, and Vicky Nicholls, eds., *Spirituality, Values, and Mental Health: Jewels for the Journey* (London: Jessica Kingsley Publishers, 2007); Beverly Musgrave and Neil J. McCettigan, eds., *Spiritual and Psychological Aspects of Illness* (New York: Paulist Press, 2010); P. Scott Richards and Allen E. Bergin, eds., *Handbook of Psychotherapy and Religious Diversity* (Washington, DC: American Psychological Association, 2000); and John Swinton, *Spirituality in Mental Health Care: Rediscovering a Forgotten Dimension* (London: Jessica Kingsley Publishers, 2001). Consider also the *Journal of Spirituality in Mental Health*, started in 2007, and the Association for Spirituality and Mental Health (htpp://spiritualityandmentalhealth.org) which promotes interaction, collaboration, *education*, research, care, and advocacy in the domains of spirituality and mental health.

[14] See, for example, the following texts: Jamie D. Alten and Mark M. Leach, eds., *Spirituality and the Therapeutic Process: A Comprehensive Resource from Intake to Termination* (Washington, DC: American Psychological Association, 2009); William R. Miller, ed., *Integrating Spirituality into Treatment: Resources for Practitioners* (Washington, DC: American Psychological Association, 1999); Thomas G. Plante, *Spiritual Practice in Psychotherapy: Thirteen Tools for Enhancing Psychological Health* (Washington: DC: American Psychological Association, 2009); and Scott P. Richards and Allen E. Bergin, *A Spiritual Strategy for Counseling and Psychotherapy*, 2nd ed. (Washington, DC: American Psychological Association, 2005) and Richards & Bergin, *Handbook of Psychotherapy and Religious Diversity*.

[15] An important contribution is, Jean Stairs, *Listening for the Soul: Pastoral Care and Spiritual Direction* (Minneapolis: Fortress Press, 2000). It must be noted, however, that what Stairs calls "soul" I call "spirit," as explained in my chapter, "The Heart of the Matter." Stairs says: "By *soul* I mean the spiritual essence of one's existence expressed through body, mind, or any other facet of one's being ... the essential self in relationship to God" (10).

[16] David W. Augsburger, *Counseling Across Cultures* (Philadelphia: Westminster Press, 1986), 17–47; Emmanuel Y. Lartey, *In Living Color: An Intercultural Approach to Pastoral Care and Counseling*, 2nd ed. (London and New York: Jessica Kingsley Publishers, 2003), 163–77.

the broader field of counseling.[17] At the same time, the uniqueness of interfaith spiritual care must not be underestimated to the extent that visions of reality, life and death, suffering, healing, wellness, and the good life, tend to become more readily and explicitly the focus of attention in the pastoral and spiritual caregiving relationship. Therefore, in the near future, practitioners and theoreticians focusing on intercultural care will in turn likely benefit from the systematic contributions of, and engagement with, those of us who work primarily in the field of interfaith spiritual care.

Fifth, research reconfirms the assumption that the caregiver's theology matters clinically, and especially so in interfaith situations. That is true because theologically conceptual and inherently normative frameworks significantly condition the form and quality of care made available to care seekers. For example, chaplains who hold an exclusivist Christian view of faith and salvation are often seriously limited in their ability to care well for patients of other faith traditions. At the same time, we can readily document ways in which caregiving practices duly reflected upon can correct, revalidate, and reshape the caregiver's theology. Indeed, spiritual caregivers have a unique opportunity, professional duty, and ethical imperative to flourish as reflective practitioners and pastoral theologians.[18] They can also do so with explicit reference to their religious tradition and theological convictions[19] while upholding the professional, legal, ethical, and institutional standards which safeguard care receivers' rights and the very integrity of the relationship of care in any given setting.

Sixth, the views and practices of interfaith spiritual care look different in diverse regional and cultural contexts. Recent writings document significant variations represented, for example, in countries such as Brazil and the Netherlands. Not unlike most other places in Latin America, interfaith care in Brazil has not yet been intentionally and systematically implemented and developed; it rarely exists on formal institutional and ecclesiastical levels and tends to be personal and informal and

---

[17] Derald Wing Sue and David Sue, *Counseling the Culturally Diverse: Theory and Practice*, 5th ed. (Hoboken, NJ: John Wiley and Sons, 2008), 42–52.

[18] See Leah Dawn Bueckert and Daniel Schipani, "The Chaplain as Reflective Practitioner and Pastoral Theologian" in *Spiritual Caregiving in the Hospital: Windows to Chaplaincy Ministry*, ed. Bueckert & Schipani, 239–53; and Daniel S. Schipani and Leah Dawn Bueckert, "Explorations I: Applying an Interpretive Framework," and "Explorations III: An Exercise in Pastoral Theological Imagination," in *Interfaith Spiritual Care: Understandings and Practice*, ed. Schipani & Bueckert, 89–98, 105–12.

[19] See, for example, John Peterson, "A Lutheran Chaplain's Nine Thesis on Interfaith Care," in *Interfaith Spiritual Care: Understandings and Practices*, ed. Schipani & Bueckert, 69–80.

spontaneous.[20] At the other end of the spectrum, spiritual care in the Netherlands deliberately addresses the multifaith social realities of the country; it seeks to make spiritual care accessible to people of diverse religious traditions and faith or philosophical orientations, and calls for specialized training on the part of caregivers also representing diverse spiritual identities and viewpoints.[21]

Seventh and finally, research persuasively suggests that progress in understanding and practicing interfaith spiritual care is transferable in several ways. Insights we have gained in the practices of interfaith counseling and chaplaincy, as well as in supervision received and given in those two forms of care, can be mutually beneficial. For their part, spiritual caregivers of diverse traditions soon discover that the very attitudes, knowledge, and skills necessary to care well for people whose traditions are different than their own, are also indispensable for care of those whose beliefs, values, and practices stem from a different religious, spiritual, or theological stream or denominational background, even if their religious affiliation appears to be the same. Further, all caregivers can soon realize that, ultimately, all relationships of care can be viewed as both intercultural and interfaith interactions. Therefore, training in interfaith care always, without exceptions, enhances the caregivers' general competence and professional wisdom.

The next section consists of summaries of the remaining chapters of this book. It provides an overview of multifaith views in spiritual care that suggest a rainbow[22] of blessing. In fact, the beautiful double rainbow on the cover of this book is meant to symbolize hope and the promise of life and transformation. It was some time after colleagues representing seven traditions had accepted my invitation to contribute essays for this project that I started imagining their perspectives and views on spiritual care as a wonderful rainbow of blessing. Indeed, our collaborative work can represent the sunlight of Wisdom and Grace refracted and reflected in a spectrum of living colors!

---

[20] James R. Farris, "Interfaith Spiritual Care: A View from Brazil," in *Interfaith Spiritual Care: Understandings and Practices*, ed. Schipani & Bueckert, 171–90.

[21] Ari van Buuren, Mualla Kaya, and Bart ten Broek, "The Junction of the Sees: Interfaith Spiritual Care in the Netherlands," in *Interfaith Spiritual Care: Understandings and Practices*, ed. Schipani & Bueckert, 279–313.

[22] It is well known that a rainbow is a color spectrum that appears when sunlight shines on the water drops at low altitude angle. It is formed by the refraction and reflection of sunlight in raindrops when a ray of light enters a raindrop, "bends," and is separated into its constituent colors (red, orange, yellow, green, blue, indigo, and violet). It is also known that rainbows are the focus of many mythologies. In the biblical tradition, the rainbow is a sign and token of God's covenant with the earth (especially humankind and "every living creature") after the great destructive flood, according to Genesis 9:12–13.

## Abstracts of the multifaith views[23]

### Journey toward Creator and the realm of peace: Two voices on Aboriginal spiritual caregiving
By Melody A. McKellar and Roger Armitte

Aboriginal spirituality is grounded in the belief that everything and everyone comes from Creator and will return to Creator. Life emerges from the Spirit World, takes human form on this earth, and returns to the Spirit World at the time of death. Death is not something to be feared for it is in the Spirit World that one is truly alive and whole. All of nature—whether human beings, rocks, or trees—is supported by Mother Earth, has spirit, and is interconnected; therefore everyone and everything is to be treated with equal respect. Community has a high value in the Aboriginal tradition, and decisions are made based on what is best for the whole community.

Elders are the traditional spiritual caregivers who teach and live out the seven Sacred Teachings: love, respect, courage, humility, truth, honesty, and wisdom. Elders pass along the wisdom they have received from oral tradition, as well as revelations they receive through dreams or visions. The Medicine Wheel is a key guide to life as it describes who and what people are. It is believed that there is a reason for everything, including sickness, so Elders help others to discover the lesson in their particular life circumstance. Elders tend to the sick and dying through traditional rituals and ceremonies such as drumming, singing songs, smudging, and sweat lodge ceremonies.

While there is a place for formal education and skill development is encouraged, more value is placed on the caregivers' ability to be a comforting, nonjudgmental presence to others in their time of need with an ability to listen with their whole being. Aboriginal spiritual caregivers are able to care for those of other faiths because they seek to focus on the fundamental commonalities among human beings and hold to the foundational belief in the worth and equality of all of life.

### The world is one family: Principles of Hindu spiritual care
By Dinesh C. Sharma

*Sanatana Dharma*, meaning "the law," and the name by which many Hindus refer to the religion, is a universal, comprehensive, and inclusive philosophy. The core beliefs of Hinduism include faith in a triune God, the divinity of all living beings, the sacred writings as foundational, the

---
[23] Special thanks go to Alicia Buhler for her assistance in preparing this section.

cyclic and eternal nature of creation, the theory of karma, the immortality of the soul and reincarnation, and the benefit of a *guru*'s guidance in achieving self-realization. There are ten *Vedic Yama* (restraints) and ten *niyama* (practices) which are also central to realizing a full life.

The practice of *Ayurveda* (knowledge for long life) addresses the three sacred dimensions of human life—mind, body, and spirit—holistically. It is believed that health is the human being's natural state; therefore, when illness is experienced, willpower, positive energy flow, right breathing, and the recitation of mantras are all to be used by care receivers for their own healing. The role of the spiritual caregiver, then, is to be present, perhaps recite mantras, and coach the care receiver in these practices, as demonstrated in the case studies.

Core competencies for fruitful spiritual care in the Hindu tradition are summed up in the caregiver being "capable, available, and of unquestionable character"; these three covenants form the basis of the *Ayurveda*. Caregivers need to pursue both action and knowledge—knowledge of the material world (*apara-vidya*) and knowledge of the divine (*para-vidya*)—and the right balance of action and knowledge yields holistic presence which is therapeutic in and of itself. Quietude is a particular way of listening to and being present with care receivers and is effective in building the care receiver's willpower. Seeing the divine in all living things and serving others as though serving God allows the Hindu spiritual caregiver to provide care in interfaith encounters.

### Three *yanas* for wise caring: A Buddhist perspective on spiritual care
By Danny Fisher

Buddhism is comprised of many streams of practice and tradition. The one universal thread that is woven through all streams of Buddhism is compassion as the highest ideal. The *yanas* (vehicles) are paths of practice that deepen compassion as one negotiates *samsara* (life, death, suffering) and *nirvana* (awakening; end of suffering).

Three *yanas* are important to the foundation and practice of spiritual care. The first is *Shravakayana* (Vehicle of the Hearers/Disciples) in which the Buddha's Four Noble Truths inform our existential condition and how suffering may come to an end. The second is *Mahayana* (Great Vehicle), where *bodhisattva*, or a being oriented toward enlightenment, is of primary importance. Through cultivation of the "awakened heart-mind" (*bodhichitta*), a compassion is developed for other human beings which motivates one to aid in one another's enlightenment. The *Mahayana paramitas*, or "six perfections," are essential in this enlightenment process; they include generosity, discipline, forebearance, exertion, meditation, and wisdom. More than virtues, these *paramitas* engage one with the interconnectedness of life. Generosity (*dana-paramita*) is outlined as an essential belief and practice through which Buddhist caregivers offer interfaith spiritual care. The third *yana* is *Vajrayana* (Adamantine Vehicle) which sees symbol as a way to get to pure relative truth, the *mandala* (sacred circle representing "orderly chaos"), being one example.

Those three *yanas* are interconnected and yet progressively build on one another, all moving the practitioner toward compassion and enlightenment. In terms of core competencies of Buddhist interfaith spiritual caregivers, the chapter highlights the following: a dedication to their own awakening and truth-telling; they practice what they preach; devotion to their teachers and lineage; openness to all people; *bodhichitta*; and they do not consider financial gain in exchange for care.

**Vulnerability as a path to the Divine: Jewish spiritual care**
By Mychal B. Springer

A foundational belief of the Jewish tradition is that God is the ultimate healer, and human beings join in partnership with God in that healing work. A communal understanding of redemption is central; while we may pray for a particular individual's healing of both body and soul, there is an understanding that any particular healing moves us all toward communal wholeness.

In the midst of vulnerability, prayer opens our heart and is healing because it connects us with God. The Torah tells the human story of exile and return, and reveals that God's way of caring for those in exile is to *be with*. Therefore spiritual caregivers seek to be present to the ill and suffering, offering them the comfort of presence. In order to join with God in being present to those suffering, caregivers must experience their own exile and recognize that their return is interconnected with the other's return from exile. Hope is born when people are heard into speech, and redemption is found in the interconnectedness of both divine and human, and human and human.

The competent Jewish spiritual caregiver is shaped by the tradition and places story at the center. Proficiency in one's own theology, and translation between traditions is key. Concretely emulating God's presence by being present to others in their exile, recognizing the divine likeness in all of humanity, and extending loving kindness is the heart of Jewish pastoral care. One partners with others and with God in the passionate pursuit of truth and wholeness. Traditional Jewish practices of visiting the sick, spiritual assessment, interpreting the law, witnessing lament, and hearing into speech are some of the essential practices. Competent spiritual caregivers also know how to engage in self-reflection, assess their effectiveness, be aware of interpersonal dynamics, collaborate with many other spiritual caregivers, and engage in ethical decision-making.

**Do justice, love kindness, walk humbly: A Christian perspective on spiritual care**
By Kathleen J. Greider

Christian spiritual care encompasses many practices in diverse settings. Christianity is characterized by diversity; however, it is recognized that much harm has been inflicted in its name. The Wesleyan quadrilateral outlines four main sources of authority in Christianity: Bible, tradition, reason, and experience. And the "streams of living water" metaphor taken from Richard Foster serves well to demonstrate how diverse traditions within Christianity co-exist. These traditions include contemplative, pietistic-holiness, charismatic, social justice, evangelical, and incarnational streams, each of which has gifts to offer the field of spiritual care. A Christian pastoral theology for interfaith spiritual care is then offered in terms of a set of normative convictions as personal credo.

The framework presented for interfaith spiritual care is once again rooted in diversity. This framework acknowledges the need for a multifocal lens, draws from the diverse traditions, or streams, of spiritual care, has multiple paradigms (spiritual, personal, communal-contextual, intercultural), multiple functions (healing, sustaining, guiding, reconciling, liberating, nurturing, and empowering are commonly recognized), and a plethora of images.

Practices of interfaith spiritual care are broken down into three stages of encounter. First, *anticipation of encounter* emphasizes maturing our personhood and involves communal-contextual self-care, intercultural self-care, personal self-care, and spiritual self-care. Second, *encounter* emphasizes maturing engagement with others and involves responsive presence, emergency care, spiritual companionship, and ritual. Third, *refreshment for re-encounter* emphasizes maturing our learning and involves self-assessment, consultation, reassessing faith stance, and continuing education. Considered together, these practices create an action-reflection cycle. Christian wisdom contributing to interfaith spiritual care is summed up as doing justice, loving kindness, and walking humbly. The purpose of these foundations, frameworks, and practices of spiritual care is to mature humanness.

## The Crescent of compassionate engagement: Theory and practice of Islamic spiritual care
By Nazila Isgandarova

The *Qur'an* is the primary textual source of Islam. This sacred text along with the *Sunnah* and *hadith*, which outline the example and teachings of Prophet Muhammad, are the essential foundations of Islamic spiritual care. Forms of care in Islam include the practice of visiting the sick (*'Iyâdah*), the approach of exemplary kindness and care (*rifq*), and doing what is beautiful as the optimal state in which spiritual care is offered (*ihsân*). Islamic spiritual care is not in tension with but rather encourages the use of conventional medial intervention when necessary.

A literature review reveals the few in number yet important contributions of Muslim scholarship to spiritual care. The author presents the case for Muslim caregivers to integrate Islamic practice and theological foundations with the theory and practice of social science in order to offer effective spiritual care. Solution Focused Brief Therapy is used in the case study to offer an example of such integration. Muslim spiritual caregivers are able to offer care to people of other faiths by recognizing the diversity and richness in the social and religious context of our time. As spiritual companions, Muslim caregivers are able to offer care to others not by offering answers to their suffering but rather by recognizing the universality of suffering and existential questioning.

The core competencies of Islamic spiritual care include mercy, respect, forgiveness, and listening. These competencies are developed through faithfulness grounded in the *Qur'an* and the *Sunnah*, following the Prophet as a role model, consistent participation in a Muslim community, and nurturing a healthy spirituality.

## *Worldviewing* competence for narrative interreligious dialogue: A Humanist contribution to spiritual care
By Hans Alma and Christa Anbeek

*Worldviewing* is a process that utilizes intrapersonal and interpersonal dialogue which constitutes identity in order to give existential meaning to life. Ninian Smart's seven dimensions of religion—narrative and mythic; doctrinal and philosophical; ethical and legal; ritual; experiential and emotional; social and institutional; and material—are applied to compare humanism to other religious systems as a source for spiritual care. Humanism emphasizes human experience, creativity, diversity, and responsibility, and contributes most directly to the narrative, philosophical, ethical, and experiential dimensions of religion.

In an effort to find meaning, existential counselors encourage clients to share their life's narrative. The case study presented demonstrates how sharing personal stories in a group setting allows for the rich diversity of stories presented to aid in creating connections and new frameworks for meaning. *Narrative interreligious dialogue* focuses on relationship between human beings rather than on differences in worldview, and, as such, it is an essential component of interfaith spiritual care. Another important component of interfaith and intercultural dialogue is the field of *ecosophy* which emphasizes unity in diversity and is concerned with our "common responsibility for a viable global society."

The overarching competence for the humanist spiritual caregiver is a *worldviewing competence*. Worldviewing competence is a caregiver's ability to understand the client's experience, especially in terms of how they create religious and/or existential meaning and then relate the care receiver's story to their own resources. Under the umbrella of worldviewing competence are three core competencies: a hermeneutic competence which includes both knowledge and process of application, self-reflective competence, and heuristic competence, which refers to a caregiver's attitude toward a client or patient.

## The heart of the matter: Engaging the *spirit* in spiritual care
By Daniel S. Schipani

The word *health* is related to the Anglo Saxon word from which *healing*, *holiness*, and *wholeness* are derived. While keeping that connection in mind, the question, what is "spiritual" about spiritual care? can be addressed by reflecting on how mental-emotional health and spiritual health are related. That reflection must take into account scientific, philosophical, and theological perspectives that inform the notions of mental and spiritual health; it must also consider the ideological, sociocultural, economic, and professional-political factors involved in current understandings of health and in health care practices as such.

A theologically grounded tripartite anthropology views humans holistically as embodied, animated, and spiritual beings (spirit, psyche [soul], body). In light of this view, the psychological and the spiritual dimensions of the self are understood as distinct yet integrated and inseparable. It is then possible to appreciate ways in which psychological factors affect the experience and the expressions of spirituality and vice versa in terms of intra-self dynamics.

The unique contribution of spiritual caregivers consists in their need to view and work with care receivers holistically while primarily engaging the spirit and, therefore, the psychological and spiritual dimensions of their self. They must develop the competence of "bilingual proficiency" in the sense of understanding the languages and resources of psychology and other behavioral and social sciences together with those of spirituality and theology, religion, or existential philosophy; further, spiritual caregivers must be able to employ that understanding and those resources in spiritual assessment and all other forms of verbal and nonverbal (e.g., rituals) caregiving practices. A related key competency is holding a four-dimensional view of reality which, in addition to viewing care receivers in light of their social contexts, recognizes and addresses the existential and spiritual dimensions definable in terms of the threat of nonbeing and the promise of new being.

**Epilogue: Core competencies for wise interfaith care**

Competencies are those dispositions, capacities, and capabilities necessary to care well in interfaith situations. They include the qualities or assets with which caregivers meet specific standards of practice in a variety of caregiving settings. A number of core competencies can be identified within the interrelated domains of "knowing," "being," and "doing" resulting in a portrait of excellence, or *professional wisdom*, for interfaith care. Further, those sets of competencies can be synthesized respectively in terms of the broad categories of *understanding*, *presence*, and *companioning*.

The holistic formation of spiritual caregivers calls for spiritual, religious, and theological training together with clinical and ministerial education. Viewed in terms of the portrait alluded to above, holistic formation includes three interrelated areas—academic, personal-spiritual, and vocational-professional. Therefore, programs aiming at preparing for, supervising, and enhancing the practice of interfaith spiritual care must include complementary pedagogies of interpretation and contextualization, formation, and performance.

We are now ready to take a closer look at how spiritual caregivers representing seven traditions perceive their task in light of the foundations that inform their frames of reference and inspire their practice. Readers are thus invited to appropriate the twofold purpose of this project: to deepen appreciation for the uniqueness and special gifts of those traditions together with a richer understanding of commonalities and differences among them; and to encourage collaboration among spiritual care practitioners and scholars.

# Journey toward Creator and the realm of peace
## Two voices on Aboriginal spiritual caregiving

*Melody A. McKellar and Roger Armitte*

Native spirituality is indistinguishable from Native cultural life. It is a holistic way of life that has evolved over centuries and has been transmitted primarily through oral tradition from one generation to the next. Cultural and spiritual life are grounded in the belief in the fundamental interconnectedness of all forms of life and all natural things with primary importance given to the land, "Mother Earth." Native spirituality is further characterized by a strong experience of community in direct contrast with the key values of individualism and private ownership of things and wealth in the dominant North American cultures. In this tradition, therefore, health care always has strong spiritual and communal dimensions. These and other features of spiritual care in an Aboriginal perspective are presented in this chapter, which is divided into two parts with the reflective testimonies of two Aboriginal Elders.[1] Both of them share from the wellsprings of wisdom and experience as professional spiritual caregivers.

## Melody A. McKellar

*It is late in the afternoon, and I receive a call from the nursing staff on one of the wards. An elderly man with dementia is very restless, and his family won't be able to sit with him until early evening. This man is slowly making the transition from this world to the spirit world. As I enter the room, my eyes*

---

[1] Wisdom is the main virtue and competence of Aboriginal (or First Nation) Elders, acknowledged as such by their communities. Elders may be either women or men. They all have authority to perform different kinds of ceremonies; however, some Elders might have special gifts for interpreting dreams, for applying herbal remedies, or to heal in a sweat lodge (see below).

*gaze upward to the eagle feather that his family has placed on the wall and the dream catcher[2] beside it. I greet him and ask his permission to sit with him for a while. We hold hands and I offer a prayer for his peace of mind, body, and spirit. His restlessness continues as he looks about the room and tries to climb out of the bed.*

*A nurse comes in and considers giving him a medication to decrease his restlessness and asks for my opinion. I suggest that we wait and see how he is doing while I sit with him. When the man and I are alone in the room, I bring out my traditional hand drum and begin to softly sing him a "traveling song." This will help his spirit make the transitional journey home when the time is right and when he is ready.*

*The sounds of the gentle heartbeat of the drum must bring some comfort as I note he is slowly beginning to relax. He understands the words of the sacred song because they are sung in his language. Regardless, his spirit understands and recognizes the prayer song no matter the language.*

*The fire marshal for the health care institution comes to the door of the man's room to let me know they have isolated the smoke alarm in his room, and they have shut it off for the next hour. (When I had arrived on the ward, I had asked the nursing staff to request that the smoke alarm be shut off.)*

*I take out my smudge bowl and prepare the ceremony as our ancestors have prepared it for millennia. I take out my eagle fan and ever so gently smudge this elderly man with the smoke from the shell. As I do so, I offer prayers of blessing and comfort. He has now fallen asleep. I find a CD of fiddle music in the lounge and leave it playing softly in the background for a man who loved to play the fiddle for his family.*

*A teaching from the Dakota people says that there are only two sacred times in a person's life: the moment we are born and the moment we die. It is I who receive such a blessing as to be able to sit with one who is ready to make the journey back to Creator. I leave the elderly gentleman sleeping peacefully while a nurse on the ward comes to sit with him when it is my time to move on.*

*I would have time to sit with him once again before he passed. For now his mind, body, and spirit are peacefully taking a rest . . .*

I am a Métis woman, one of the Aboriginal groups in Canada, and have French and Mohawk roots. I have lived most of my life in the province of Manitoba although my birth relatives come from Quebec. I am very thankful to have had amazing Elders who have guided me on my adult Aboriginal spiritual journey. They are Métis, Ojibway, Plains Cree, Swampy Cree, and Dakota. In what follows I highlight first of all some of

---

[2] See description of the dream catcher below.

the main beliefs and values dear to my tradition. I then make reference to the practice of spiritual care from my perspective and identify some of the core competencies necessary to care well for all people.

## Foundations

All things originate from the Creator and have been given life and a purpose for existence. In the Medicine Wheel teachings, it is Creator who is in the Centre of the circle of life and from which all of life revolves. One of my former Elders spoke of the fact that it is only the human race that has forgotten our purpose. All other parts of Creation—the willow tree, the tiny ant, the hawk, the water, the grasses, and every other part of Creation—are still carrying out their original instructions given by the Creator. The main difference between us as humans (or two-legged creatures) and the rest of Creation is that Creator has given us the ability to make choices.

All of Creation is interconnected and all parts rely on one another. If the waters or the trees disappeared on the planet, could we as humans survive? What if all the animals disappeared? What if we, two-legged beings on the earth, disappeared? What would happen to the rest of Creation? There are so many times when we as human beings see ourselves as the most important part of Creation out of our own arrogance. We are not the most important living creatures in the Universe. We are just one part of Creation, no more or any less important than any other part of Creation.

We often refer to other parts of Creation as our relatives. This helps us remember our place in the Universe and that we are related to every living thing. We will refer to the earth as our mother or the rocks as grandfathers/grandmothers, the sun as grandfather, and the moon as grandmother. We may call the bear our brother/sister. We know that there are parts of creation much older than we are, and so we refer to them as our relatives, "All Our Relations." It is a reminder of the teachings of Respect for all of life. We cannot take any part of Creation for our own use without the offerings of prayers and giving something in return. We would never think of picking a plant without first offering our prayers and letting the plant know our purpose for using it and giving thanks for its medicine. We have certain teachings that we need to follow when we use other parts of Creation for health and healing.

We have travelled from the Spirit World to this physical world and will return to the Spirit World upon our death. When we take our last breath on earth, our next breath will take place in the other dimension. I have never heard of the concept of "hell" in our traditional spiritual way. When we return to the Spirit World, we will have a chance to "review our choices" that we made in this physical plane and have an even greater understanding of how our choices affected those around us (including the rest of Creation). While we are living in this physical plane, we should admit to mistakes we have made and ask forgiveness from those we have hurt. It is a sign of a humble person to be able to own one's mistakes and then to learn from those mistakes to make different choices. That is a part of our spiritual growth while we are in the physical form. Our greatest teachings come from our challenges.

Regarding the seven Sacred Teachings also mentioned in the second part of this chapter—love, respect, courage, humility, truth, honesty, and wisdom—we claim that we cannot know any of them without having known their opposite. Those things that we see as painful, difficult, or challenging will sometimes have the deepest meanings for us later on in our journey. For example, I cannot know what love is unless I have experienced the opposite of love. It is only then that I can begin to understand the teaching of love.

Community is essential to us. I often hear people from the dominant society talk about "I" or "me," and it seems as though the world should revolve around their individual wants and needs. This is not how we as Aboriginal persons understand community. Each infant, child, woman, man, and elder has a significant role and part in the development of our communities. Again, no one is less or more important, for all have a role to play. When a person is ill or injured, extended family and community members gather round for support. That is often difficult to understand for those staff in hospitals who are not part of an Aboriginal community. Decisions are to be made for the welfare of the whole community.

In Aboriginal communities, one of the greatest attributes a person can offer is the gift of sharing with others. In traditional societies, the hunters shared the meat amongst Elders and children first, then other community members. Sharing what you have, even if it is your last, is important. When you are in need, then there should be others to share with you as you have shared with them.

We have many ceremonies that we can use to help us in our healing journey. There are several natural ways of healing: sweating, talking, yelling (in the form of releasing energy; this does not mean yelling at someone else), shaking, crying, laughing, and yawning. Any healing that occurs is not through the power of the man or woman leading the ceremony. All healing comes from the Creator, who uses the leader of the ceremonies as a conduit.

Our Elders are given teachings and wisdom from their Elders. In this way teachings, stories, songs, and ceremonies are passed down through oral tradition from generation to generation. Stories are shared that hold wisdom for how one might live life or learn from the experience of an animal in the story. Our Elders are very connected to the spiritual realm and are shown things in a variety of ways: dreams, visions, etc. Our ancestors knew that people with a paler skin were coming to our lands before the very first Caucasian person arrived. They were shown these things in ceremonies, dreams, and visions.

There are many of our Elders who share their wisdom and teachings with us about the coming times and how we should be preparing and living. When we need to work on an aspect of ourselves that needs some healing, we respectfully seek out those Elders who have such knowledge and understanding. An Elder does not push him/herself on you but will wait for you to come and seek help when the time is right. The Elders know the ceremonies to offer in order to seek the guidance and direction from the Spirit world. Elders know other Elders who might "specialize" in a specific area, as they have been given those gifts by Creator.

The old adage, "you can't change anyone but yourself," is so true. We must work on ourselves to facilitate positive change. That is our responsibility. When we do that, we help facilitate positive change for our communities. When we are able to live in balance and harmony with ourselves, then it becomes easier to live in balance and harmony with all living things and to emanate love and respect.

## Caregiving practice

As a spiritual care provider, I work with all peoples regardless of race, creed, nationality, etc. One of the most important foundations for me in my everyday walk is to show respect and to be present. I ask Creator to work through me so that I may be open to whatever is needed in the moment. I need to ensure that I remain centered and grounded in my work. That is why it is important for me to continue to work on my own healing so that I can be present for others. Sometimes people just need someone present with them and to hold the sacred space for them so that they might be able to cry or share their hurt or pain. Oftentimes, the answers will come to them as to their next step. Sometimes I will provide a ceremony that will help facilitate the space needed for the answers to be given.

Traditional medicine and ceremonies can work alongside allopathic medicine. I would never advise persons to leave allopathic medicine or their allopathic physician. When I myself had a serious illness a number of years back, I made certain that my physician knew I was using traditional medicine and attending traditional ceremonies alongside the allopathic modality.

Our traditional practices are very rich in experiential and sensory forms. We remain connected to the earth and all of Creation. For many persons that connection has been forgotten when they live surrounded by pavement and cement. The "re-membering" of connection to the land assists our spirit and energy to re-connect to the life cycles and natural rhythms of the universe. If you ask folk to remember back to their fondest times in their lives, they often recall the times of connection to community and to the land, in whatever form that takes.

**Qualities of spiritual caregivers**

Spiritual caregivers need to live out the seven Sacred Teachings of love, respect, courage, humility, truth, honesty, and wisdom. These seven Sacred Teachings are foundational for any culture. We must practice from the heart and not offer spiritual care from the head. It is through the heart that we connect with one another.

It is essential for spiritual caregivers to be grounded and to have some life experience. They must have worked on their own healing journeys and continue to do so. Although they are solid in their own practices, it is important to be open to others, thereby having flexibility for what might be required in the moment. Knowledge does not always come in the form of a PhD. The recognition of life experience and wisdom passed down through oral traditions is equally important. Living out the seven Sacred Teachings from any spiritual practice is vital.

Spiritual caregivers need to be able to listen fully, not just with their ears, but with their whole being. They must be nonjudgmental. I have only walked in my shoes, no one else's. Although I may have similar experiences to others, I cannot possibly know everything that has led to this moment in this person's life. To that essential guideline, I wish to add that to become competent spiritual caregivers they must:

- be open, accepting, and respectful;
- practice patience and compassion (sometimes it may seem like a revolving door when working with persons in a health care setting. When I see the same person coming over and over again through the emergency department, then it is probable that support systems, social services, and other needs may be missing in that persons' life);
- communicate well, both verbally and in writing;
- know ourselves, both gifts and limitations;

- continue to work on our own healing journey and admit when we have made a mistake.

Spiritual caregivers need to be trained in their calling. That does not always mean in a formal educational system. Most of our traditional Elders have a PhD in life experience; they just do not have the paper hanging in the frame. It is important to recognize that and to know that their unique qualifications will contribute to the health care team in a special way. In any event, it is important for all spiritual caregivers to further their education as they practice spiritual care. As days are set aside for medical staff to take continuing education, so it should be for spiritual caregivers. Counseling skills and ability are an important aspect of spiritual care, and formal training in these areas is indeed an asset. Having some formal training in the area of interfaith care is also beneficial, as the following vignette illustrates.[3]

*A young non-Aboriginal woman approaches me in my office to ask when I will offer another sweat lodge ceremony. We talk about the possibilities open to her in light of her scheduled appointments with various professionals in the health care facility. She has been in the facility for nearly a year and has found that Aboriginal spiritual ceremonies bring her peace and comfort for her mind, body, and spirit.*

*This will be her eighth sweat lodge ceremony since I have come to know her. We have a separate sweat lodge on the property just for women. Since the building of the women's lodge, many of them come to my door to ask specifically for a ceremony.*

*Like so many others, this young woman comes with a history of having suffered various forms of violence and abuse. It has been difficult for her to find a place in the world where she is accepted for who she is and where she feels she "fits in" without judgment. Self-harm is still very evident and is part of the past cycle of abuse.*

*She clearly demonstrates a deep inward knowing of when it is time for her to participate in a sweat lodge ceremony. Being able to request that for herself is a positive step in her recovery and an indicator of growth in self-confidence.*

*Healing work is not for the faint-hearted, and the road to recovery is often a long one that requires great patience. One step forward, two steps back, two steps forward, one back. Spiritual care is vital. The physical body mends itself much more quickly than the mental, emotional, and spiritual dimensions of our*

---

[3] The vignette is meant as a testimony of my being available and willing to offer spiritual care to any care receiver, with resources from my Aboriginal tradition. It shows the potential value of those resources to help care receivers in terms of their own spirituality or faith.

*selves. For today, this young woman, like so many others, has taken another small step toward her road to recovery. Tomorrow she may experience another fork in the road. Whichever direction she moves, there will be spiritual care offered and we will once again travel the road together . . .*

## Roger Armitte

### Foundations

As a Medeowin, I believe that everything that exists has life and comes from the Creator—everything and everyone. The earth is our mother, our provider. The sky is our father, providing water. Both supply what is necessary for life. Everything has a spirit. Each tree has a spirit. Therefore, we ask the spirit of the tree for permission and forgiveness before we chop it down. And we tell it that we are grateful for it. We follow this procedure when we hunt and fish, when we pick medicines, or cut grass. We say "thank you, we are grateful," and we ask for forgiveness and permission. Even rocks are seen as a life-form; they too have a spirit. In the sweat lodge,[4] for example, even the rocks are considered "grandfathers" or "grandmothers." We are all connected. We are all one. We are related to the four-legged as well as the two-legged creatures, and to all the creatures of the air and water. Although humanity is the only species that is able to know, no species is superior to, or less than, any other—all have gifts. Some may have more and some may have fewer, but all have equal value. Some people literally bow to me because I am an Elder, which I do not like at all. If a child bows to me, I know that I may have more knowledge than that child at the time, but that does not mean that the child will not have equal or greater knowledge as they grow up.

Our belief is that we all originate in Spirit, spend some time in human form, and then return to Spirit. We believe that we are only partially alive on earth. When we die our spirit is released and we are freed to return

---

[4] The sweat lodge is one of the fundamental ceremonies consisting in a purification procedure which precedes spiritual quests. Many lodges are for communal prayer purposes, but others are for healing. Usually a sweat lodge is required both before and after the fast. An appropriate site is a virginal section of ground which has not been desecrated by the trampling of feet or the disposal of waste matter. After an Elder has selected a site, it will be blessed with tobacco and sweetgrass. Construction details vary from tribe to tribe and can only be considered on an individual Elder basis. It takes about one and a half hours to erect a five-foot high, igloo-shaped structure from bent willow branches tied together with twine. The structure is covered with canvas or blankets to exclude all light. It can accommodate eight persons at a time. Stones are heated outside the sweat lodge, traditionally in a fire. Four stones are admitted four times each to the sweat lodge, representing the four directions. There are prayers and singings as well as pipe smoking during the two-hour ceremony. Ontario Multifaith Council on Spiritual and Religious Care (OMCSRC), *Multifaith Information Manual*, 5th ed. (Toronto: OMCSRC, 2011), 274.

to the fuller realm of Spirit. When we return to the Spirit World, we reclaim our full lives and selves. Therefore, we do not see death as final. On the contrary, death is only a beginning, a transition. In fact, in most Aboriginal languages a word or term for death simply does not exist. Death is not a punishment but a reward. As a young child, I was not afraid of death because I was taught to not be afraid of death but rather to embrace it. Children were taught that we had more to fear in life than in death. Death is a transformation. I celebrate the transition from this life to the next, and accompany people on their journey into the Spirit World, from the first breath to the last within this cycle of life. Aboriginal experience of the Spirit World is very present and practical. Dreams and visions play an important part in this. There are various traditional, ritual, and symbolic approaches to the end of life. They include use of grandfather/mother rocks, cutting of hair, star blankets for burial, and the symbolism of colors of clans and of beading.

We believe that our destiny is already laid out for us. Everyone is born with certain tasks that we are given to complete in this life. Even though it is laid out for us, we can change our destiny by the choices we daily make. We are in control, to a certain degree, and can strongly influence the course of our own lives. For example, many in my culture have a hard time understanding that alcohol is taboo. It is not beneficial for life, and the body does not require it. It is a choice. We understand it to be a poison, yet so many are affected by it. Some studies have even suggested that Aboriginal people might have a gene which makes us more susceptible to alcohol.

We do not see ill health as a punishment but as a natural part of our life cycle. Everything gets diseased, including trees, fish, air, and earth. Ill health is part of the flow of nature. We believe that we are all responsible for our own health. When we are sick, we can look to ourselves and question ourselves—what did I do or not do? Sickness does not just happen—there is a reason for it, perhaps even a purpose.

Community is a big part of our society. Ill health and dysfunction ultimately stem from lack of community. Community is our foundation, our structure, our connection to life. We have a responsibility to members of our community. All members are equal, and all communities are equal. All play a part—one within the other. All contribute to life. There are several fundamental beliefs that are central to our communal culture's worldview, as briefly presented below.

**The Medicine Wheel**

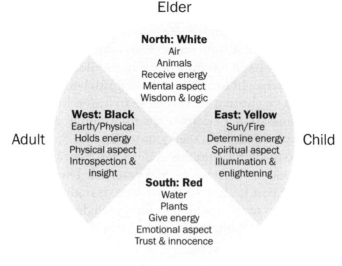

We hold that each of us has a Medicine Wheel that describes who and what we are.[5] It represents the four directions, the four seasons, the four races (yellow, white, red, black), the four stages of life, and the four areas of our human self—physical, mental, emotional, and spiritual. Used as an analytical tool, the Medicine Wheel can function as our guide to life; and when considered properly from the time of our birth, it can help us live a life free of major problems. There is a reason for everything in life—a root cause. The Medicine Wheel helps us stay centered and balanced. Take, for example, a toothache. If we do not attend to it, the physical pain can begin to affect us emotionally and even spiritually. If we care for the root cause, we can avoid the pain growing into the other areas. If we return to it and pay attention to it, we are healthier in all dimensions of life. Life never stays the same, and we are changing every second. If we are out of balance, our emotions can also affect our physical well-being.

**Sacred Teachings**

We hold to seven central Sacred Teachings: love, respect, courage, humility, truth, honesty, and wisdom. The importance of the Sacred

---

[5] The Medicine Wheel is an ancient symbol arising from within many Aboriginal communities, and there are diverse Aboriginal views and practices related to it. The Medicine Wheel can be adapted to many uses; however, the emphasis is always on the need for harmony and balance within oneself, with others, and with all creatures on earth. It provides a graphic reminder that change is inevitable, life is a developmental process, and seeking wholeness is a most valuable goal.

Teachings is to direct our life well and lead us to a good outcome if we follow them. Following these teachings leads to a balanced path. It is important to live one's life in light of all seven teachings—spiritually, physically, and psychologically (that is, emotionally and mentally). All are equally important and interconnected. All seven teachings should be equally balanced in life. None should be neglected. The teachings are a guideline and offer instructions as to how we should live our lives. Different peoples have similar, though somewhat varied, sacred teachings. These vary between tribal groups. Often the Sacred Teachings are spoken of at rituals and ceremonies—sometimes one or two are focused on. These Sacred Teachings are introduced in childhood. As we mature, we take them to the next level. For example, a child's concept of love is different than an adult's—but as the child grows older and more mature, their conception of love expands and develops as well.

**Oral teachings/life teachings of Elders**

Life—how does one live and how does one view life itself (work, sleep, eating, drinking, interaction with people and with land)? A big part of First Nations belief is that we spend a lot of time connected to the earth because the earth is our mother, the mother of everything. The earth sustains our life. Many First Nations people have traditionally not been formal gardeners, because we believe that everything we need the land provides. Food can come directly from her, and does not need to be planted by our own hand. Likewise, we will not cut down a tree if we can wait for it to fall on its own or use wood from a tree which has already fallen.

**Dream catcher**

The dream catcher is a tool that was given to First Nations people through a vision, to assist the children in separating bad dreams from good dreams. Dream catchers hang over babies in cradles and over young children in their beds. The webbing in the dream catcher allows the good dreams to go through and the bad dreams to get caught and held there. The webbing catches nightmares, which filter down and get caught in the feathers hanging below. And then these nightmares get burned by the sun when its rays touch the feathers in the morning.

I was told a story about a Kokum (grandparent) who was taking her little grandson for a walk. They walked along the path for a while, and then the boy saw a spider web along the side of the path. The boy picked up a stick and was ready to break the web. But the boy's Kokum said, "No," and explained that this web was Grandfather Spider's home, and that it was important to let Grandfather Spider live in peace. Later that night, Grandfather Spider came to the home of the Kokum and her grandson while the grandson was sleeping. He gave the dream catcher to the Kokum in thanks for saving his home from the little boy.

**Drum**

The sounding of the drum is the heartbeat of Mother Earth. Its rhythm reconnects us to the earth, our own mother, each time we hear it. The drum is a sacred object, and we use the drum often. There are specific drum teachings and singings that we use to assist with healing. In addition to the drum, rattles and whistles are often used in healing ceremonies.

**Life**

Life is sacred. We are dependent on it. It is not to be taken for granted. The sun, air, water, fire, and all elements of nature are essential to life. I see cities, sidewalks, and concrete as scabs on Mother Earth. They prevent Mother Earth from breathing well; they smother her. A sacred prediction talks about the eighth and final fire; that within that time the earth will become sick, children will be attacking parents and vice versa, earth will crumble, and waters will rise. This will start in the east and proceed around the earth, to the north. Earth will be cleansed and renewed. First Nations people will reclaim their sacredness. Others will seek them out to rebuild equally. Some traditional people have been preparing for this.

The sources of our beliefs and values come from revelations. These revelations come to Elders and to medicine men and medicine women. They are then passed along. Much wisdom is contained in sacred scrolls which are held by shamans. One of these scrolls resides in the Manitoba Museum.

My Kokum (grandmother) first introduced me to the teachings as a young boy. Kokum would tell me these stories from the same rocking chair. She would sit down in that chair and ask for a cup of tea, and I knew that that meant it was "story time." So I would come and sit with her and listen, and the rest of my family would leave us alone. My Kokum would tell me stories knowing that I would not understand fully until later. Wisdom from these stories did come to me as I grew. Over time, I learned also from others' grandparents, and then from connecting with people in the world, and from other Elders, shamans, and medicine people.

I had a strong awareness of being on the "Elder path" from a fairly young age. This was why intentional wisdom was shared with me by my

Kokum, who had this awareness of my "Elder path" as well—though I had to grow into it. The status of Elder is never sought; it is bestowed. Although I knew for many years that this was my path, I was surprised when the title was bestowed upon me. I was not sure I was yet ready for it.

Our history is based almost entirely on oral tradition—stories and songs—handed down to others via the elders. Teachings regarding healing and wholeness depend somewhat on the various tribal groups or societies (i.e., I am from the Medeowin Society). These rules and wisdom teachings are handed down by the elders, including teachings about healthy living—i.e., how to live, build a home, ensure the home is balanced and well, and not sick. Teachings about how to be healthy and stay healthy are embedded in our wisdom. The Medicine Wheel encompasses all teachings, and they all interlock and speak of health.

Each person is equally important, and has duties and commitment to life to be the best they can be. It is good to be reminded to live life to the fullest and to keep in mind the balance of wellness. Take water for instance. It is essential to remember its importance and how it nourishes us. Understanding and appreciating the simplicities of life are also very important. The sun rises every day, the moon sets every day. We should let life flow. But we always want to alter, change, or fix it. Because we are not happy with ourselves, we want to change our surroundings. We think it is easier to change our surroundings than to change ourselves. We would be wise to leave nature alone and live in harmony with it, rather than trying to conquer it.

**Caregiving practice**

There is an assumption that I work only with First Nations people. That is not the case; I offer care to anybody who needs it. Many Aboriginal teachings actually apply to everyone. People are human. We take care of people as much as we can with the tools that we have. I look at similarities rather than at differences. We all have similar needs and wants. I can provide spiritual care for all. Many people are spiritual but not religious, and there is a difference.

Some specific teachings are geared primarily to First Nations (similar to how Sacrament of the Sick is a ritual of Roman Catholics). I try to be there to provide emotional, physical, psychological, and spiritual support. I perform numerous ceremonies. These include medicine smudging, the pipe ceremony, the naming ceremony, the clan-giving ceremony, and the giving of traditional names. I care for people in trauma, for those who face difficult diagnoses, for those who often suffer from loneliness. I often care for those facing end of life issues and assist the dying in traveling to the other side, through traditional songs and rituals. The traditional drum often plays an important part of the ceremonies. I care for the drum and provide for patient access to the drum. I am also involved in certain rituals for the hospital, such as naming of the library section for Aboriginal works. Apart from performing the traditional Aboriginal ceremonies, I basically practice just as other Spiritual Health Specialists.[6] When Aboriginal patients are reluctant to follow the suggestions of the health care, I also stress the importance of modern medicine in balancing traditional care.

It is never impossible for me to provide spiritual care as a Traditional Aboriginal person, yet there are challenges. It is only difficult when we allow certain things to interfere. I need to remember that I am just the conduit for the Creator. A true healer or medicine man or woman will not identify as such. I just need to be calm and care for anybody who needs my care.

It is hard sometimes to deal with the build-up of pain. I feel this very strongly on behalf of my people, especially youth and the incidence of suicide among them. I find it hard to know that so many are born into unhealthy environments full of despair, where the only means of escape is, unfortunately, escaping from the family, which then creates new problems. It is painful to watch this cycle which repeats itself in terrible ways. I want to say to my people: "Let's not do it this way. Let's not have our children killing themselves. We can rise as a community."[7]

There are numerous ways that the Aboriginal tradition can enrich and supplement the field of spiritual care. The Aboriginal tradition brings a balance and simplicity and overall comfort; also, the emphasis on ritual is particularly enriching, as illustrated in the following vignette.

*One day in the early fall, I was paged to companion and provide support to a family whose loved one was a patient in our Medical Intensive Care Unit. The patient was a brother, a husband, a father, and a grandfather to those gathered around the bed, and was clearly also a friend to many who were unable to be present with him in the ICU. The family gathered was a close-knit family, and it was obvious that the patient in the bed was beloved to each one of them, and that they were already feeling the ache of his dying.*

*As the patient was nearing the end of his life, and was not conscious, the*

---

[6] Spiritual Health Specialist is the name of spiritual caregivers at the Health Sciences Centre, the largest health care center in Winnipeg, Manitoba.

[7] On a personal level, I must add that from time to time I also experience racism from hospital staff. It is subtle—reflected in a look, in actions, or in speaking.

family was pleased to have me lead them in a ritual for this gentle man. I invited them to gather around him in a circle and place their hands on him, or on one another. I offered a traditional prayer and sang a song in Ojibway. The ritual then became a time of laughter, tears, and storytelling as I invited all present to share memories and words of their time with him. We heard a story from a ten-year old grandson, who talked about walking down the country roads with his grandpa and what it felt like to hold his grandpa's hand for so many quiet walks together. We heard various family members share words and stories of the time they had known and loved him. After each one had offered words and memories, the patient's granddaughter sang a song in Ojibway that her grandpa had sung to her many times.

We then moved to the Hope Room,[8] where the ritual continued. I continued singing, chanting, and drumming, as the family gathered and prepared for the ceremony. In honour of the patient's life, and to help him along on his journey, we joined together in a smudging ceremony. I began singing a Traveling Song,[9] and the family joined in. All together, the family's voices joined as one as they sang their love to him, and as they sang their support for his journey into the next life.

Finally, we ended with each of them saying Ki-wa-ba-min, or, "we'll see you later." We left the Hope Room, returned to the MICU, and gathered once more around the bed. Once more I sang to the patient in Ojibway—and the family moved in very close. There was so much love around that bed! Twenty minutes later the patient passed away, and again we said, Ki-wa-ba-min. "We'll see you later."

The Aboriginal tradition is about being very open and nonjudgmental. It allows a person to tap into their own spirit. Awareness of our purpose and place in life and in nature is important. It offers a unique perspective and a different kind of grounding. The Tradition also provides enriching contributions to the field of spiritual care in these ways: awareness of, and emphasis on, dreams and the meaning one might find within them; awareness of our connectedness to the earth, and remembering the sacredness of all that is around us; awareness of the cycles—of the seasons, of life, of the Medicine Wheel; following the cycles of nature as part of the natural rhythm; and remembering we are not here to subdue or change

---

[8] The Hope Room is a room adjacent to our Sanctuary space and is used often in ceremonies and rituals of many kinds. The Hope Room has direct ventilation to the outdoors, so smudging in this space occurs frequently.

[9] The Travelling Song is meant to accompany the patient on his walk toward Creator and as he prepares to enter the Spirit World.

or affect nature—but that nature is what we follow. We will never succeed at changing the world; rather, we must look to ourselves to change.

## Qualities of spiritual caregivers

As I see it, there are several essential qualities of heart that a spiritual caregiver must have. They must have a pure heart that is willing to be there for anyone, with genuine love and concern, as well as respect and honor for all people. They must not be selfish, but genuinely respectful and comfortable with themselves for who they are, acknowledging their own gifts. They must believe that we are all here for a reason and have a place in life. They must be mindful that not all people are alike, but that we all have much in common. A spiritual caregiver must live with integrity and honesty.

A spiritual caregiver must have a good knowledge and understanding of what life means to them, while being respectful to all. They must understand that life is sacred and that their lives are intertwined with those of other people, including those to whom they are giving care. They must not seek to "take advantage" of life but to be receptive to where life leads. They must be respectful and especially be aware of respect that is owed to others, such as Kokums and the elderly. They must also be careful to respect the life journey of the patient and remember that they too could be in the same position someday. They must be willing to share their own knowledge and experience and realize that sickness can also be a teaching; that it is there for a reason. In any given setting, a spiritual caregiver must possess the qualities and skills of being nonjudgmental, open, accepting, kind, polite, compassionate, versed in "people skills," able to listen (not just hear), and able to see (not just look at) someone.

Though there is no "training" to be an Elder per se, deeply rooted knowledge and life experience is crucial. Also crucial is training in communication skills, empathy, perseverance, understanding of human behavior, and counseling skills. A spiritual caregiver must seek education in these things, which can come in a variety of ways. They should seek formal training in many of these areas.

We are all human. We must move forward beyond our differences and our labels. No one is exempt from pain or sickness. We all have a responsibility to our fellow human beings regardless of whether we are rabbis, priests, or elders; that is what makes us human. We are one.

# The world is one family
## Principles of Hindu spiritual care

*Dinesh C. Sharma[1]*

Rooted in such practices as *pranayama*,[2] meditation, and yoga, Hinduism has much to offer both spiritual caregivers and receivers, and to those within the faith tradition as well as to those coming from other or no faith backgrounds. To begin, I will briefly describe the core beliefs of Hinduism pertinent to spiritual care. I will then consider principles of Hindu caregiving, including practical illustrations. Finally, I will highlight key competencies for effective care.

### Core beliefs of Hinduism

To appreciate why Hinduism has something unique to offer spiritual caregiving, it is helpful to have a basic understanding of a few of the religion's core beliefs, as listed below:

- There is only one triune God.
- All living beings are divine.
- The sacred writings of Hinduism are foundational to the religion.
- The nature of creation is cyclic and eternal.
- The theory of karma—that is, "as you sow, so shall you reap"—teaches us that a balance exists in the universe, and that, to some extent, we are masters of our destiny. We create karma through our thoughts, words, and actions.
- The soul is immortal and will return to live in a new body after death of the former through reincarnation. The ultimate goal of

---

[1] Pandit Dinesh C. Sharma wishes to pay his oblation to the lotus feet of his guru (spiritual teacher), and all sages, and dedicates this essay to them.

[2] Pranayama is a Sanskrit word meaning "extension of the *prana* or breath," or "extension of the life force," and can be simply defined as "rhythmic control of breath."

human life is to attain *moksha* (liberation), or to know God, and this is possible only when all karmas are dissolved.
- According to Hindu scriptures, it is easier to achieve self-realization, that is, divine knowledge, with the help and guidance of an able guru (spiritual teacher).

In addition to those key beliefs, Hindu scriptures prescribe ten *Vedic Yama* (restraints) and ten *niyama* (practices). The ten Vedic restraints include *ahimsa* (non-violence), *satya* (always speak the truth), *asteya* (refrain from stealing), *brahmacahrya* (chastity or divine conduct), *kshama* (patience and forgiveness), *dhriti* (steadfastedness), *daya* (compassion), *arjava* (honesty), *mitahara* (moderate appetite), and *shaucha* (purity or external and internal cleanliness).

The ten Vedic practices include remorse, contentment, charity, faith, worship, scripture listening or reading, cognition, *vrata* (sacred vows), *jap* (recitation of God's name, sometimes aided by a rosary), and austerity. Those who follow the discipline, practices, and principles just highlighted are likely to live a healthy, happy, and long life.

## Sacred writings

Followers of Hinduism refer to the religion as *Sanatana Dharma*—meaning "the eternal law." The foundation of Sanatana Dharma rests on four pillars, each known as a Veda, meaning "divine knowledge" or "ultimate reality." The mantras in the Vedas are the words revealed to sages by God. Originally, the Veda was a single oral collection of mantras, but, over time, the single tradition was divided into four books—*Rig-Veda, Yajurveda, Samaveda,* and *Atharvaveda.*

Four *upavedas* (or "sub-vedas") also exist, though lists vary somewhat as to what is included. The most pertinent upaveda to our topic of spiritual caregiving is the *Ayurveda* (*Ayur* means "life"), dealing with the prevention of disease and preservation of life. Alongside the Ayurveda, the *Charanavyuha* includes three other upavedas: the *Dhanurveda*, associated with combat skills; the *Gandharvaveda*, relating to music and dance; and the *Sashtrashastra*, affiliated with military science.

## God in Hindu philosophy

Though Vedic philosophy holds that there is only one God—and that this God is eternal, unchangeable, omnipresent, omniscient, and omnipenetrating—it is not possible to give a comprehensive definition of God within the framework of Hinduism, as people see God in different forms and by different names. God is the inner soul of every being, and every human is part of the Divine consciousness. God is infinite (Atharvaveda 10.8.12); God is immortal (Rigveda 10.48.5); God is beneficial and a judicious friend (Yajurveda 36.9). We might also talk about God by understanding what God is not, which is known as Neti neti ("not this, nor that")—God cannot be seen, cannot be specified, is without color, and without eyes or ears.

While many Hindus believe in roughly 330 million gods and goddesses, this is not contradictory to the monotheistic faith. According to the Rigveda (1.164.46), "God is one, though sages call God by different names." In general, Hindus believe in the trinity of the *Brahma* (Creator), *Vishnu* (Preserver), and *Shiva* (Destroyer).

## Hinduism and community

Consistent with the recognition of God as one, though with many names, *Sanatana Dharma's* philosophy and traditions are universal, comprehensive, and inclusive. The prayers, mantras, principles, and guidelines from the Hindu scriptures are meant for the benefit of all humanity, not just for Hindus. A well-known mantra from the *Brihadaranyaka Upanishad* models this universality:

*Om sarve bhavantu sukhinah*
*Sarve santu nir-aamayaah*

*Sarve bhadraanni pashyantu*
*Maa kashchid-duhkha-bhaag-bhavet.*

May everyone be joyful!
May everyone be healthy!

May everyone look to the good of others!
May no one in the world suffer!

Historically, members of any given community were classified into four categories based on vocation, as found in Bhagavad Gita, 18.41–45—the *Brahmana* (teacher), the *Kshtriva* (protector), the *Vaishya* (nourisher), and the *Shudra* (worker). Rohit Mehta states, however, that "this is a functional classification of humankind, but behind it one can see the comprehension of the psychological attitude of man. The fourfold classification has both a social and an individual significance. In its social setting, it indicates an ideology of social integration."[3]

The mantra of Vasudhaiva Kutumbakam affirms that the entire world is one family—a bold and powerful statement. Every human being is a temple in which God resides, and any help or service rendered to a fellow being is considered as service to God.

## Spiritual care practice
### Health and healing: Origin of Ayurveda

The practice of *Ayurveda*, or "the knowledge for long life," is a holistic treatment, and includes caring for the mind, body, and spirit—the most sacred three dimensions of human life. As the name suggests, Ayurveda is a science of life as well as an art of living, and is applicable to all human beings. It is based on the premise that the universe is made of five elements: air, fire, water, earth, and ether. These elements are represented in humans by three doshas, or energies: *Vata* (air and ether elements), *Kapha* (water and earth elements) and *Pitta* (fire and water elements). Ayurveda endeavors to restore harmony of the above doshas through cleansing, palliative measures, and the treatment of underlying cause.[4]

Health is a natural state of existence—in fact, according to the Taittiriya Shaka of the Krishna Yajurveda (2.3.11), every human being is born with the innate potential for living a healthy life of one hundred years or more. The teachings of Swami Satchidananda instruct us to keep our bodies strong, to care for them gently, and to live in such a way that makes them healthy. He says, "The body is a vehicle of divine expression, as are all forms of creation. To become a good instrument of the divine, maintain your health. Have an easeful body, a peaceful mind, and a useful life."[5]

Illness, however, can come from the type of food we eat, lifestyle choices, or the environment we find ourselves in. Prevention of illness and maintenance of good health go together in life. Hindu philosophy, however, affirms that each human body is capable of healing itself. While a physician can aid in the healing of the body and the spiritual caregiver can help in restoring peace of mind, it is the care receiver who plays the

---

[3] Rohit Mehta, *From Mind to Super Mind: A Commentary on the Bhagavad-Gita* (Delhi: Motilal Banarsidass Publishers Private Limited, 1995), 186.

[4] N. A. Murthy and D. P. Pandey, *Ayurvedic Cure for Common Diseases* (New Delhi: Orient Paperback, 1997), 1, 29.

[5] Cited by Swami Sarvaananda, "The Hindu Chaplain," *Hinduism Today* (Magazine Web Edition: July, August–September, 2009). Swami Sarvaananda, PhD, BCC, became the first Hindu chaplain in the United States in 2001. She is a disciple of the late Swami Satchidananda. [E]

most vital role in their own healing. Dr. R. L. Kashyap observed that there are four basic methods of healing found in the Hindu scriptures: the willpower of the person, openness, recital of mantras, and communication.[6] He explains that in order to have a happy and fulfilled life, we must make use of and nourish our willpower, fortitude, and quietude. These resources, however, need replenishing, and the mantras, discussed later, can help us in this restoration.[7]

### Willpower

A patient's thoughts can be both their greatest resource in overcoming illness and their greatest obstacle. In harnessing control of thoughts, willpower plays a vital role in the recovery of any person. According to Hindu scriptures, humans are made by their belief—what they believe, they are. Sri Aurobindo asserts, "Disease is needlessly prolonged and ends in death more often than is inevitable, because the mind of the patient supports and dwells upon the disease of the body.[8]

Helping patients uncover a sense of strength in themselves will help them recover more quickly. Reverend Mother from Sri Aurobindo Ashram, India, writes that everything you do should be done in "a spirit of complete surrender." You should do your best, while still placing the final outcome in the hands of the Divine.[9]

### Positive energy and pranayama

Often, the problem a patient suffers from is the result of negative energy affecting a part of their mind, soul, or body. In most cases, unfortunately, the person in need of care does not know how to harness positive energies, often due to lack of faith and the negative attitude that generally accompanies illness or traumatic situations. Helping patients develop a positive attitude and faith in their capacity to help themselves greatly assists the healing process.

While helping to build the self-esteem of patients is a longer-term undertaking, pranayama is a breath tool that might immediately affect overall health for any given patient, for everyone is always breathing and will do so until the end. In order to assist a patient in this way, we should guide the patient to think positive thoughts, reminding them that, with each breath, illness leaves their body while healing power enters in. As

---

[6] Dr. R. L. Kashyap, *Shanti Mantras* (Bangalore: Institute of Vedic Culture, 2009), vii, xi, 17.

[7] Ibid.

[8] Mother Aurobindo Ghose, *On Thoughts and Aphorisms* (Sri Aurobindo Ashram: 1984), 324.

[9] Ibid, 327.

we become more confident in assisting patients with their breathing, we might further train them to hold different postures so that good energy might flow through their bodies and on to specific areas.

Another way of assisting the patients in their breathing is to actually match one's breath to that of the care receiver, who might be breathing either too slowly or too quickly, and then slowly change our breathing to the appropriate pace.

**The power of mantras**

The next step after right breathing involves the power of mantras. I strongly believe that mantras and prayers have healing powers, though science has not yet found a fully satisfactory explanation. My belief in the effects of prayer is only strengthened by my personal visits with patients. In the following paragraphs, I will provide a few examples of the healing power of prayer that I have witnessed in caregiving situations.

One afternoon, I received a call that a lady in her early sixties had a brain hemorrhage. When I reached the hospital she was unstable and speaking out of context. Her forty-year-old son was in tears and holding her hand. I first consoled the son and asked permission to sit beside him. "Uncle," he said, "she went shopping and felt very sick. Immediately she called for an ambulance and now here she is." The elderly woman mumbled something difficult to understand. With the son's permission I took her left hand in mine and started to chant a few mantras, and, to the amazement of her son, she calmed down quickly. Because the chanting of the mantras brought the woman some measure of peace, I began daily visits, sometimes even coming multiple times in the same day. After brain surgery, the woman fully recovered, and I believe this was largely due to the miraculous nature of prayer.

At another time, I was approached by the family of a young woman after she had started her fourth treatment of chemotherapy. My wife and I visited their home the same day. I talked to the parents first and then to the young woman. I listened, showed empathy, and comforted the care receiver. A bit scared and uneasy, I invoked my guru's spiritual powers and started to pray while my wife held the patient's hand. The following verbatim on this caregiving situation further illustrates my views and the practice of spiritual care from a Hindu perspective.

**Case study**

A young woman in her early twenties sat in her bedroom, in both distress and pain. A small dog was by her side and her father was present. We knew this family through our local temple, and it was at her parents' request that my wife and I visited the family. We learned that she was suffering from cancer and had already had four therapies. Despite all her pain and discomfort, she appeared receptive and eager for our visit.

C = Care receiver
S = Spiritual care specialist
F = Father

The father received us at the door and directed us to the living room.

F   Namaste, Mrs. and Mr. Sharma.
S   Thank you, John, for inviting us to your home. We are glad we can be with your family at this time.
S   If you don't mind, please tell us a little bit about your daughter's health condition.
F   Mr. S. (He was holding back his tears, and I tried to comfort him with a slight pat on his back.) Mr. S., my daughter was fine until she noticed a small growth on her neck. We went to the family doctor, and he prescribed an antibiotic that she took for a month, but it didn't help. (He continued to narrate the ordeal that the family was going through, including their many sleepless nights.)
S   I can understand your feelings, John . . . it is hard to believe that your own child is so sick. (I touched his hand, comforted him, and requested that he pull himself together, especially in front of their daughter—I asked him whether a glass of water would help.)
F   Thank you, Mr. S. I feel relieved talking to you.
S   We would like to talk to your daughter, if you don't mind.
F   Sure. (He pointed toward a room upstairs, and we followed him into their daughter's room.)
S   Hello, P., I am Dinesh Sharma, a spiritual caregiver, and this is my wife, R.
C   Hi uncle, I know you from the temple.
S   Is it OK with you if my wife stays here?
C   Yes, by all means. (She was speaking in a mild voice, and her pain was tangible.)
S   I just talked with your father about your illness. Do you mind speaking with us for a few minutes?
C   Of course I will speak with you.
S   Please tell me about your health.
C   One morning I found a lump in my neck, so my parents took me to

our family doctor. He prescribed some medicine, but it did not help, so my father insisted that I see a specialist. (There was a moment of silence. I tried to comfort her by holding her hand.) Finally, I was diagnosed with this dreadful disease.

S  I am very sorry to hear about your ordeal.
C  Do you think I will survive this cancer? (Her father had left the room, and I was surprised by the directness of the question but maintained composure.)
S  I am not a doctor, but I have seen many patients recover from cancer ... I am confident that you will be fine with the quality medical care you are receiving.
C  Hmm (as if she was not sure.) ... It is good to talk to you, but I am tired. Would you mind saying some prayers for me? (I read the Sanskrit prayers in English: "God takes us from the non-being to true being, from the darkness to the light, from death to immortality. Om! Peace! Peace! Peace." It appeared that she liked the tune of the mantra and smiled faintly.)
C  Please do come again.
S  Thank you, I will. Take care.

After leaving the young woman's room, I talked to the father and agreed to come daily for at least a week and once a week thereafter. I left with a heavy heart and recited a mantra to care for my own distress. The next day, I received notice that the girl wished to speak with me again.

*2nd Visit*

The young woman was finishing her breakfast in her bedroom. She insisted that I have some coffee, an offer I accepted.

S  How are you feeling today?
C  Not well.
S  Was there a reason you called for me?
C  Yes, I have two questions on my mind. First, what if I do not recover from this illness? And, second, I am concerned about my studies. (She was in her second year at the university.)
S  Yesterday I reminded you that you are getting the best treatment available in the medical field. Rest is important—only you can help yourself.
C  How might I help myself?
S  Think only about your health, and do not focus on the cancer. You can believe that you are getting better day by day. Have you heard

about the rule of 20/80?
C  I'm not sure. Would you mind telling me?
S  The rule of 20/80 is that twenty percent is what has happened to you, and eighty percent is how you react to the situation. Instead of focusing on "why me?" you should focus on overcoming this disease.
C  Thank you, but how do I do this?
S  You should make a promise to yourself that you will be happy and always focus on your health. Do not worry about your studies right now. For now, you should concentrate on getting better.
C  Thanks, that really takes the burden off of me ... Uncle, please suggest some prayers that I might recite.
S  You can recite many prayers, but it is best to recite "Om Gum Ganpate Namaha," (meaning, "I pray to Eternal Supreme consciousness, Ganesh. He is beyond the three attributes of humans. It is by contemplating on Ganesh, in the heart, that Brahama creates, Vishnu preserves and Rudra absorbs the creation") and ask for good health.
C  Thank you. I feel much better. (I thanked her and wished her good luck.)

I continued to visit this young woman from time to time, and she has shown remarkable progress and gratitude. I always reminded her that her recovery was due to her positive attitude and continued focus on self-care. To everyone's great surprise, the young woman's level of pain and unease was reduced significantly after the next chemotherapy treatment. The woman survived the illness and resumed her normal daily life. Both the patient and her family firmly believe that the guru's grace and the powers of the mantra were essential to her healing. I also believe that the family's deep commitment and faith played an important role in the young woman's recovery.[10]

---

[10] Nalini Tarakeshwar and colleagues studied and sought to measure religious coping—that is, the function of religious beliefs and practices in times of crisis—among Hindus. They found that, similar to results obtained with other religious traditions, religious coping for Hindus serves five main functions: finding meaning, gaining control, gaining comfort and closeness to the Divine, gaining intimacy with others, and achieving life transformation. Those researchers developed a Hindu Religious Outcome 20-item scale assessing the degree to which involvement in Hindu pathways lead to valued outcomes (e.g., "Practicing yoga/meditation brings me mental peace and stability"). They also created a 27-item scale assessing degree of involvement in four Hindu pathways: devotion, ethical action, knowledge, and restraint (e.g., "How often do you perform puja in honor of your deity?" [Path of Devotion]). N. Tarakeshwar, K. I. Pargament, & A. Mahoney, "Initial Development of a Measure of Religious Coping Among Hindus," *Journal of Community Psychology* 31, no. 6 (2003): 607–28; and, by the same authors, "Measures of Hindu Pathways: Development and Preliminary Evidence of Reliability and Validity," *Cultural Diversity and Ethnic Minority Journal* 9, no. 4 (2003): 377–94.

Commitment to follow-up, evident in the case studies provided above, enables the professional caregiver the ability to monitor the effect of therapy and the healing process. It may also help to avoid the relapse of the ailment and provides material for later assessments.

## Competencies for fruitful spiritual care

Spirituality is an integral part of ancient Indian health, both in philosophy and practice. In providing health care, there are three basic covenants in the Indian system that provide the foundation of *Ayurveda*—that one is capable, available, and of unquestionable character. Caregivers should have thorough knowledge of the subject, as well as purity of both heart and body. They should be free from vanity, egotism, and boastfulness and should show regard for decent behavior, speech, and dress. They should be respectful to patients as well as to their patients' conditions.

A true and professional spiritual caregiver should be courteous, self-controlled, compassionate, abstemious, modest, and have a passion for learning. In the Hindu practice of spiritual care, knowledge and action are complementary to each other. Knowledge without action is futile, and action without knowledge can be dangerous. According to Hindu scriptures there are two types of knowledge which any good spiritual caregiver will both seek and acquire: *apara-vidya*, which involves the knowledge of the material world; and *para-vidya*, or knowledge of the divine, leading to self-realization. In fact, Hindu philosophy holds that spiritual healing occurs when the soul is finely in tune with the Brahman (Creator).

Hindu scripture describes the qualities a caregiver should have:

> He who knows only the theory but is not proficient in practice gets bewildered on confronting a patient, just as a crowd feels afraid on the battlefield. Only the wise person who knows both theory and practice is capable of obtaining success, just as only a two-wheeled chariot is useful in the battlefield.
> —Sushruta Samhita[11]

Caregivers should have, again, both knowledge and practice, theory and action. A good caregiver will know how to provide spiritual care in diverse situations and circumstances. They will have a wide knowledge in related realms, including the emotional and socio-spiritual fields. Practically, they will model a healthy self-esteem, which will convey a positive image to the care receiver. They should show empathy toward

---

[11] David Frawley and Ranade Subhash, *Ayurveda: Nature's Medicine* (Twin Lakes, WI: Lotus Press, 2001), 193.

the values and beliefs of the patient, as well as sensitivity to the social and cultural beliefs of others. A good caregiver will communicate well and behave in such a way that care receivers feel comfortable and understood. They must also have the ability to hold their own beliefs with integrity and without compromise, while not imposing or super-imposing their own personal beliefs or values onto the patient.

> That person alone is fit to nurse or to attend the bedside of a patient who is cool-headed and pleasant in his demeanor, does not speak ill of anybody, is strong and attentive to the requirements of the sick, and strictly and indefatigably follows the instructions of the physician.[12]

Similarly, Charaka wrote that any attendant should "be devoted to the patient, have purity of mind and body, and be intelligent or clever."[13]

## Action

As mentioned previously, we must have a desire and a plan if we hope to have good health, and remembering the effects of karma might assist us in maintaining that desire and creating a plan, even in dire circumstances. In care and counseling, the understanding that each action has a reaction that will somehow, someday, bring balance makes it easier to understand and accept a situation one has not caused directly—such as the impending death of a loved one. Remembering the balance of karma might help individuals have greater acceptance and even assist them in surrendering to what unfolds. When we remember that there is a reason behind everything, it becomes the person's duty to deal with the present and not resort to pondering the "what ifs" of the past that might have changed the present. Instead, plans can be made, action taken, that all might move forward.

Holistic presence might come about when action and knowledge come together and under the right circumstances. This presence might help the care receiver feel safe, comfortable, protected, and understood, and often results in a sensed connectedness and hope. Holistic presence that is a byproduct of appropriate knowledge applied during a care visit is not a complementary therapy, but is rather the correct, complete, and cohesive therapy, often able to produce overall satisfaction. In the words of Rohit Mehta, "right action is possible only if there is right perception.

---

[12] Ibid.

[13] Vern L. Bullough and Bonnie Bullough, *The Care of the Sick, the Emergence of Modern Nursing* (London: Neal-Watsin Academic Publication Inc, 1979), 24.

And right perception . . . is that condition of the human mind in which it is capable of total and undistracted attention, freed from confusion of thought, and not caught in the play of opposites."[14]

### Communication through quietude

In Hindu spiritual care, it is believed that it is best for a caregiver to be in a state of silence and deep quietness, or *quietude*. This quietude is the state in which the mind is focused on listening to the other person empathetically, and is often called "active listening." Effective listening will help build the care receiver's will-power and self-confidence and creates an overall positive attitude. Inner-stillness—just being, not doing—is a great healing force and essential in assisting patients and families as they deal with turbulent emotions. Inner-stillness brings with it outer stillness.

Hindu caregivers in North America may encounter particular communication challenges, especially in issues of culture and language. An important example is that, though first-generation Hindu immigrants may have a good understanding of English, our patients may not always understand our speech. In any event, we caregivers need to make an extra effort to communicate clearly.[15]

### Challenges in interfaith spiritual caregiving and what Hinduism might offer

It is my belief that basic traits are held in common by all faith-based spiritual care systems. On the surface, individuals look different, but we are all human and of equal value—we are all made of the same basic elements. In the same way, the spiritual needs of different faith groups are similar but with a few external differences. All care receivers need unconditional comfort and understanding, regardless of their religious tradition. Indeed, Swami Vivekananda has stated that we should let the poor, the illiterate, the ignorant, the afflicted, be our God; we must know that service to them alone is the highest religion. In other words, any caregiver should provide services to a patient in need as if they were serving God, regardless of their religion or lack of religion.

The fundamental Hindu principle that "truth is one; though seers express it in many ways," is a cornerstone for good interfaith spiritual

---

[14] Mehta, *From Mind to Super Mind*, 186.

[15] For a helpful discussion of caring for Hindus in Canada and the United States in light of specific challenges related to cultural differences and family and marriage in particular, see Anu R. Sharma, "Psychotherapy with Hindus," in *Handbook of Psychiatry and Religious Diversity*, ed. P. Scott Richards & Allen E. Bergin (Washington, DC: American Psychological Association, 2000), 341–65.

care.[16] The caregiver must respect religious differences while acknowledging that there is an essence of sameness, believing that truth, joy, love, and light might be found on any path.

Diversity does exist, however, and always presents an opportunity for learning. In these situations we need to practice mutual respect and understanding. The best approach in multifaith interactions is to try to know and understand those other traditions and backgrounds and accept them on their terms. Hindu chaplains or spiritual caregivers should have a working knowledge of other faiths and, especially, Judeo-Christian spiritual care, as the majority of care receivers in North America are from the Judeo-Christian tradition, broadly speaking. Consequently, acquaintance with Judeo-Christian beliefs and rituals is imperative. When I meet care receivers who are non-believers, I seek to listen and, whenever possible, talk to them about using the inherent energy flowing through every living creature that might help them meet any challenge.

Finally, it is the nature of a chaplain's work to care for anyone impacted by crisis on a daily basis. We help individuals face transitions, assist survivors in coming to terms with grief, handle mundane matters that accompany death, and find ways to walk with the living as they move ahead in their lives, and all this on a daily basis. It is beneficial for every individual, regardless of faith background, to have assistance in finding meaning, hope, and moving forward.

In conclusion, I would like to share a teaching of my spiritual guru: "It is said that a healthy mind and an enlightened spirit will certainly help to create a healthy body. In my opinion, spiritual health care is more a philosophy of healthy living, love, empathy, happiness, peace, trust and enlightenment, rather than a philosophy of religion." *Om Shanti . . . Shanti . . . Shanti*—let there be peace within us and among us.

---

[16] Rig Veda Samhita 1.164.46.

# Three *yanas* for wise caring

## A Buddhist perspective on spiritual care

*Danny Fisher*

One of the misconceptions in the popular understanding of Buddhism is that it is a monolithic tradition—pretty much the same thing whether you are practicing as a *zendo*, a *vihara*, or a *gompa*.[1] In fact, Buddhism is made up of a constellation of schools, communities, traditions, and groups so vast and varied that many in the field of Buddhist Studies have begun to make a rhetorical switch to talking about Buddhist *religions*. For years, *The Buddhist Religion*, first authored by Richard H. Robinson and then co-authored by Willard Johnson in subsequent editions, has set the gold standard for textbooks on the subject. The most recent edition, which added Thanissaro Bhikkhu as an author, took the bold step of changing the title to *Buddhist Religions*.[2] From my vantage point as a theological educator and chaplain, this reality of Buddhist diversity makes doing any kind of systematic work inordinately difficult and often yields specious results; it is better, I think, as some new young scholars have argued, to speak of Buddhism in broad denominational terms.

### Foundations

My own spiritual home is the Rosemead Buddhist Monastery in Rosemead, California, just down the road from where I teach at the Fo Guang Shan Buddhist-founded University of the West. The monastery is the headquarters of the Los Angeles Buddhist Union (LABU) and home to my

---

[1] For the readers ease, diacritical marks have been removed from Sanskrit, Pali, and other languages terms. In some cases, these terms have also been phoneticized.

[2] Richard H. Robinson, Willard L. Johnson, and Thanissaro Bhikkhu, *Buddhist Religions: A Historical Introduction* (Belmont, CA: Wadsworth, Cengage Learning, 2005).

primary teacher Bhante Chao Chu, who has a deep and sincere commitment to Buddhist ecumenicism. As an ordained lay Buddhist minister in the International Order of Buddhist Ministers—which is overseen by Bhante Chao Chu and operates under the auspices of both the LABU and the intrafaith Buddhist Sangha Council of Southern California—my responsibilities include observing the ten precepts and rules of conduct that have been devised, and supporting the LABU in its work of presenting "the universal truths of Sakyamuni Buddha's teachings as recorded in the Pali Canon" and mission to "promote practice in meditation, mindfulness, Dharma study, and community engagement." This involves serving and being of support to Buddhists of all kinds (and others) however I can. This approach has been the defining characteristic of my time in and preparing for Buddhist ministry.

By virtue of my education at the Shambhala Buddhist-founded Naropa University in Boulder, Colorado, the Shambhala Buddhist tradition has been very important to me in my spiritual journey as well. Shambhala Buddhism has roots in the Kagyu and Nyingma schools of Tibetan Buddhism, and was established as a unique Buddhist path by the noted teacher Chögyam Trungpa Rinpoche (1939–1987). In traditional Tibetan Buddhism, the kingdom of Shambhala refers to a mythical, idealized place. Trunpga Rinpoche, however, taught that Shambhala could be conceived of as a vision for a very possible enlightened society. The key to realizing enlightened society, he suggested, was touching in with our own basic goodness, fearlessness, dignity, and compassion. Rinpoche believed that these qualities were the outcome of a deep and mature Buddhist practice. He also taught that Buddhism did not have a monopoly on the ability to cultivate them; on the contrary, he noted that we could see "spiritual warriorship" in many different places. It can be found in all the world's wisdom traditions, from the code of the samurai to the experiences of the desert mystics to the deeds of the knights errant to the Native American way of life, and so on. In a bit of wisdom that I think is applicable to the practice of professional chaplaincy, Rinpoche once said:

> While everyone has a responsibility to help the world, we can create additional chaos if we try to impose our ideas or our help upon others. Many people have theories about what the world needs. Some people think that the world needs communism; some people think that the world needs democracy; some people think that technology will save the world; some people think that technology will destroy the world. The Shambhala teachings are not

based on converting the world to another theory. The premise of the Shambhala vision is that, in order to establish an enlightened society for others, we need to discover what inherently we have to offer the world. So, to begin with, we should make an effort to examine our own experience [and help others to do the same], in order to see what [is there] that is of value in helping ourselves and others to uplift their existence.[3]

Trungpa Rinpoche's ideas and the Shambhala principles have permeated much of my education. At the end of the day, however, my own deepest commitments are to Buddhist ecumenicism, interfaith understanding, and professional spiritual care and counseling. Part of working toward this has been my training and work as a chaplain.

Despite my own approaches to both Buddhism and religion broadly as incredibly diverse phenomena, I am moved by an observation from Lewis R. Lancaster, the mighty and prolific Buddhist scholar (and University of the West colleague) who was the first-ever recipient of the PhD in Buddhist Studies from the groundbreaking program at the University of Wisconsin-Madison. He says:

> The frustrating thing . . . about the Buddhist tradition is that at every level, whenever we define it, we have already lost it. I ask myself how people can know that they are Buddhists. The one thing that all forms of Buddhism hold as their highest ideal is compassion. That seems as close to a universal answer as I can find . . . Buddhists, when they talk about compassion, say that if you are enlightened, you will have a deeper response to suffering. If insights do not lead to compassion, then it is not what the Buddha experienced at his enlightenment. This view makes an enormous difference.[4]

The Tibetan traditions which have been so helpful to me—and which are often said to contain the entirety of Buddhism's diverse teachings—certainly share this view. It is important, though, to point out that there is a gradual deepening of our understanding of compassion as we progress through the *yanas* (literally, vehicles), or paths of practice, within this system.

The Buddha himself said he taught only two things—suffering and the end of suffering. In understanding the *yanas*—not to mention developing

---

[3] Chögyam Trungpa Rinpoche, *Shambhala: The Sacred Path of the Warrior* (Boston: Shambhala Publications, 2003), 10–11.

[4] Dairyu Michael Wenger, *Dharma Days* (Petaluma, CA: Pomegranate Communications, 2009).

what might be called a "Buddhist pastoral theology"—it is helpful to remember this fundamental aspect of Buddhist pedagogy. Compassion is the highest ideal of all Buddhists as they negotiate *samsara* (the painful cycle of life, death, and rebirth) and *nirvana* (awakening, freedom from that painful cycle). In the first *yana*, known as the *Shravakayana* (or, the Vehicle of the Hearers, or Vehicle of the Disciples), the Buddha's original teachings on the Four Noble Truths are of primary importance. These teachings articulate our existential condition and how it is that our suffering can end. They are: (1) the truth of the stress and dissatisfaction that come from realities that characterize our human condition; (2) the truth of the origins of this suffering in our grasping and craving; (3) the truth that the cessation of our suffering depends on giving up our self-centered grasping and craving; and (4) the truth of the path leading to the cessation of suffering (which is known as the Noble Eightfold Path). The Four Noble Truths explicitly detail our situation, as well as present us with options—awakening is possible, and there are certain methods for living this life more fully. Those methods are encapsulated in the Noble Eightfold Path: right view, right intention, right speech, right action, right livelihood, right effort, right mindfulness, right concentration. These eight can be whittled down into three categories, or three trainings: *shila* (morality/ethics/virtuous conduct; this includes right speech, right action, right livelihood), *samadhi* (meditation/mental development; this includes right effort, right mindfulness, right concentration), and *prajna* (insight/wisdom; this includes right view and right intention). These three trainings undercut a sense of self and serve as the antidote to suffering by offering a path—a way to make a relationship with our suffering, a way of changing our entire experience of ourselves and our world, a way of experiencing ourselves and our world with the knowledge of no-self and the other realities taught by the Buddha. The three trainings are a path presented to us so that we might learn to settle into the truth of things as they are, and that we might minimize the amount of suffering we perpetuate in ourselves and upon others. This is why it is said in the *Samyutta Nikaya* and the *Visuddhimagga* that "when a wise one, well established in *shila*, / develops *Samadhi* and *prajna*, / then as a *bhikkshuni*, ardent and sagacious, / she succeeds in disentangling the tangle."[5]

A key soteriological tool in this endeavor to minimize and ultimately end one's own suffering—and then be of greatest benefit to others—is the cultivation of awareness through the practice of mindfulness meditation,

---
[5] Quoted by Acharya Judith Simmer-Brown on September 29, 2003.

which is simply bringing our attention to the present moment with the help of an object such as the breath. Taught by the Buddha as the very foundation of the path toward the cessation of suffering, mindfulness meditation has proven to be enormously useful outside of Buddhist religious contexts as well.[6] Mindfulness also plays a vitally important role for Buddhists engaged in professional chaplaincy work, as the following example demonstrates:

*As they come into the morgue, the EMTs are delicate and deliberate—breaking the silence with the softest of whispers, and only when they absolutely must. Once inside, the gurney is gently positioned beside the cold chamber, where the small body beneath the sheet will be stored after all of the intake paperwork is finished. Chaplains are always present in these situations, and that is how I've found myself here—a fly on the wall.*

*Standing there, watching over the team as they wait, I catch myself turning away from what lies before us all. I gaze down at surgical instruments or look around the room for something else to distract me. Child fatalities are difficult to bear, even if you see them from time to time—indeed, they can be too much even to look at. Being close to such a loss is affecting, no doubt about it, and there is an impulse to turn away.*

*But I bring my attention back to the gurney and those in the room, remembering that it's my job to not turn away from suffering. As a chaplain, I'm there first and foremost to bear witness. I can offer care and counsel, of course, but I won't be able to do either of those things very well if I'm actively avoiding that which arises. Chaplaincy is about looking closely and listening deeply—trying to understand people and situations exactly as they are.*

*This is certainly consistent with my own Buddhist practice. In my spiritual life, I do my best to reduce unhelpful and harmful habitual tendencies and cultivate beneficial, truly compassionate qualities. I do this by trying to bring my attention to the present moment with deliberate, nonjudgmental awareness. It behooves my professional life to carry this discipline through to my work with others.*

*I recognize, too, the potential in staying with and exploring that unbearable feeling. When I'm able to just be with the feeling instead of avoiding it, I am able to understand it and then learn not to fear or try to avoid it. I turn into the suffering so that I might become braver and of greater benefit to others . . .*

---

[6] In 2007, for example, the National Center for Complementary and Alternative Medicine, one of the National Institutes of Health, found that more than 20 million Americans had used meditation techniques derived from Buddhist or Hindu traditions for various health reasons in the previous twelve months.

In the second *yana*, the *Mahayana* (or, Great Vehicle), the *bodhisattva* ideal, is of principal importance. A rough translation of the term bodhisattva gives us "a being who is oriented towards enlightenment."[7] According to one of my teachers, Acharya Judith Simmer-Brown, bodhisattvas are characterized by a number of important qualities.[8] First, they do not think of things in terms of attainment; we may have certain goals or ideas of attainment that we apply to our spiritual practice such as becoming a more "peaceful" or "nice" person, but bodhisattvas are operating on another level entirely. Second, they "abide by means of *prajnaparamita*"—the "Perfection of Transcendent Wisdom," the way that has no sense of duality and no emotional or conceptual obscurations of mind. In other words, they do not abide in a particular *place* but in a particular *way*. Third, and on a similar note, they transcend that which is false, such as the notion of duality. Fourth, they are fearless—they properly confront that which is frightening; they have the courage of lions.[9] Fifth, they attain complete *nirvana*, *anuttara samyak sambodhi* ("unsurpassable, true, complete enlightenment"). To put it in Acharya Simmer-Brown's words, it is this awakening that gives the bodhisattva her ability to "make light where once was dark." Finally, a bodhisattva is joyful—they enjoy freedom, and their spontaneous action is joyful.[10]

The bodhisattva derives these qualities through her cultivation of *bodhichitta*—the "awakened heart-mind," the basis for enlightenment in the *Mahayana*. When we speak of *bodhichitta*, we are speaking of two aspects: absolute and relative *bodhichitta*. Absolute *bodhichitta* refers to wisdom—the recognition of *shunyata*, emptiness; an understanding of the interdependent and transitory nature of all things. Relative *bodhichitta* refers to the practice of great compassion. Although these two aspects seem separate, they are, in fact, inexorably linked. If we can learn how to touch into absolute *bodhichitta*, we can learn how to make sense of relative *bodhichitta*—the absolute is directive in terms of the relative.

---

[7] Damien Keown, *Dictionary of Buddhism* (Oxford and New York: Oxford University Press, 2003), 38.

[8] This information comes from a series of courses taught by Acharya Judith Simmer-Brown at Naropa University, Boulder, CO.

[9] I am reminded of the "demon story" told in the tradition, in which a great yogi takes the seemingly counterintuitive approach to an evil spirit: if one experiences fear, he bravely looks at what scares him and requests that it be his teacher.

[10] Here, I always think of His Holiness the 14th Dalai Lama, whose happy spirit has inspired millions, within and outside of Buddhism.

When we talk about the practice of compassion in relationship to *bodhichitta*, we are generally referring to particular practices, such as the four immeasurables, *tonglen*, and especially *pranidhana* (the bodhisattva vow). The bodhisattva vow is one's formal commitment to work for the awakening of others. It is a promise to be helpful in leading others to the experience of *nirvana*. Again, this is an important undertaking for the bodhisattva in that they realize the interconnection of all beings and that no one is free until everyone is free. This being the case, other beings offer us precious opportunities to work toward this highest form of awakening; without them, there is no chance of Buddhahood. It follows, then, that we should be grateful to others for the opportunity that they offer. Hence, a famous statement from the great practitioner Dilgo Khyentse Rinpoche, who said, "The immediate causes for attainment of Buddhahood are other beings: we should be truly grateful to them."

The "great compassion of the bodhisattva" also refers to all the myriad, beneficial ways in which the bodhisattva actively extends herself out to others. It is limitless compassion, rooted in the bodhisattva's understanding of the interconnection of all beings. It is a feeling of empathy that is tempered by the wisdom of emptiness—an open-heartedness that knows no territory and is rooted in the aforementioned ethic that says no one is free until everyone is free. The practice of limitless compassion is said to be more difficult than the practice of lovingkindness; the rationale behind this provocative statement is that unlike lovingkindness, limitless compassion takes us into the realm of problems that may be unsolvable—it is simply bearing witness in the face of suffering. To put it in the terms of *Mahayana* practice, this is why it is often said that "the *Shravakayana* transcends *samsara*, but the *Mahayana* transcends *nirvana*." In the *Shravakayana*, we are conducting a precise examination of our confusion in order to curb confusion in the future, while, in the *Mahayana*, the bodhisattva re-enters confusion with the noble heart of compassion. In the *Mahayana*, the focus is less on the confusion itself than it is on the quality of wakefulness available in each situation. Wakefulness is there first, argues the *Mahayana*—confusion is merely contingent. In the *Mahayana*, we must go "through" the confusion with compassion.

This is very different from what Tibetans call "idiot compassion," which is enmeshed in confusion. It is the same feeling of empathy but without the benefit of wisdom. The bodhisattva goes beyond conventional, suffering-inducing notions of what is helpful, confronting confusion with compassion *and* wisdom. Or, as James Whitehill puts it:

Moral virtue without *shunyata*, or transforming liberation, may be shallow and weak; but *shunyata* without moral virtue is blind and dangerous. She who has accomplished awakened virtue, the merging of skilled, well-disposed, rational moral agency with self-transforming spirit, is, in contrast, deep, strong, ever-maturing, and rational...by her character and deeds she reduces suffering and promotes friendliness, compassion, joy, and peace.[11]

One way for the bodhisattva to achieve the balance of these two is through the practice of the *paramitas*. *Paramitas* literally translates "that which has reached the other shore."[12] When we speak of the *Mahayana paramitas*, we are talking about the "six perfections," or "attributes of Buddha activity," essential for a sentient being practicing on the bodhisattva path: *dana-paramita* (generosity), *shila-paramita* (discipline), *kshanti-paramita* (forbearance), *virya-paramita* (exertion), *dhyana-paramita* (meditation), and *prajna-paramita* (wisdom).[13] As His Holiness the 14th Dalai Lama of Tibet explains, the original Sanskrit implies a transcendent quality to these activities in that "unlike ordinary generosity, etc., [the six *paramitas*] are untainted by attachment and other negative emotions."[14] When one practices generosity, there often can be an egoistic edge to the undertaking. If we are practicing the virtues to be "nice," for example—so that we might be liked or impress others or make someone stop doing something that makes us uncomfortable—then we are not practicing them as *paramitas*. Similarly, we might think that the practice of the virtues will make us "good" people. If this were the case, we would again be practicing these activities for egoistic reasons.

Certainly, the conventional practices of generosity, etc., do not always come from a corrupt place. However, the conventional practices of the virtues do differ from the practice of the six *paramitas* in a very significant way. When a sentient being practices the virtues as *paramitas*, she is actively working toward dropping her sense of duality and strengthening her sense of interconnection. In other words, the bodhisattva practicing

---

[11] James Whitehill, "Buddhist Ethics in Western Context: The Virtues Approach," *Journal of Buddhist Ethics* 1 (1994), accessed February 10, 2006, http://jbe.gold.ac.uk/1/white1.html.

[12] Ingrid Fischer-Schreiber, Franz-Karl Ehrhard, and Michael S. Diener, eds., *The Shambhala Dictionary of Buddhism and Zen*, trans. Michael H. Kohn (Boston: Shambhala Publications, 1991), 169.

[13] Chögyam Trungpa Rinpoche, *Mudra* (Berkeley & London: Shambhala, 1972), 102.

[14] Tenzin Gyatso (His Holiness the 14th Dalai Lama of Tibet), *A Flash of Lightning in the Dark of Night: A Guide to the Bodhisattva's Way of Life*, trans. Geshe Thupten Jinpa (Boston & London: Shambhala Publications, 1994), 134.

the *paramitas* is deliberately chipping away at her ego. His Holiness continues, "When generosity and so forth are practiced as *paramitas*, are practiced with an understanding that the subject, object, and the action itself are all devoid of true existence, these acts become very profound and completely transcend ordinary generosity and so on."[15] Implicit in this statement is that the bodhisattva must have the proper ground and path if this is to be realized. Whitehill explicates further:

> The center of Buddhist tradition affirms that moral effort, mainly through practicing the *paramitas*, must be conjoined with meditative and transformative practices to be ultimately effective for oneself and for others. It also affirms that the practices of awakening have little foundation and less result, for oneself or others, without the frame, skills, and habit of moral practice.[16]

The following paradigm draws from the wisdom of the *Mahayana*; when we extend ourselves to others, the real inner-work deepens considerably. Working in service of her fellow sentient beings, the student/ *bodhisattva* discovers that it is impossible to be truly generous, ethical, patient, perseverant, mindful, or insightful unless she is willing to look deeply at her intentions, motivations, fears, sorrows, and growing edges. But perhaps nothing is as effective in developing this awareness at the heart-level as working with and for others. The *bodhisattva* must engage. She has to start work immediately. Of course, she needs a view, a path, guidance, support, and care, but she must come up against the sufferings and needs of others if she is going to "wake up" and support others as they attempt to do the same. To learn and grow, the *bodhisattva* has to be in community, working for the benefit of others, trying to do the very best she can with what she has each and every moment.

It seemed fitting, then, that when we began our Clinical Pastoral Education (CPE) internships we would also study and practice the *paramitas* in considerable depth as part of our Applied Theology I, a course I taught in tandem with CPE. As I worked with the *paramitas* during my rotation as a chaplain intern at a local hospital, I found that the teachings spoke to me like they never had before. The distinction between the conventional practice of the virtues and the practice of them as *paramitas* became much clearer. In struggling to practice the *paramitas* as *paramitas*, it became apparent to me just how difficult an undertaking this

---

[15] Ibid., 117.

[16] Whitehill, "Buddhist Ethics in Western Context."

was. Moreover, it became painfully obvious just how often I mistook the conventional practice of the virtues for *paramita* practice. I recognized both of these subtleties immediately.

### Interfaith practice

By way of answering whether and to what extent *Mahayana* practices, and Buddhism more broadly, make it possible to offer *interfaith* spiritual care in the sense of caring for people of other faiths, we do well to look at one example in the *paramitas*: the example of *dana-paramita* (generosity). As Acharya Simmer-Brown, has written:

> [This kind of] generosity is the virtue that produces peace, as the sutras say. Generosity is a practice which overcomes our acquisitiveness and self-absorption, and which benefits others.[17]

In this way, *dana-paramita* proves to be crucial for Buddhists doing pastoral care and counseling in a religiously plural context...

*I, a chaplain intern, sit in the room of a young male graduate student who has recently been in a car accident. I'm not assigned to his floor, but the pastoral care department put us together thinking that he might like to talk to another young male graduate student.*

*We talk about the accident. He's struggling to make meaning of this accident, even though he knows that his is not the first car accident at that horrible, complicated intersection. I invite him to tell me more about what he's thinking. He starts big, telling me about his belief in God—that He is all-knowing, but more importantly all-loving. He believes that everything happens for a reason.*

*Then he starts talking about the accident. "Is this a punishment? It's punishment, right?" My immediate impression is that this is a good guy, and here he is, this poor good guy, wracking his brain for reasons why God would put him through a car accident as retribution.*

*This is a classic, textbook case of why professional chaplaincy can be hard on Buddhist chaplains. Most professional chaplains hail from the Abrahamic faiths, and quite a lot of patient concerns revolve around the beliefs and worldviews of those traditions.*

*Not much of what this young man is saying resonates with me personally. I could reach for the things from my own tradition that help me. I could try to dispel the notions I hear that have not served me personally. But that's not right. It's not care.*

---

[17] Judith Simmer-Brown, "The Crisis of Consumerism," Mountains and Rivers Order of Zen Buddhism, accessed January 9, 2010, http://www.mro.org/mr/archive/21-3/articles/crisisofcon.html.

*What can I give this young man that really benefits him? I wonder.*

*I come back to that most fundamental, most important, of chaplaincy skills: listening. There's a disparity I can hear in what he's saying. Perhaps if I reflect that back . . .*

"I heard you say before that God is all-loving," I say.

"Yes. He loves everybody. He doesn't hate anybody."

"He loves them just as they are. He's not a judgmental, spiteful God?" I ask.

"No. Not at all. I don't believe it when people say God's like that. That's wrong. God is love."

"So then does God love everybody but you? Why would an all-loving God punish you, but love everything else in creation?"

He's gob-smacked. Clearly this loophole in his thinking has never occurred to him before.

"You know, I never noticed that . . ." he says, looking back at me, his eyes moistening.

"If God is love, I'm pretty sure that includes you too."

*I can see that he's really hearing this, and that it's affecting him—benefitting him.*

*This is dana-paramita, I think. It's like this.*

The third *yana*, the *Vajrayana* (or, Adamantine Vehicle), is the most difficult to talk about in many ways. As Reginald A. Ray writes, "In *Vajrayana* Buddhism, we are directed toward pure relative truth through the language of symbol. The [specific] symbolic language that is used in the *Vajrayana* to suggest the actual way in which the world appears is that of the *mandala*, 'sacred circle.'"[18] There are many abstruse explanations of *mandala* and the principle to be gleaned from it. For me, though, Chögyam Trungpa Rinpoche's description of the *mandala* principle as "orderly chaos" is most helpful. "It is orderly because it comes in a pattern," he writes. "It is chaos, because it is confusing to work with in that order."[19] I understand this in two ways. First, the mandala principle is a way of making sense of our relative experience of *samsara* and *nirvana*, building on everything that has come before it in the context of the three *yana* journey. Just as there are distinct ways of relating to *samsara* and *nirvana* in the *Shravakayana* and the *Mahayana*—in the *Shravakayana*, we try to understand and uproot our destructive habitual patterns, and, in the *Mahayana*, we cultivate *bodhicitta*—so too are the methods distinct

---

[18] Simmer-Brown, "The Crisis of Consumerism."

[19] Chögyam Trungpa Rinpoche, *Orderly Chaos: The Mandala Principle* (Boston: Shambhala Publications, 1991), 3.

in the *Vajrayana*. The *mandala* is the *Vajrayana* mode of organizing or systematizing the various and interconnected manifestations of wisdom and neurosis in ourselves and in the relative world. In a sense, it is in itself a profound teaching on buddha-nature. It shows us the inherently awakened quality of the seemingly chaotic relative world, as well as demonstrates the wisdom aspects of neurotic qualities of mind. The *Vajrayana* teaches us that some of our trouble comes from our attempts (in gross and subtle ways) to solidify that which is intangible—what Ray defines as "the ultimate truth of the emptiness or non-substantiality of phenomena, and of pure relative truth, pure appearance, ineffable phenomena, arising in a relational mode, based on causes and conditions."[20] Because the phenomenal world of pure appearance is beyond the scope of our traditional understanding, a new way of communicating about this experience is needed—hence the *mandala*.

Second, I understand Rinpoche's comments as pointing toward tantric practice, a unique new method of practice on the three *yana* journey. While the *yanas* are certainly interconnected, continuously developing and clarifying the wisdom of one another in a reflexive sort of way, they are nonetheless progressive—each building on the wisdom of the *yanas* that precede it, as well the progressive turnings of the Wheel of Dharma. Thus, the practitioner's work evolves from *yana* to *yana*. Ray explains: "Having attained some fruition in the [*Shravakayana*] and having trained in the *Mahayana* through taking the *bodhisattva* vow and practicing the *paramitas*, the tantric practitioner aims to fulfill his or her *bodhisattva* commitment through a path of yoga, meditation, and retreat practice."[21]

### Core competencies

In terms of a profile of wisdom in spiritual care by identifying core competencies—attitudes, knowledge, and skills—that define professional excellence, I would like to use a rubric introduced by Judith Simmer-Brown. It is her list of the six qualities of a spiritual friend in terms of the *Vajrayana* tradition.[22] In the more than five years since I encountered these teachings, they have continued to be instructive for me as I have "taken my seat" as a spiritual caregiver and counselor.

---

[20] Reginald A. Ray, *Secret of the Vajra World: The Tantric Buddhism of Tibet* (Boston: Shambhala Publications, Inc., 2002), 129.

[21] Ibid., 68.

[22] Introduced in class on March 15, 2005, and inspired in part by textual sources in the *Vajrayāna* tradition.

*The person is dedicated to your awakening—they tell you the truth*

As lay Buddhist ministers, my colleagues in the International Order of Buddhist Ministers and I are neither monastics nor formal teachers *per se*. Though we are often asked to teach and always do so when asked, our ministries are primarily about service—benefiting others however we can, from sweeping a floor to teaching dharma, and everything in between. Though the Buddhist Sangha Council of Southern California often speaks of us as being like historic *upasakas*, I see us as having more in common with the lineage of dharma protectors. As Chögyam Trungpa Rinpoche said of members of Shambhala International's "Vajra Guard," so we could say of the Council's Buddhist ministers: "Your role is maintaining the strength and dignity in a situation, making sure that, when the buddhadharma is presented, it is presented in a proper atmosphere, a clear atmosphere."[23] Given the interfaith nature of chaplaincy work, this might be translated to mean that we must carefully tune in to the needs of others—always seeking to truly understand them on their own terms as best we can, and be of benefit by helping them draw strength, inspiration, and guidance from their own beliefs and values. This is certainly a guiding principle for me both in chaplaincy and in my work as a pastoral educator.

In both higher education and ministry, another important part of communicating with those we serve is responding in genuine, sometimes very direct ways to what we discover—"telling the truth." Trungpa Rinpoche again: "If there are lots of clouds in front of the sun, your duty is to create wind so that the clouds can be removed and the clear sun can shine."[24] This, to me, is what being a good chaplain and a good professor is all about—serving others collectively and individually in such a way that "the sun can shine." Dr. Simmer-Brown once used a Ralph Waldo Emerson quote with us in the Vajrayana Texts class that I have found valuable in negotiating the critical work of the chaplain and the teacher: "Criticism should not be querulous and wasting, all knife and root-puller, but guiding, instructive, inspiring, a south wind, not an east wind."[25] Being authentic, truthful, is the only way you can "create wind"; how skillfully you can direct it depends on the quality of one's practice, which brings me to . . .

---

[23] Chögyam Trungpa Rinpoche, *True Command: The Teachings of the Dorje Kasung* (Halifax: Trident Publishing, 2005), 62.

[24] Ibid., 63.

[25] William Henry Gilman, ed., *The Journals and Miscellaneous Notebooks of Ralph Waldo Emerson* (Cambridge, MA: Harvard University Press, 1973), 88.

*They practice what they preach*

As a Buddhist minister, chaplain, and professor of chaplaincy/Buddhist theology, it is essential for me to maintain a daily practice and general "spiritual fitness." For me, this means primarily (and at the absolute minimum) keeping up with my daily practice of meditation. Obviously, one cannot attend to someone (or even really listen to or communicate genuinely with them) if he or she is not able to be right there in the present moment with that person. And, generally speaking, the people with whom one works in the context of chaplaincy will need the chaplain to be able to do this. Mindfulness meditation practice in particular is a way of cultivating an awareness of what is happening in our experience moment-to-moment. According to the Buddha himself, one who is well established in mindfulness has the following qualities:

> There is the case where a monk, a disciple of the noble ones, is mindful, highly meticulous, remembering & able to call to mind even things that were done & said long ago. He remains focused on the body in & of itself—ardent, alert, & mindful—putting aside greed & distress with reference to the world. He remains focused on feelings in & of themselves . . . the mind in & of itself . . . mental qualities in & of themselves—ardent, alert, & mindful—putting aside greed & distress with reference to the world.[26]

In this practice, we typically sit on a cushion and bring our awareness to our breath. It is learning to meet each moment on its own terms, without running away from it or trying to manipulate it or change it. It is training our mind to be present, to be there with what is. At the same time, though, we are careful to avoid the traps of samsaric mind. Trungpa Rinpoche once again:

> If you try to domesticate your mind through meditation—try to possess it by holding onto the meditative state—the clear result will be regression on the path, with a loss of freshness and spontaneity. . . . You focus your attention on the object of awareness, but then, in the same moment, you disown that awareness and go on. What is needed here is some sense of confidence—confidence that you do not have to securely own your mind, but that you can tune into its process spontaneously.[27]

---

[26] "Indriya-vibhanga Sutta: Analysis of the Mental Faculties," trans. Thanissaro Bhikkhu, *Access to Insight*, accessed November 20, 2011, http://www.accesstoinsight.org/tipitaka/sn/sn48/sn48.010.than.html.

[27] Chögyam Trungpa Rinpoche, "The Four Foundations of Mindfulness," *Shambhala*, accessed November 20, 2011, http://www.shambhala.org/teachers/vctr/fourfoundations.html.

Even a little bit of this training is beneficial in the context of chaplaincy; one of the natural results of this practice is that the practitioner is able to relate to his or her experience, and those of others, with much greater authenticity and a deeper sense of awareness. Of course, whether it is mindfulness meditation, prayer, psychotherapy, arts, sports, all of the above, or something else that gets the chaplain to this point, what is most important is that the chaplain be as fully present as possible.

At my best, I find that the work of the chaplain serves me not only to benefit others but also myself. Offering spiritual care and counseling instructs me further in becoming a truly attentive presence and careful listener in my own life. Done well, it helps me become a more present, grounded person. Indeed, over time I have found that if I want to be a truly positive spiritual presence for others, I have to give myself the gift of self-acceptance. So I come back to the cushion again and again.

*They have devotion for their teacher(s)—they are rooted with the lineage*
It seems to me that we could talk about at least three kinds of teachers in the Buddhist tradition, broadly speaking. Among these kinds of teachers, as mentioned in the Pali canon, are those in our families of origin:

> Mother & father,
> compassionate to their family,
> are called
> > Brahma,
> > first teachers,
> > those worthy of gifts
> > from their children.
> So the wise should pay them
> > > homage,
> > > honor
> > > with food & drink
> > > clothing & bedding
> > > anointing & bathing
> > > & washing their feet.
> Performing these services to their parents,
> the wise
> > > are praised right here
> > > and after death
> > > rejoice in heaven.[28]

---

[28] "Itivuttaka: The Group of Fours," trans. Thanissaro Bhikkhu, *Access to Insight*, accessed November 20, 2011, http://www.accesstoinsight.org/tipitaka/kn/iti/iti.4.100-112.than.html#iti-106.

Of course, not every person is so fortunate to have had parents worthy of such descriptions and praise. At the very least, there is a lesson to be gleaned here about the importance of family systems work—understanding from where and from whom we have come, and how our strategies for engaging and working with others have been influenced and conditioned by those relationships. Indeed, as Ronald W. Richardson has written, "past emotional [patterns] of adapting to the intensity of a relationship [continue] to affect and shape the present."[29] As chaplains, we do well then to be cognizant of our familial lineage and appreciate them, inasmuch as they have provided strengths and growing edges for our work in this very moment with others.

The second kind of teachers are those the Buddhist traditions speak of perhaps more frequently than others (and the kind that are almost certainly being referenced specifically with this particular quality): personal spiritual mentors. In all of the Buddhist traditions, one finds a good Buddhist teacher described as being someone who sees all of the student's strengths and weaknesses, and mirrors those things back to the student—even when it might be uncomfortable or even devastating. Through all of it, though, the student is nurtured and enriched in the best possible ways. As Lama Ken McLeod has written:

> When we start exploring the mystery of being, we are still mired in habituated patterns. Limited in perception to a world projected by these patterns, we do not and cannot see things as they are. We need a person, a teacher, who, standing outside our projected world, can show us how to proceed.[30]

Though the relationship is often quite challenging and difficult, the student should be experiencing support and growth on the path, inspiring a deep appreciation for the teacher. As Dilgo Khytentse Rinpoche has said so well, the student comes to recognize that "no matter what circumstances arise, the compassionate kindness of the spiritual teacher will never forsake [the student]. . . . The spiritual master is like the earth, never giving way beneath [their] feet."[31]

Third, and lastly, are all those around me. Bhante Chao Chu often tells

---

[29] Ronald W. Richardson, *Becoming a Healthier Pastor: Family Systems Theory and the Pastor's Own Family* (Minneapolis: Fortress Press, 2005), 14.

[30] Ken McLeod, *Wake Up to Your Life: Discovering the Buddhist Path of Attention* (San Francisco: Harper San Francisco, 2001), 6.

[31] Dilgo Khyentse Rinpoche, *The Hundred Verses of Advice: Tibetan Buddhist Teachings on What Matters Most*, trans. Padmakara Translation Group (Boston: Shambhala Publications, 2006), 44.

us that as Buddhist ministers we have a responsibility to serve and support the Buddhist community widely. Key to this, he says, is truly *accepting* others for who they are, not merely *tolerating* their differences. Explicit here is an attention to Buddhist ecumenicism; implicit, I think, is the suggestion of even wider, interfaith cooperation. My teacher is asking us with our training as ministers to be open and receptive and grateful for the teachers who will be put in our paths whenever we are with others. In addition, as another one of my precious teachers, Chökyi Nyima Rinpoche, has written: "Appreciate other beings with this attitude: 'With the help of these beings, I can develop the precious enlightened attitude, *bodhichitta*. With the help of these beings, I can progress toward Buddhahood. The fact that it is possible for me to train in the six *paramitas*, in the four means of magnetizing and so forth, and in the vast activities of a bodhisattva, is only possible because of other beings—so, thank you very much!'"[32] As a Buddhist, I must recognize all sentient beings as my teachers and cultivate gratefulness for them and the teachings that they offer.

*They work with people whether they are "good" or "bad"*

On the surface, this quality carries with it an instruction about working with all kinds of people: the privileged, the oppressed, the virtuous, the iniquitous, and so on. I strive to do this in my work as a Buddhist minister and chaplain, and to contribute in my own very small ways to opening higher education up in such a way that it might be available to more than just those with certain social advantages. There is also a special teaching here for those who do chaplaincy, I think. As my friend, fellow Naropa alumnus and prison chaplain Karuna Thompson often says, "The chaplain is the conscience of the institution he or she serves." Chaplains help foster and facilitate community. In order to do this effectively, they must learn to understand various perspectives—perspectives that can often be in direct conflict. As a chaplain committed to community-building, I know that I need to try to work with everyone, "whether they are 'good' or 'bad.'"

Obviously, this lesson has applications for teachers as well. As the director of the particular program for which I work, I am acutely aware of the need for our students to be presented with a range of ideas and viewpoints. For me, this diversity of perspectives takes the form of not just the material but also the other professors and the student cohorts. In this way, each individual student learns to work with all kinds of people, including those who think just like they do and those who think in

---

[32] Chökyi Nyima Rinpoche, *Present Fresh Wakefulness: A Meditation Manual on Nonconceptual Wisdom* (Berkeley: North Atlantic Books, 2004), 75.

almost the completely opposite way. Again, as Trungpa Rinpoche says, "The challenge of warriorship is to live fully in the world as it is and to find within this world, with all its paradoxes, the essence of nowness. If we open our eyes, if we open our minds, if we open our hearts, we will find that this world is a magical place. It is not magical because it tricks us or changes unexpectedly into something else, but it is magical because it can BE so vividly, so brilliantly."[33]

*They have bodhichitta—relative and absolute*

In many ways, I think the less said here, the better—it is probably more than a bit presumptuous for each of us to speak about how well we have cultivated and developed the mind of enlightenment. I think our teachers, as well as our students and the others we serve, are best suited to do that. In terms of how I understand this quality in my roles and responsibilities as a Buddhist minister, chaplain, and pastoral educator, though, I return often to a teaching by Burma's Nobel Peace Prize-winning democracy leader Aung San Suu Kyi:

> As a Buddhist, if you really want to consider what we, as human beings, are here for it's quite simple: we are trying to achieve enlightenment and use the wisdom that is gained to serve others, so that they too might be free from suffering. While we can't all be Buddhas, I feel a responsibility to do as much as I can to realize enlightenment to the degree that I can, and to use it to relieve the suffering of others.[34]

*They do not have money as a consideration*

This is perhaps the most straightforward quality, and part of the code of conduct for those of us ordained as ministers by the Buddhist Sangha Council of Southern California: we offer our services freely. Professional chaplains, of course, are generally salaried. There is, however, a more general operating principle to be drawn from this particular teaching, and it is this: be available to others. Obviously, as a chaplain, one needs a healthy sense of boundaries and the skills for good self-care, but spiritual care and counseling work should be more than just jobs for the practitioner. With this in mind, I myself try not to avoid those relatively small acts of responsibility and/or generosity that may arise by saying things

---

[33] Chögyam Trungpa Rinpoche, *Shambhala: The Sacred Path of the Warrior* (Boston: Shambhala Publications, 2007), 147–48.

[34] Alan Clements, ed., *The Voice of Hope: Aung San Suu Kyi Conversations with Alan Clements* (New York: Seven Stories Press, 2008), 195.

like "It is not in my job description" or "I am not on the clock." Trungpa Rinpoche again, to close: "If you are a warrior, decency means that you are not cheating anybody at all. . . . Decency is the absence of strategy. It is of utmost importance to realize that the warrior's approach should be simple-minded sometimes, very simple and straightforward. That makes it very beautiful: you having nothing up your sleeve; therefore a sense of genuineness comes through. That is decency."[35]

## Conclusion

"To be human is to interact with other people," writes Buddhist practitioner and psychologist Karen Kissel-Wigela in her wonderful book *How to Be a Help Instead of a Nuisance*.[36] She continues:

> Many times as we relate to others—both those we know well and count as friends and those we may never have seen before—the desire to be helpful arises in our hearts. In a way, nothing is more simple or basic, yet many times we don't know how to go about it. We may want to help, to extend comfort, support, intelligent help, but we don't know what to do.[37]

With its attention of identifying and addressing stress, dissatisfaction, suffering, and difficulty as clearly and carefully as possible, and identifying and cultivating beneficial qualities of body, speech, and mind with as much clarity and care, Buddhism offers those working in spiritual care and counseling inestimably valuable tools for "being a help instead of a nuisance." Above we have seen how each of the three *yanas* lays groundwork, sets a path, and provides a vision of fruition in terms of relating not just to others but also to ourselves.

It is perhaps not so surprising, then, that one senior chaplain colleague from another religious tradition once said to me and some of my colleagues whom she was impressed with, "What took you Buddhists so long to get to this whole professional chaplaincy party? With teaching and training like this in your traditions, it's no surprise that you're all so adept at this." Certainly Buddhist practitioners entering the fields of professional spiritual care and counseling are coming in with understandings

---

[35] Chögyam Trungpa Rinpoche, from "Perkiness," a talk given to the Directors of Shambhala Training, July 1978, available at the Shambhala Publications Blog, accessed November 16, 2010, http://live.shambhala.com/decency-is-absence-of-strategy.

[36] Karen Kissel-Wigela, *How to Be a Help Instead of a Nuisance: Practical Approaches to Giving Support, Service, and Encouragement to Others* (Boston: Shambhala Publications, 1996), 2.

[37] Ibid.

and skills that are going to serve them, their colleagues, and their patients incredibly well. Just being with what is, not turning away from suffering, reconciling dichotomies, etc.—these are things you must have to do this work, and they've already put in a lot of work on them as Buddhist practitioners. While the fields of spiritual care and counseling can learn much from the influx of Buddhist chaplains, Buddhist chaplains too can learn much from the different approaches and ideas they will encounter in their colleagues and patients. By such openness and mutual learning, we can surely go farther in our work as spiritual caregivers and counselors. As His Holiness the Dalai Lama has said, "If a harmonious relationship is established amongst societies and religious beliefs in today's multi-ethnic, multi-religious and multi-cultural world, then it will surely set a very good example for others."[38]

---

[38] His Holiness the Dalai Lama, from "Religious Harmony," a talk given to the International Association for Religious Freedom, Ladakh Group, August 2011, available at the website of the Office of His Holiness the Dalai Lama, accessed November 16, 2010, http://www.dalailama.com/messages/religious-harmony.

# Vulnerability as a path to the Divine
## Jewish spiritual care

*Mychal B. Springer*

### Foundations of the Jewish tradition

> Heal us, Adonai, that we shall be healed. Save us that we shall be saved, for You are our praise. Bring complete healing to all of our wounds.
> [Insert words of healing for a specific individual in need.]
> For You are our sovereign, steadfast, merciful healing God. Praised are You, Adonai, who heals the sick among his People Israel.[1]

This is a blessing for *refu'ah*, "healing," and comes from the *siddur*, the prayer book. The *siddur* serves as a practical guide to faith and its foundations, with layers of prayers that are drawn from the Bible, the Talmud, and medieval poets. Though liberal *siddurim* (prayer books) include modern-day prayers, those who pray with the traditional language of the *siddur* imbibe the rhythms of Jewish spiritual life, even when they wrestle with those rhythms. This particular blessing is found in the *amidah*, the multi-blessing prayer which stands at the heart of each prayer service three times daily.

This blessing for healing lays out clearly that God is the healer and savior who is responsible for the well-being of the people. On the surface it seems that people do not play a role in this healing—that the spiritual care which people need will come directly from God. Indeed, if we look at some of the verses in Jeremiah 17, which is the source of the beginning of this prayer, there are verses in that same chapter which warn of the danger of trusting in people over God. There seems to be a dichotomy between God and people as the source of help.

---

[1] Lawrence A. Hoffman, ed., *My People's Prayer Book, Vol. 2: Traditional Prayers, Modern Commentaries—The Amidah* (Woodstock, VT: Jewish Lights Publishing, 1998), 116–18.

Early on, the rabbis recognized the important role that doctors could play in partnering with God in physical healing. Strikingly, the word for "doctor," *rofeh*, which appears in this prayer, is applied to people and God alike.[2] Clearly, people can and must play a role in healing, even though the obligation is to trust in God alone. We could say that when people and God are aligned as partners, then trusting in people is an extension of trusting in God and does not pose a threat to the person's relationship with God. Because of this, doctors and spiritual caregivers alike are attuned to the essential role that ethical dialogue, grounded in religious discourse, must play when people are making life and death decisions.

A further clue about how we should properly understand the role of people in the healing process rests in the way the rabbis adapted Jeremiah 17:14 as they built the *refaeinu* prayer around it. In Jeremiah, the plea for God's healing is in the singular:

> Heal me, O Lord, and let me be healed;
> Save me and let me be saved;
> For You are my glory.[3]

In our prayer, whose antecedents appear in the Talmud, the rabbis have changed the language to the plural. One could say that this is because the communal prayer context naturally leads the blessings to be shifted into the plural.[4] But, given the centrality of the role that the community plays in Judaism, we can glean a theological reason as well. Being healed and saved by God becomes more possible when we access God as a community, when we establish that we are all in need of God's help and that we are connected to one another in that need. While the healing still comes from God, and the wisdom of the doctors comes from God, giving voice to the need for healing establishes that we are witnesses to one another's brokenness. Through this witnessing we establish ties of responsibility to one another, and God's healing becomes possible in new ways.

The language of the prayer is very literal. When it asks for "complete healing (*refu'ah sheleimah*) to all of our wounds," we are invoking a God who hears individual petitions and can respond with a miraculous cure to all that ails us. The word *sheleimah* shares a tri-letter root with the word *shalom*,

---

[2] The Wisdom of Ben Sira, 38:9–15; II Chronicles 16:12–13.

[3] Jeremiah 17:14.

[4] Ismar Elbogen, *Jewish Liturgy: A Comprehensive History*, trans. Raymond P. Scheindlin (Philadelphia: The Jewish Publication Society & NY: The Jewish Theological Seminary, 1993), 43.

"peace." With this complete healing, a person experiences a restoration to wholeness, which is a taste of true peace. In the *misheberakh* prayer, which is a prayer for healing recited in front of the open Torah scroll, the words *refu'ahsheleimah* are modified by *refu'athanefeshu'refu'athaguf*, "healing of soul and healing of body."[5] While there are some Jews who offer this prayer with a hope that the prayer will be efficacious in participating in God's moving toward granting this physical and spiritual healing, there are other Jews who do not approach this prayer in this way. For those Jews, and there are many spiritual caregivers among them, this pairing enables us to focus on the fact that even when the healing of the body is not possible, the healing of the soul is yet possible. And that the healing of the soul can take place even as the body dies.

Despite the daily affirmation of the belief that God intervenes in the world in response to prayer, the idea that God does not intervene in the manner described by the *refaeinu* prayer has been a part of Jewish thinking over the course of many centuries. Moses Maimonides, the great 13th century sage, doctor, commentator, codifier of the Talmud, and philosopher, says that this kind of intervention is exceedingly rare.[6] So what, then, does it mean to pray for God's intervention for those of us who do not expect God to respond in a literal way? This question is especially urgent, given that a central piece of chaplaincy practice involves prayers for healing with a similar beseeching for divine intervention. This question can be quite challenging for people who ask it in the comfort of their oriented lives. But when people are faced with the disorientation of dire circumstances, either their own circumstances or those they witness firsthand in the lives of others with whom they are lovingly connected, prayer often comes to life without much need for justification. It is the experience of praying, the opening of the heart in a moment of vulnerability, which reminds us why entering into the prayer itself can often be healing, quite apart from any theory of how God works in the world.

One way in which the rabbis conceptualized the human obligation to provide care for one another is grounded in the idea that people are commanded to emulate God's ways.

> The Holy Blessed One visits the ill,
> as it says, "And God visited him [Abraham]

---

[5] Jules Harlow, ed. with translations, *Siddur Sim Shalom: A Prayerbook for Shabbat, Festivals, and Weekdays* (NY: The Rabbinical Assembly, 1985), 404.

[6] Moses Maimonides, *The Guide of the Perplexed, Volume Two*, trans. Shlomo Pines (Chicago: The University of Chicago Press, 1963), 495.

in Elonei Mamreh" (Genesis 18:1),
so you too shall visit the ill."[7]

The rabbis determined that God attends to the sick by looking at the story of Abraham when he is recovering from his circumcision. In keeping with the customary usage of the word *vayera elav*, "and God visited him," the verse should continue with a verbal declaration from God.[8] But our verse is the exception, and these words are not followed by any verbal declaration at all. In looking to understand why this verse is different, the rabbis extrapolated that the point of this visit was *bikkur cholim*, "the visiting of the sick." Rashi, the 12th century commentator, drawing on the midrash, interpolates that God asked after his well-being, *"sha'al ma shlomo."*[9] Israel Kestenbaum writes that the absence of that verbal declaration comes to teach us that God's method was *to be with* Abraham.[10] There was no content which needed to be revealed, because the relationship itself, in the midst of Abraham's suffering, was the focus. Kestenbaum sees the loving gift of the relationship itself to be the source of the healing. As we look at foundational concepts of spiritual care, this insight about God's method of caring for the sick highlights the importance of presence, attunement, and drawing near, over content. In striving to emulate God in caring for others, people must strive to become as fully present as possible.

The Psalms cry out with the suffering of those who crave the healing presence of God. Psalm 27, for example, depicts a yearning to be close to God.

> One thing do I ask of the Lord,
> it is this that I seek—
> that I dwell in the house of the Lord,
> all the days of my life,
> to behold the Lord's sweetness
> and to gaze on His palace.[11]

---

[7] Babylonian Talmud Sotah 14a. See also Midrash Genesis Rabbah 8, and Joseph S. Ozarowski, "Bikur Cholim: A Paradigm for Pastoral Caring" in *Jewish Pastoral Care: A Practical Handbook from Traditional & Contemporary Sources*, ed. Dayle A. Friedman (Woodstock, VT: Jewish Lights Publishing, 2001), 57.

[8] Nahum M. Sarna, ed. and commentary, *The JPS Torah Commentary: Genesis* (Philadelphia: The Jewish Publication Society, 1989), 128.

[9] Rashi on Genesis 18:1.

[10] Israel Kestenbaum, "The Gift of Healing Relationship: A Theology of Jewish Pastoral Care" in *Jewish Pastoral Care*, ed. Dayle A. Friedman (Woodstock, VT: Jewish Lights Publishing, 2001), 4.

[11] Robert Alter, trans., *The Book of Psalms: A Translation with Commentary* (NY: W. W. Norton & Company, 2007), 92.

The image of being close to God is of being physically in God's space, the Temple. The opposite image is of experiencing God's hidden face, God's inaccessibility. The Psalmist dreads this experience of God-turned-away and pleads:

> Do not hide your face from me;
> do not turn your servant away in wrath.[12]

There is a pronounced physicality to the understanding of divine presence and absence. The physicality adds power to the cry, the beseeching. The image of the distance and the desperation to draw near takes center stage in the psalm. The dynamic of reading the psalm is that the voice that cries out demands to be heard. The Psalmist grapples with anger, the possibility that the withdrawal is due to God's anger, and the fear and anger that the Psalmist has about feeling abandoned. The lament itself is seen as faithful. Only through the lament is healing possible. As the anguish is witnessed, then the psalmist is able to experience God's face shining on him or her.[13]

The physicality of divine presence and absence translates strikingly into the realm of spiritual care. To begin with, the laws regarding *bikkur cholim*, "visiting the sick," involve the obligation to be present with the person who is sick.[14] The physical showing up, which has no measure (the more the better) echoes the Psalmist's plea to draw near. The laws about attending to the sick person's physical needs, drawn from the *aggadah* (rabbinic story) about Rabbi Akiba, who swept the floor when his student was sick, demonstrates that the realm of the spiritual must include an awareness of the larger context in which the suffering person dwells.[15] Spiritual care must include an awareness of who is shunned in our society, and the ways in which people who are perceived as not being whole continue to be devalued. Based on the assertion in Genesis that we are all created *b'tselem Elohim*, in the divine image, spiritual care begins with truly seeing the divine image in all of humanity.[16] This acknowledgement of the sacredness of humanity must be grounded in attuned relationships

---

[12] Ibid, 93.

[13] Numbers 6:25. See *TANAKH: A New Translation of The Holy Scriptures According to the Traditional Hebrew Text* (Philadelphia: The Jewish Publication Society, 1985), 216.

[14] Maimonides, *Mishneh Torah, Laws of Mourning* 14:1, 4–6; and *Shulchan Aruch, Yoreh Deah* section 335.

[15] Babylonian Talmud Nedarim 40a; see also, Ozarowski, 65.

[16] Genesis 1:27.

with particular individuals. By offering our presence to another we value that person, we bear witness to his or her story and reality. By turning our face toward the other, we alleviate his or her suffering.

But the physicality of wanting to draw near also reminds us of the pain of God being beyond reach in ways that cannot readily be repaired. The destruction of the First and Second Temples in Jerusalem (another word with the same root as *sheleimah* and *shalom*) echoes the expulsion from the Garden of Eden and also the experience of being sent into slavery in Egypt. While the theme of exile as punishment for sins certainly exists in the tradition, the promise of return is just as firmly in place. Exile provides us with a chance to examine our ways and become reoriented on a path of right living, even as we have to grieve the losses that are involved.

Beyond the destruction of the Temples, the language of exile captures a truth about human experience which resonates apart from the specific historical events. The human condition itself is a condition of exile, of alienation. Inside religious narratives we live with the hope of return, in its largest sense. Michael Fishbane sees "movements from disorientation and chaos to orientation and cosmos at a sacred center" as the central narrative of the Bible.[17] This narrative captures human experience on a profound level. Lurianic mysticism, which emerged in the sixteenth century in response to the Jewish expulsion from Spain, understands exile as "a metaphysical symbol for all that is wrong, out of joint, imperfect, or unredeemed in creation."[18] While biblical prophets warn that the destruction will be the result of the people's sins, once the destruction of the Second Temple happens, we begin to see a non-retributive justice approach to Israel's sufferings. The Talmud teaches that each time God's people have gone into exile, *Shekhinah*, "God's presence," went with us. And that when we will be redeemed, *Shekhinah*, "God's presence," will be redeemed with us.[19] This teaching affirms that in the face of great suffering, presence in its fullest sense is the source of comfort. (From a gender perspective, it is noteworthy that the *Shekhina* is God's feminine aspect.) But the passage goes even further in looking at the theological dynamics

---

[17] Michael Fishbane, "The Sacred Center: The Symbolic Structure of the Bible" in *Texts and Responses: Studies Presented to Nahum N. Glatzer*, ed. Michael Fishbane and Paul M. Flohr (Leiden, The Netherlands: E. J. Brill Publishers, 1975), 23. This paragraph draws on Mychal B. Springer, "Exile and Return Retold: Theology Theory," *Journal of Supervision and Training in Ministry* 18 (1997): 166–67.

[18] Neil Gillman, *Sacred Fragments* (Philadelphia, PA: The Jewish Publication Society, 1990), 265–66.

[19] Babylonian Talmud, Megillah, 29a.

involved. Here we see that our longing for return and redemption is shared by God. An aspect of God joins us in our brokenness.

A line from the *hoshanot* liturgy—prayers of supplication for salvation offered during *Sukkot*, the holiday of Booths—echoes this idea and can help us to understand the dynamics more fully. These prayers have their origins in the circumambulation of the altar in the Temple period. In the prayer "Save Yourself and us!" which is recited daily throughout the holiday, we chant:

> As You saved the chorus who sang out "God saved!"
> And You who gave birth to them were saved with them, help us now.[20]
> As You freed them declaring: "I will bring you out,"
> which our sages interpreted: "I went out with you," hoshana! Help us now...
> As You accompanied the people You sent into Babylon,
> Journeying into exile with them, help us now.[21]

In the first couplet, we see that God saved the people and was somehow also saved with them. The Savior is in need of salvation. There is something about the process of human beings being saved that contributes to God's restoration. We could say that this hints at the limitation of God's power. Or we could say that the human experience is intimately bound up with the divine experience. If we return to the idea that we have to emulate God, we might almost see this as a variation which understands that God's experience in the world, as it were, is only possible in relationship with human beings. So when people are saved, God is also saved. This idea is further substantiated in the second couplet, where God is the one who brings the people out of Egypt, and yet God is also brought out of Egypt (*hutzeiti eetchem*) in the process. Finally, in the third couplet, God sends the people into exile and God goes, too. In the Hebrew, the verb is *shulachti*, "I was sent," conveying that God was sent into exile along with the people, not just that God chose to accompany them. The interconnectedness of human experience and divine experience conveys great love. Somehow, human and divine stories depend on one another. So it is not too much of a stretch to say that when we attend to

---

[20] Abraham Joshua Heschel, *Heavenly Torah: As Refracted through the Generations*, ed. and trans. with commentary by Gordon Tucker (NY: Continuum, 2005), 107. This line is based on an early midrash taught by Rabbi Meir on Exodus 14:30.

[21] Harlow, *Siddur Sim Shalom*, 201. I would like to thank Rabbi Jason Rubenstein for first calling my attention to these lines. See Heschel, *Heavenly Torah*, 110–11.

another person, we attend to God. When we help restore another person to a sense of cosmos, we help restore the Holy One to cosmos. This is what is meant when Lurianic mysticism teaches that the sparks of the *Shekhinah* are scattered throughout the world, and in our exile we must gather up the sparks, through religious acts, so that God and the world can be restored to wholeness.[22] In this way, the healing of spiritual care is linked to redemption not just of the individual but of humanity, the divine, and the cosmos itself.

By accompanying us into exile, God is functioning in a healing way. The aspect of God which is broken, in need of redemption from exile, is the aspect of God which is most available to us when we ourselves are in exile. In the depths of our suffering, it is not the transcendent aspect of God which offers the greatest comfort. Back to the imagery of Psalm 27, the glory of being in God's temple is not an option. Our only hope is to experience God's face shining on us. And the face we yearn to see has to be with us in our exile. The face cannot be removed, seemingly unaffected by the trauma of our overturned lives. By understanding that God is sent into exile with us, the rabbis underscored that God's healing power is tied up in God being with us. And, therefore, in order to emulate God, we must have access to our own brokenness as well. In order to offer spiritual care to others, we must make space for our own experiences of exile and know that we can only participate in their coming out of their Egypt when we know that our own experience of coming out of Egypt is bound up in their story as well.

Estelle Frankel quotes Rabbi Menachem Mendel of Kotzk saying, "Nothing is more whole than a broken heart." She offers her interpretation of what this means:

> If we can find a way to hold and embrace our pain gently, recognizing that brokenness is simply part of the human condition—in a sense, nothing special—then we may begin to feel empathically connected to all other beings. This is the broken heart that makes us whole.[23]

The God/*Shekhina* who models going into Egypt with us, shows us that we cannot remain separate from the suffering, or we become irrelevant. Spiritual healing begins with joining with the other, even as

---

[22] Gershom G. Scholem, *On the Kabbalah and Its Symbolism* (New York, NY: Schoken Books, 1969), 116.

[23] Estelle Frankel, *Sacred Therapy: Jewish Spiritual Teachings on Emotional Healing and Inner Wholeness* (Boston: Shambhala, 2003), 21.

we maintain our separate identities.

One very dramatic way in which the reality of brokenness and the need for healing is highlighted inside of Jewish tradition and practice is through the marking of *Tisha B'Av*, the Fast of the 9th of Av, which commemorates the destruction of both Temples in Jerusalem and the expulsion from Spain. By including this day in the liturgical calendar, the rabbis emphasized that the experience of suffering must be grappled with regularly, that brokenness is central to our communal experience and our understanding of our relationship with God. The restrictions of the fast day convey that *Tisha B'Av* is both a day of atonement and a day of mourning.[24] As a day of atonement, it makes us grapple with the responsibility we bear for how we function in this world. Spiritual caregivers need to be equipped to help people reflect on their lives and sort through the ways in which they have gone astray, which is the first step of turning in *teshuvah*, "repentance," and seeking forgiveness. As a day of mourning, it makes us recognize that the human need to tell the story of our losses is key to our being able to move toward wholeness.

The book of Lamentations is read in the Synagogue on *Tisha B'Av*. The book tells the story of the destruction of the Temple in vivid language and draws the reader/listener into the story as a witness. Kathleen M. O'Connor reflects on the ways that the book of Lamentations orients us in spiritual care.[25] She speaks about the function of the lament. The lament is the crying out for "the Absent One, the God who hides behind the clouds." Precisely because God is not available, the lament can be fully articulated without being minimized.[26] O'Connor gleans a theology of witness from the book of Lamentations:

> Lamentations can shred the heart and spawn despair, but, paradoxically, by mirroring pain it can also comfort the afflicted and open the way toward healing. It can affirm the dignity of those who suffer, release their tears, and overcome their experience of abandonment.[27]

The witness plays a key role in helping the sufferer heal. In the face of overwhelming suffering, it is the crying out itself, and being heard by

---

[24] I would like to acknowledge that I am drawing from David Kraemer's annual phenomenal teaching about Tisha B'Av to the Clinical Pastoral Education students.

[25] Kathleen M. O'Connor, *Lamentations & The Tears of the World* (Maryknoll, NY: Orbis Books, 2002), 84; and Lamentations 3:44.

[26] O'Connor, *Lamentations & The Tears of the World*, 85.

[27] Ibid., 96.

the witness, which provides the possibility of redemption, which makes hope possible. "Although lamenting the truth in even a partial way can take generations, there is no way forward without bringing suffering to voice."[28] Spiritual care rests on being able to hear the other into speech. This process can feel overwhelming to the caregiver, who needs to grapple with his or her own pain in order to see the pain of others most fully.[29] By confronting our despair, we come to renewed life and the establishment of a more robust community.[30]

At the end of *Shabbat*, when it is dark outside, traditionally Jews recite *havdalah*, the ceremony which distinguishes between *Shabbat* and the rest of the week, the holy and the everyday. In the *havdalah* ceremony we say: "Behold, God is my salvation. I will trust and not be afraid."[31] This verse, taken from Isaiah 12, asserts that trust will enable us to overcome fear. It is the fear of the dark, of the chaos of night. I love this verse because the assertion about trusting reminds us that we have reason to be afraid. The trusting is necessary precisely because the fear is real. Spiritual care offers us the place to explore the fears while we cultivate the relationships, human and divine, which strengthen our capacity to trust—the relationships which cultivate our hope in the transforming power of God and God's partners in our lives.

### Jewish spiritual care tradition in caregiving practice

A middle-aged Jewish woman, Stephanie, whose husband is dying, met with me recently. She wanted me to give her guidance about how the Jewish tradition could help her travel through the period of his dying. She began by seeking information. This is often how pastoral contact with clergy begins. The temptation is to answer the question, to be polite. But if we return to the idea that the essence of *bikkur cholim*—attending to the sick, and by extension, attending to those who love them—is being with them, then we need to invite the one we are caring for to move away from the content, to make room for a fuller connection. I invited Stephanie to put the resource question on hold for a moment, assuring her that we would return to it. I did not want her to think that I was not mindful of her expressed need, but I needed to help her learn how she could draw

---

[28] Ibid., 94.

[29] Ibid., 107.

[30] Ibid., 108–09.

[31] Jonathan Sacks, trans. and commentary, *The Koren Sacks Siddur* (Jerusalem: Koren Publishers, 2009), 724.

on me as a resource in a fuller sense than she had expected. As we began to talk, she told me about her relationship with her husband and some of what his illness had been like for her and their family. She conveyed that she knew his time on earth was very limited, and she had a sense that others had gone through this before her, so she wanted to benefit from the wisdom of others. Her impulse came from wanting to overcome the isolation of going through a profoundly disorienting experience. Although she could not avoid the disorientation in its largest sense, she had enough positive experiences inside the Jewish community to know that our tradition could ease the suffering by holding her up as she went through it. She proclaimed herself a reader in search of material to read, and I did give her references to a couple of books. (We are, after all, the people of the book.) I also told her about some communal resources, such as the Jewish Healing Center, which offers spiritual counseling and support groups. But our time together went beyond these resources.

I recognized that Stephanie felt inadequate in the face of having to travel this road. She wanted to know how experts would advise her to do it, since she felt she did not have internal resources sufficient for the task. After listening to her describe how she had navigated her husband's illness so far, it was clear to me that she was a highly competent woman who had already risen to many challenges, yet the final stages of preparing for her husband's death had left her feeling self-doubt. The problem with my giving her even great answers would have been that doing so would have exacerbated her greatest challenge—coming to believe that she has what she needs or will find what she needs—to survive even this most devastating loss. So one strategy that I chose was to tell her that most ideas about what to do at this stage in life are really very simple, if she just lets herself think of them. I gave her an example. She told me that her husband loves piano music but that he's too weak to play the piano anymore. I suggested that perhaps she could work with her husband to make a CD with his picks of piano pieces, with his favorite pianists for each piece. Once she got the idea, that she could look for ways to make his legacy concrete through his passions and his commitments, her creativity began to flow. This idea of legacy ties in with the afterlife. Judaism has a traditional belief in the afterlife, though there are diverse takes on this belief among Jewish thinkers throughout the centuries and in our own day. While some Jews believe in a literal afterlife, others focus on the ways in which the person lives on in this world through his or her legacy.

We then moved on to thinking about Stephanie's connection to aspects of the Jewish tradition that she could draw on. I asked her if there was anything in the *siddur* (the prayer book) or any Jewish practice or teaching which is particularly significant to her. She responded that, even though her husband was too sick to accompany her, she chose to go to synagogue on *Yom Kippur*. We talked about what drew her to be there, and she described the pull of the community and the familiar melodies. Given that she did not like going anywhere alone, this was the beginning of her accepting that as her husband declined and eventually died, she would need to function alone in the world. The synagogue provided a context in which she could begin to experience herself in new ways, with a sense of protection.

I wondered if there were any *Yom Kippur* prayers in particular which stood out for her. She responded that she has always loved the *piyyut*, the liturgical poem "As clay in the hand of the potter." *Mahzor Lev Shalem*, a High Holy Day prayer book, offers the heading "Human Vulnerability" for this prayer. Without even realizing it, Stephanie had called up the perfect religious resource for herself. The opening verses are:

> As clay in the hand of the potter, who thickens or thins it
> at will, so are we in Your hand, Guardian of love;
>> *Recall your covenant; do not heed the accuser.*
> As stone in the hand of the mason, who preserves or breaks it
> at will, so are we in Your hand, God of life and death;
>> *Recall Your covenant; do not heed the accuser.*[32]

At this moment of her husband's complete vulnerability and her own tremendous vulnerability, she had gravitated to a prayer which depicts the human condition as being fundamentally one of vulnerability. Clay in the hand of the potter evokes the image of not being in control, of life as delicate, of God holding us, in the most tactile terms. When we began to discuss the meaning of her *piyyut*, Stephanie was amazed to discover how much wisdom her own heart possessed in its choice of liturgy. By bearing witness to Stephanie's internal reality, through her engagement with this text, Stephanie and I were able to connect in a deep way. That experience of presence led Stephanie to touch gingerly on a raw place—the looming prospect of becoming a widow, with all that that meant for her. A name she didn't want. A life she didn't want. The words of the refrain, *la brit habet*, translated here as "recall Your covenant," literally mean "look to

---

[32] Edward Feld, ed., *Mahzor Lev Shalem for Rosh Hashanah and Yom Kippur* (NY: The Rabbinical Assembly, 2010), 227.

your covenant."³³ The plea for God to look—to see, to witness—enabled Stephanie to hold God accountable for seeing her reality, for not turning God's face away, for staying bound to her no matter what lay ahead. That was the eternal promise of the covenant.

In the end, Stephanie gave me guidance about how to journey with a dying husband. In order for me to connect with her in her competence, self-doubt, fear, and yearning to be held by God, I needed to make room in my heart for the dreaded reality that someday—and who knows when—my husband and I will be separated by death. While the language of our conversation gave voice to her story, the texture of my presence was given form by my willingness and ability to experience myself as vulnerable alongside her. If I kept Stephanie at a distance, feeling secure in my own life, then I could not enter into the space of truly accompanying her. I must go into exile with her, in the sense of recognizing that we share a destiny as human beings, and we are fundamentally connected in that destiny. Stephanie felt lifted up in the experience of being heard as she gave voice to her reality, better equipped to bear the suffering that she cannot avoid.

My experience with Stephanie was enhanced by our both being Jewish, because Stephanie came into the conversation with the expectation that I could help her, and our common language facilitated our connection. My expertise in Jewish theology, texts, and practice meant that I could help her deepen her awareness of how she could draw on the resources she already possessed. Nevertheless, I have also experienced that this very commonality can make spiritual work more difficult, since patients can be afraid that one of their own will judge them; therefore, they may feel safer with someone outside their community. One example of this kind of situation was with Jerry, a Catholic man who reclaimed his sense of spirituality during an extended stay in an isolation room. When I presented myself to Jerry as the chaplain, he was interested in meeting with me precisely because a clergywoman, and a Jewish one to boot, was outside his realm of experience. I didn't know it at the time, but Jerry's acceptance of me was in some ways bound up with his own alienation from the church. He loved the freedom to explore aspects of his spirituality which resonated with the spirituality of other traditions. As an outsider, I could be present for Jerry without having a personal stake in his reconciling with the church.

But, as a rabbi, I also have a strong sense of the importance of com-

---

[33] Marcus Jastrow, compiled, *Dictionary of the Targumim, Talmud Babli, Yerushalmi and Midrashic Literature* (NY: The Judaica Press, Inc., 1985), 868.

munity. So as I listened to Jerry, I witnessed his pain at being cut off from the church. My healing connection with Jerry had helped him to realize that clergy and religious community could be partners with the divine in the healing process. As I reflected that back to him, I sensed that he was interested in becoming reconciled in the church, as long as he didn't have to sacrifice his principles in order to do so. At this point in my care for Jerry, I recognized that I needed to bring in a Catholic member of the team to attend to Jerry's unique Catholic needs. Jerry was surprised to discover how much it meant to him to come home again at the end of his life. Meanwhile, I was able to continue to support Jerry in the spiritual work which centered on his experiencing a call, like Moses in the wilderness, during this period of facing his own death. I listened to Jerry give voice to the narrative of his life, seeing it as holy, even though it wasn't lofty and even though it was ending much too soon. Despite the disorientation of illness, Jerry found a new sense of orientation before he died.

My own experience of being supervised in Clinical Pastoral Education (CPE), in the process of becoming a certified chaplain, was so transformative and religiously essential for me that I decided to become a CPE Supervisor. The fact that most of my supervisors were Christian had a profound impact on me. When I entered CPE, a year away from ordination as a rabbi, my spiritual life was in disarray, and I was struggling to make my peace with an agnosticism which bordered on atheism. Engaging in pastoral work and receiving expert supervision began to reawaken my believing self. As I got my bearings, I leaned on the religious wisdom of my supervisors, anxious at times that I would not be true to my own tradition. But their acceptance of me and their willingness to engage me even at my most resistant kept me on a steady path. Over time I learned to draw on my own religious tradition in ways that were essential for me and deeply effective for patients.

As a supervisor, I focus on helping students do the hard work of unpacking their own suffering and learning to tell their own stories more fully so that they can access themselves for effective attunement and the kind of deep presence on which spiritual care depends. When I worked with Judith, a Jewish woman, I paid attention to the ways in which she professed love for the patients but was often caught up in her judgments about them. As we explored this paradox in supervision, I worked to make a connection with Judith. I paid attention to the verbal and nonverbal ways in which she pushed me away. I allowed myself to feel the distance between us, even as I committed myself to cultivating more connection. One of the ways that I cultivated this connection was by drawing on my own history of feeling judgmental, which was intertwined with my experience of feeling judged. In supervision I shared with Judith the following sacred story of my own, which grew out of a moment in which I fell short in a dramatic way and felt great shame.

One *Yom Kippur*, I stood in services in the late afternoon, fully aware of my own falling short, and participated in the recitation of the prayer of supplication, *Avinu Malkeinu*, "Our Father, Our King." Although I had recited those words many, many times, it was as if I heard them for the first time.

> *Avinu Malkeinu*, have mercy on us, answer us, for our deeds are insufficient, deal with us charitably and lovingly, and redeem us.[34]

Our deeds are insufficient. In the face of all my trying to measure up and falling short, I had always felt the weight of God's judgment. But this prayer was teaching me that I could never measure up through my deeds. Literally, the prayer says *ein banu ma'asim*, "we have no deeds." God's relationship with us is determined by God's *chesed*, God's love for us. Despite the importance of taking responsibility for our acts, ultimately God's love is a promise, is unwavering. I felt flooded with God's love as I stood in my community. And a weight was lifted from me. I was overwhelmed with gratitude and hope. This experience changed the way I related to others. Filled up with God's love, I felt able to access love toward others much more fully, and issues of my feeling judgmental and judged melted away dramatically.

As I shared this story with Judith, she felt joined in her struggle with judgment, and she felt embraced and worthy despite her shame. While she had a history of feeling loved by God, she had much less familiarity with feeling loved and accepted by people. By exposing my own vulnerability, Judith saw me as a sister traveler toward whom she could draw closer, with the hope that the loving embrace would be healing. I also invited her to be real with me about her reactions to me and our work, positive and negative, which she increasingly risked doing. As our relationship blossomed, we witnessed that her relationships with patients began to shift. The judgment receded, and increasingly Judith was actually able to feel the loving feelings—echoes of God's love—with the patients. The patients embraced her care and her loving presence as the gift that it was. I know that I would not have been able to supervise Judith in this way if I had not received the gift of loving presence from my own supervisors.

---

[34] Feld, ed., *Mahzor Lev Shalem for Rosh Hashanah and Yom Kippur*, 391.

They played an essential role in bringing me to my *Yom Kippur* revelation and in helping me to draw on that revelation, both dynamically and overtly, in supervising students. In the world of spiritual care, the truth of interconnectedness, divine and human, and human-human, remains miraculously redemptive.

## A profile of wisdom in Jewish spiritual care

Core competencies of Jewish spiritual care derive from the foundation of the Jewish faith tradition's concepts and practices. They can be divided into competencies of knowing, being, and doing.[35]

### Knowing

Competent caregivers must have mastery of their own approaches to Judaism and in-depth familiarity with how those approaches shape the role and identity of the spiritual caregiver. This mastery must be coupled with the capacity to celebrate the unique ways in which *Torah* (Jewish wisdom in its broadest sense) emerges from the experience of giving and receiving care. They must comprehend the ways that *halakhic* (legal) and *aggadic* (narrative) frameworks of Judaism serve to organize religious and spiritual experience. The diversity of Jews' relationship to *halakha*, which can range from complete adherence to the practice of traditional Jewish law to complete lack of adherence in any overt way, must be embraced in order for spiritual caregivers to serve others without feeling a mandate to change the other. At Sinai, God spoke in one voice, but people heard God's voice in many languages.[36] The underlying basis for *halakha* and *aggada* is the multi-layered textual tradition which ultimately rests on the narrative of God's relationship to human beings, which shapes how we aspire to behave on earth. The *aggadic* tradition, specifically, places narrative at the center, valuing the ways that stories shape our lives and highlighting the importance of spiritual caregivers being able to hear the stories of others as sacred texts.

Spiritual caregivers must have a proficiency in exploring theological dynamics. Expertise in working with embedded theologies, with ability to facilitate the construction of deliberative theologies when appropriate, is essential.[37] Caregivers must possess an ability to recognize the

---

[35] Here I follow the model of core competencies proposed by Leah Dawn Bueckert and Daniel Schipani, *You Welcomed Me: Interfaith Spiritual Care in the Hospital* (Kitchener: Pandora Press, 2010), 169–76.

[36] Exodus Rabbah 5:9.

[37] Carrie Doehring, *The Practice of Pastoral Care: A Postmodern Approach* (Louisville, KY: Westminster John Knox Press, 2006), 112–18.

ways in which theology is functioning in people's lives in life-affirming and life-denying ways, especially theologies of reward and punishment. Attunement to the dynamics of *el hai vekayam*, "the ever-living God," is also part of the caregiver's proficiency in theological dynamics.[38]

Competency in functioning in translation with a range of other approaches to Judaism as well as with other religious traditions is a skill of the competent spiritual caregiver. This skill of translation grows out of the experience of living in exile, which has required Jews to be able to thrive in foreign lands and speak foreign languages, like Joseph in Egypt. This capacity to function within multiple frames of reference also equips spiritual caregivers to translate between different disciplines as part of a multi-disciplinary team. Furthermore, it informs the practice of spiritual care as a discipline which has been enriched by the interplay between psychology and religion.[39]

## Being

Competencies of being include being present with another with a high level of attunement. A quality of this presence includes orientation toward *shleimut*, "wholeness," understood as a state of integration of faith and doubt, exile, despair, brokenness, missing the mark, forgiveness, hope, love, redemption, and return. In order for caregivers to be attuned to the other's wholeness, they must embrace their own stories of exile and return, their own disorientation, brokenness, and experiences of reorientation. Only then can there be genuine ability and willingness to enter into the disorientation of exile in order to journey with another, with the hope of participating in some aspect of return. The caregiver, however, must be practiced in establishing appropriate boundaries between self and other when impulses to rescue or flee get triggered.

A caregiver must be able to recognize the *tselem Elohim*, "divine likeness," in all people, and connect with them with an appreciation of their sacred qualities, even when that *tselem Elohim* seems to be in eclipse. Ability to emulate God's practices of *gemilut chasadim*, "loving kindness," is an essential trait of the competent caregiver.

Jewish spiritual caregivers must have a love of *hiddush*, "new insight," and the ways that Torah is made new through people's lived experience. They must be proficient in the *hevrutah*, partner learning model of the

---

[38] Daniel 6:27, in the Aramaic.

[39] See the works of Aviva Zornberg, for example, *The Beginning of Desire: Reflections on Genesis* (NY: Image, Doubleday, 1995) for exquisite examples of Torah commentary steeped in psychological insight.

*beit midrash* (the study house), which understands that passionate engagement leads to the uncovering of truth. The caregiver must also have an appreciation that *elu v'elu divrei Elohim Hayyim*, "These and these are the words of the ever-living God," which leads to a multiplicity of interpretive possibilities. A mandate for the spiritual caregiver is to listen with respect to the wisdom which each person derives in the process of wrestling with the reality of his or her life.[40] Finally, competent spiritual caregivers must see themselves as God's partners, participating in the redemption of the world through *Tikkun Olam*, the human contributions to the repairing of the world.

### Doing

The practices of a competent Jewish spiritual caregiver are based on an expertise in concretely emulating God through the establishment of loving, healing relationships. This includes competence in establishing pastoral relationships with care receivers, with skill in an array of pastoral strategies. Dayle Friedman conceptualizes this in the language of the Jewish tradition by designating four levels of spiritual care, as framed by the word *Pardes*, a traditional acronym for four kinds of hermeneutics, which literally means "orchard."[41] The four are as follows:

> **Peshat:** the level of fact; giving voice to the story. This level is particularly important for someone who is processing a traumatic event and is working to reconstruct it in language so that it can be absorbed by the brain.
> **Remez:** the level of emotion; listening and responding to feelings with empathic attunement.
> **Derash:** the level of meaning; listening to the person's narrative with an ear for the ways in which that person's sense of the meaning of his or her life, and the theological frames which shape his or her understanding, are embedded.
> **Sod:** the level of soul; this level of connection is a gift of God's chesed, "love."

Caregivers must be committed and skillful in creating relationship with and caring for those who are marginalized or shunned, recognizing that they, too, are created *b'tselem Elohim*, "in the divine image."

Competent Jewish spiritual caregivers have a familiarity with

---

[40] Babylonian Talmud, Tractate Eruvin 13b.

[41] Dayle Friedman, "PaRDeS: A Model for Presence in Hitlavt Ruchanit" in *Jewish Pastoral Care*, ed. Friedman, 44–50.

traditional Jewish practices of *bikkur cholim*, "visiting the sick," and other *halakhot* (Jewish laws) which facilitate healing. Ability to facilitate a Jewish spiritual assessment,[42] proficiency in witnessing others' laments as an essential part of the process of moving toward hope and healing, and hearing people into redemptive speech when they are in the pit are all key practices. Proficiency in providing care receivers with interpretations of Jewish law, practice, and theology when appropriate is also an essential skill. Caregivers must have a capacity to draw on religious resources, including prayer, in creative collaborative process with care receivers, as well as have expertise in recognizing issues of guilt and pathways of fostering processes of *teshuvah*, "repentance/return."

Internalization of a professional level of ongoing reflection on spiritual care practice, assessing effectiveness of interventions, being attuned to when the caregiver has missed the mark, being able to explore dynamics of intertwined stories (transference and counter-transference) in a non-defensive way with self and colleagues are all essential to the practice of good spiritual care. Finally, skillfulness in collaborating with other Jewish religious leaders and leaders of all faiths to support care receivers in ethical decision-making, especially at the beginning and end of life, is key to competent spiritual care practice.

---

[42] See Marion Shulevitz and Mychal Springer, "Assessment of Religious Experience: A Jewish Approach," *The Journal of Pastoral Care* 48, no. 4 (Winter 1994): 399–406; see also Zahara Davidowitz-Farkas, "Jewish Spiritual Assessment" in *Jewish Pastoral Care*, ed. Friedman, 104–24.

# Do justice, love kindness, walk humbly
## A Christian perspective on spiritual care

*Kathleen J. Greider*

In this chapter we reflect on interfaith spiritual care through the lens of caregiving in Christianity. Three realities are obscured by this goal and the limitations of space. First, no one chapter can do justice to the history of spiritual care in Christianity. Referred to early in Christian history as *cura animarum* (Lat.)—cure of souls—it is known now by numerous names that reference many specialized practices in diverse settings: care of souls, pastoral care, spiritual care, congregational care, care of congregations, spiritual friendship, spiritual direction, pastoral counseling, Christian counseling, biblical counseling, social service/advocacy, and chaplaincy in hospices, hospitals, law enforcement, fire and other emergency services, the military, prisons, schools, and workplaces. A rich tradition lies in the background of this chapter's limited examination.

Second, Christian diversity and divisions can barely be acknowledged, especially given this volume's assumption of the value of interfaith spiritual care. Christianity is so characterized by diversity that it is possible to speak of Christia*nities*.[1] Even beliefs about Christianity's inspiration, Jesus of Nazareth, demonstrate profound differences.[2] Only the fallacy of essentialized identity can generate "the" Christian point of view. I strive to show the diversity in Christian traditions, but it is not our focus.

Third, harm inflicted by Christians shadows every claim made about Christian care. Through crusades, colonization, coerced conversion, and

---

[1] See, for example, Bart D. Ehrman, *Lost Christianities: The Battles for Scripture and the Faiths We Never Knew* (New York: Oxford, 2003).

[2] See, for example, Gregory J. Riley, *One Jesus, Many Christs: How Jesus Inspired Not One True Christianity, but Many: The Truth about Christian Origins* (New York: Harper San Francisco, 1989).

other forms of invasion, Christians have committed violence against bodies and souls. Moreover, Christians in many regions of the world enjoy the privileges of Christianity's sociocultural and political dominance, and some use religion in divisive and oppressive ways, often without apparent awareness or care regarding the costs to other people and communities. Lewis Schlosser's argument that the dynamics of Christian privilege bear similarities to white privilege and male privilege deserves careful consideration,[3] though it is beyond the scope of this chapter. Christians also harm each other in the name of religion. Both "liberals" and "conservatives," fearing diversity and dissent, deal harshly with nonconformity. Almost without exception, Christians and former Christians I encounter carry wounds inflicted by other Christians through judgmentalism. Harm done in the name of religion is not unique to Christianity, of course. Nonetheless, repentance, confession, and reparation for the harm we do have central importance in Christianity. I offer this chapter in that spirit.

## Locating the discussion

A multiplicity of locations comprises the narrative of my Christian life. I was born into a pietistic, evangelical community that for two decades formed me as a Christian. My Christian identity was made more multi-layered in college and graduate school by religious studies and theological education. Especially relevant regarding interfaith care was study of other religions, particularly Buddhism and its view of suffering, Judaism's theology of G-d, and study of Christian liberation theologies, which still provide primary motivation, focus, and standards for my life and vocation. Ordained in the United Methodist Church, I served through parish ministry, chaplaincy in medical and psychiatric settings, spiritual direction, and pastoral psychotherapy until 1991, when my ministry became education. I teach practical theology, spiritual care, and spiritually integrative counseling at Claremont School of Theology, in the interreligious Claremont Lincoln University consortium.

Put too simply, my primary methodology is an ongoing action-reflection-action cycle in practical and pastoral theology where, with care as motivation and orienting standard, wisdom from lived experience and interdisciplinary resources—including, of course, religion and spirituality—are brought into mutually analytical dialogue to revise praxis, in service to the common good. I expand later on my theological location

---

[3] Lewis Z. Schlosser, "Christian Privilege: Breaking a Sacred Taboo," *Journal of Multicultural Counseling and Development* 31 (Jan. 2003): 44–51.

but begin here by stating that my first loyalty is to Divine Mystery,[4] which, largely due to my birth into a Christian context, I have glimpsed most consistently through Jesus of Nazareth. Thus, I strive in my beliefs and practices to emulate the humility, extravagant welcome, and evangelical boldness[5] exemplified by Jesus as he embodied G-d on earth.

This discussion is limited to the U.S. context and English-language literature. "Spirituality" is the religious or non-religious search for meanings, values, and modes of living that address matters of ultimate, profound significance and serve the common good. "Care" is offered by persons or institutions with intent to convey respectful concern and to advocate for abundant life for all; care seekers sometimes experience it as such, though not necessarily. "Spiritual" care is respectful concern offered by persons of mature faith (religious or nonreligious) with the intent to support others in their spirituality. "Interfaith" spiritual care is such concern offered in relationships characterized by validation of spiritual and/or religious difference and grounded in caregivers' support of freedom of/from religion. Thus, by definition, proselytization is not part of interfaith spiritual care. This claim is not primarily semantic, however—it has a Christian pastoral theological rationale (elaborated below) that includes restraint of the power and cultural privilege accorded in the United States to Christian caregivers.

Interfaith spiritual care is never nonsectarian.[6] Spiritual care is always rooted in the spiritual specificity of the participants in a multifaith relationship. Moreover, at this point in history, education, practices, and professional certification in spiritual care remain significantly tied to Christianity.[7] The history and standards of Western European and North American Christian care have been globalized, while the international-

---

[4] When referencing divinity, I use a variety of designations (for example, Divine Mystery) in order to practice respect and humility; symbolize the incapacity of humans to know the divine completely (for example, the tetragrammaton YHWH or the formulation "G-d"); and avoid any one name becoming an idol.

[5] John H. Thomas, "Extravagant Welcome, Evangelical Boldness," in *Come as You Are: United Church of Christ 2004 Annual Report*, accessed July 24, 2011, http://www.ucc.org/about-us/pdfs/annual_report_2004.pdf. See also J. Bennett Guess, "Evangelical Courage," *UCC News*, June–July, 2005, accessed July 24, 2011, http://www.ucc.org/ucnews/junjul05/courage.html.

[6] See, for example, Christian ethicist Grace Y. Kao's demonstration of this claim in relation to prayer in the context of the US military in "Mission Impossible: 'Nonsectarian' Prayer in the Military Chaplaincy," *Political Theology* 11, no. 4 (2010): 577–606.

[7] The challenges of and slow evolution toward taking religious pluralism into account can be seen in two organizations that have a Christian heritage but are now credentialing chaplains from other traditions: the Association of Professional Chaplains and the Association of Clinical Pastoral Education, Inc.

ization and indigenization of spiritual care in any religious tradition has barely begun.[8] Much research remains to be done before we will understand how the spiritual specificity of the participants influences interfaith spiritual care, but I assume such influence.

For example: How does it affect spiritual care by Christians that in most of our communities the terminology of "pastoral" care remains in common use? And what of the effect of other Christian specificities? Though offered by laypersons, "pastoral" care by clergy has special significance. It includes interpersonal care of congregants and families but is also effective when offered to congregations and other groups. Pastoral care is offered not only through conversational counsel but also through preaching, liturgy (including sacraments), small groups, education (especially Bible study), concrete and crisis care within and beyond the congregation (provision of food, shelter, financial assistance, etc.), home visitation, and enjoyment of one another in community life. Christian readers especially are equipped to consider why some practices have had disproportional influence in both "pastoral" and "spiritual" care.

Further, contemporary Christian caregiving is widely characterized by affirmative relational qualities—respect and compassion, for example. At the same time, Christian caregiving tends also to be characterized by concern for another's wrongdoing and efforts to spur care seekers to change. Historian John McNeil comments on the history of this tendency: "Lying deep in the experience and culture of the early Christian communities are the closely related practices of mutual edification . . . and fraternal correction."[9] These early practices have not disappeared but continue in conscious and unconscious impulses within Christian caregivers who seek the betterment of another's belief and behavior. Unfortunately, much of the value of these early practices has been lost, their reciprocal and enriching qualities too often having degenerated into one-sided efforts at altering others. Finally, when Christians speak of "spiritual" care, we cannot escape being influenced by specific Christian meanings—Christianity's notion of the human spirit (and soul), for example, and Christian trinitarianism that yields the Holy Spirit as an aspect of the Divine.

The remainder of the chapter is divided into three main sections: a

---

[8] Emmanuel Y. Lartey, "Globalization, Internationalization, and Indigenization of Pastoral Care and Counseling," in *Pastoral Care and Counseling: Redefining the Paradigms*, ed. Nancy J. Ramsay (Nashville: Abingdon, 2004), 87–108.

[9] John T. McNeil, *A History of the Cure of Souls* (New York: Harper, 1951), 85. This enduring tendency likely has its genesis in response to persecution at the time of Christianity's origins, which gave rise to concern that Christians would be tempted to renounce "right" belief and behavior.

discussion of theological foundations vital for interrelating Christianity and spiritual care, especially in interfaith caregiving; description of selected frameworks and practices in Christian spiritual care that have potential for interfaith care; and, a distillation of what these Christian foundations, frameworks, and practices suggest for wisdom in interfaith care.

## Theological foundations

I have selected three approaches to help convey how Christianity's theological complexity might illuminate interfaith spiritual care: the Wesleyan quadrilateral, "streams of living water," and credo—a Christian pastoral theology for interfaith spiritual care.

### The Wesleyan quadrilateral

Rooted in the writings of theologian and pastor John Wesley, founder of the Methodist tradition in Christian Protestantism, the image of a quadrilateral portrays the interrelatedness of sources of authority for Christians. The four-sidedness of the quadrilateral represents four main sources—Bible, tradition, reason, and experience. Lines between the points of the quadrilateral represent the interplay between the sources—each source informs the others. A quadrilateral may have sides of equal or unequal length; this flexibility in the symbol represents that among Christians the four sources have different degrees of influence. Especially, Christians tend to give differing weight to the Bible. Still, the quadrilateral helps us see more concretely what Christian spiritual care demonstrates—that among Christians, virtually all dimensions of the creation have potential to be valuable sources of foundational wisdom for spiritual caregiving.

### "Streams of living water"

Richard J. Foster offers a framework for comprehending and valuing the interrelationship between diverse traditions within Christianity.[10] Inspired by a biblical metaphor—"Out of the believer's heart shall flow rivers of living water" (Jn 7:38)—Foster argues that Christianity's multiple traditions are all "streams of living water." They are all part of a "deep river of divine intimacy, a powerful river of holy living, a dancing river of jubilation in the Spirit, and a broad river of unconditional love for all peoples."[11] Only when taken together can the diversity among Christians adequately embody the richness of Christianity: "It is a little

---

[10] Richard J. Foster, *Streams of Living Water: Celebrating the Great Traditions of Christian Faith* (New York: HarperSanFrancisco, 1998).

[11] Foster, xv.

like the Mississippi River, which gains strength and volume as the Ohio and Missouri and many other rivers flow into it."[12] A Christian addressing Christians, Foster identifies six "streams" discernible in the life of Jesus of Nazareth, six "great traditions" of the Christian faith:

- The contemplative tradition emphasizes a prayer-filled life, modeling our lives on the importance of prayer and intimacy in the life of Jesus.
- The pietistic-holiness tradition emphasizes a virtuous life, modeling our lives on purity of heart as exemplified by Jesus.
- The charismatic tradition emphasizes a Spirit-empowered life, modeling our lives on Jesus' life in the Spirit.
- The social justice tradition emphasizes a compassionate life, modeling our lives on justice and shalom as Jesus practiced it.
- The evangelical tradition emphasizes a gospel-centered life, modeling our lives on the good news Jesus proclaimed for all, even as he was drawn to suffering and marginalized persons.
- The incarnational tradition emphasizes a sacramental life, imitating Jesus' reverence for each moment.

**Credo: A Christian pastoral theology for interfaith spiritual care**

In Christian Protestantism, "pastoral" theological reflection is a study of the interrelatedness of human experience and scholarly wisdom, especially religious and/or spiritual resources, in which care is the motivation and orienting standard for theory and practice. My experience of the interplay between Bible, tradition, reason, and experience has gradually yielded pastoral theological warrants for the theology of religious pluralism and care I have discerned is required of me as a Christian. Born in community, and perhaps shared by others, the theological claims I sketch in this section are not more than a portion of my credo, as best I can speak it at this juncture in my life.[13] It is not prescriptive for others; I hope instead it invites conversations that further illuminate for me life together in Divine Mystery. I grasp and practice these assertions imperfectly, but they orient my efforts in interfaith care of souls.

- Most fundamental is Divine Mystery: that so much of origins, ultimacies, values, and meanings are unknown by humanity, or

---

[12] Ibid.

[13] A broader statement is found in Kathleen J. Greider, "Pastoral Theological Reflections on Caregiving and Religious Pluralism," *Pistis e Praxis: Theologia e Pastoral* 3, no. 2 (July–Dec. 2011): 449–65.

known but unpracticed, constitutes for me mystery of a divine order, a sacred enigma evocative of my wonder and respect. Biblically expressed: G-d's thoughts are not our thoughts (Is 55:8). No religious system comprises the unknowability of Divine Mystery.

- My right to think, speak, and/or act in relation to Divine Mystery rests on a spirituality of humility and *via negativa*, well-expressed in theologian Peter Rollins' explication of his book's title: *How (Not) to Speak of God*.[14] The same is true of my use of all holy writings, especially the Bible, and all sacred practices.
- I most often glimpse Divine Mystery in multiplicity, ambiguity, and paradox. Thus, I strive to give them preference over human certitude, except where they contribute to unnecessary violence, which is sin.[15] This "both/and" quality of life is conveyed in Eccl 3:1–8: "for everything there is a season . . ." Accordingly, I prize the multiplicity of religions and spiritualities, except where they are used to rationalize unnecessary violence.[16]
- Humanity is made in the image and likeness of G-d (Gn 1:26–27). Thus created in and empowered by relationality with Divine Mystery, humans are responsible above all else for wise stewardship of the power invested in us.
- My first loyalty is to Divine Mystery. Accordingly, I take seriously warnings about idolatry and serving other gods (Ex 20:3–4; Dt 5:7–8). I strive not to take as idols any particular religion, scripture, theology, denomination, congregation, or human leader. I strive not to proselytize, religiously or otherwise, because to do so would be idolatry.
- I cannot repay the gift of my life, but I can express my gratitude for it by combating violence and contributing to that which is lasting and essential: "What does YHWH require of you but to do justice, and to love kindness, and to walk humbly with YHWH?" (Mi 6:8). Right relationship in the face of oppression, compassion where there is suffering, and self-examination in the face of that

---

[14] Peter Rollins, *How (Not) to Speak of God* (Brewster, MA: Paraclete, 2006).

[15] Marjorie H. Suchocki, *The Fall to Violence: Original Sin in Relational Theology* (New York: Continuum, 1994), 16.

[16] Though beyond the scope of this chapter, this claim indirectly affirms religious multiplicity in persons and communities. For discussion of this human reality common in many regions of the globe, see Kathleen J. Greider, "Religiously Plural Persons: Multiplicity and Care of Souls," in *Pastoralpsychologie und Religionspsychologie im Dialog/Pastoral Psychology and Psychology of Religion in Dialogue*, ed. Isabelle Noth, Christoph Morgenthaler, and Kathleen J. Greider (Stuttgart: Kohlhammer, 2011), 119–35.

which is most sacred—this is my responsibility in relation to the reality of sin and evil and the hunger for loving relationships.
- The "Golden Rule" is authoritative for my relationships with others because it is taught in my own and many other religious traditions. I especially appreciate statements of it that advise restraint, as in Buddhism: "Hurt not others in ways that you yourself would find hurtful" (Udana-Varga 5,1).
- Born into Christian culture and communities, Christianity is my native religious language and the Jewish rabbi Jesus my primary spiritual teacher. Just as I have learned Christianity from the Jewish Jesus, I have been challenged and nourished by beliefs and practices in other faiths, into which I could have been born.
- My salvation is centered not on my beliefs in Jesus but in my fidelity to Love and right relationship. No religion monopolizes the love of which Jesus spoke when asked a trick question about which commandment is greatest: "love YHWH with all your heart, soul, and mind and your neighbor as yourself" (see, for example, Mt 22:34–40). Since this is the greatest commandment, I understand it to supersede the "great commission" (Mt 28:16–20).
- Conversion is part of Divine Mystery, the work of G-d. On the one hand, I am obliged to be open to be converted, should this be part of the Divine Mystery, perhaps to a more passionate embodiment of Christianity. On the other hand, I am obliged to strive toward living a life more persuasive of the possibility of Love and Justice. The relationship between conversion and evangelization is for me well-illuminated by the writer May Sarton: "We convert, if we do at all, by being something irresistible, not by demanding something impossible."[17]
- Stories of Jesus in relationship show me profound ways of caring, especially in interfaith encounters: his love of questions more than answers; his desire that all persons have abundant life (Jn 10:10); his savvy with regard to the dynamics of power and privilege; his warnings against judging others (Jn 8:7); his sense of humor, which peeks through his use of parables; his emphasis on taking the initiative to seek reconciliation when another is troubled by us (Mt 5:21–26); and, not least, his wise guidance regarding the ambiguity of humans—be wise as serpents and innocent as doves (Mt 10:16).

---

[17] May Sarton, *The House By the Sea* (New York: Norton, 1977), 57–58.

## Frameworks and practices for interfaith spiritual care

Though spiritual care is never nonsectarian, it is intriguing to note that numerous Christian frameworks and practices for spiritual care are not predicated on Christian belief. There are obvious exceptions—Christian sacraments, prayer "in the name of Jesus," use of the Bible and other resources with Christian interpretation and intention, Christian counseling. Nevertheless, there are frameworks and practices for spiritual care that, though developed in Christianity, are not the property of Christians. We proceed cautiously, since research on interreligious spiritual care has barely begun. However, as in the practice of medicine, where relief of human suffering sometimes requires physicians to try untested treatments, we sometimes have no option but to offer untested expressions of interfaith spiritual care. We proceed cautiously, venturing into uncharted waters for urgent, pragmatic reasons.

In this section, I briefly describe five conceptual frameworks for interfaith spiritual care—multifocal lenses, streams of living water, paradigms, functions, and images—and then illustrate them in my discussion of several practices. At the end of the section, I indicate how these frameworks and practices might work in interfaith spiritual care in relation to a common human situation of need.

### Frameworks

I begin with a framework in the form of a metaphor—that of a multifocal lens—by which we can imaginatively conceptualize how spiritual caregivers might engage the ever-increasing ways of knowing available to and required of us. Such a lens on their cameras equips photographers to see how different focal points render the scene differently, more nuanced than when seen with the naked eye. Imagine how the "naked eye" of our overall point of view on a caregiving situation is enhanced with a multifocal lens! Five uses of our metaphorical lens immediately present themselves. The metaphor helps us imaginatively engage the interdisciplinary work essential in practical and pastoral theology and in care: various academic disciplines—anthropology, psychology, sociology, medicine, for example—are multiple focal points within our overall point of view that enhance our comprehension of and response to human situations. The relationship between and use of premodern, modern, postmodern, and postcolonial points of view and analyses are multiple foci in the analytical lens that informs appropriate response.[18]

---

[18] Carrie Doehring calls for the use of a "trifocal lens" in her discussion of the necessity in pastoral care for premodern, modern, and postmodern points of view. See Doehring, *The Practice of Pastoral Care: A Postmodern Approach* (Louisville: Westminster John Knox, 2006), 1–8.

Analysis of the dynamics of power and privilege so foundational to postmodern and postcolonial analyses—and always in the foreground or background of human relationship—requires a multifocal point of view. For example, a multifocal lens reveals that nearly every group of humans has been both target and agent of oppression;[19] and, at the same time, it reveals that some forms of oppression are more deadly and insidious than others, some forms of privilege more valuable and unassailable than others. Multiple religious perspectives present in interfaith spiritual care situations could be understood as different focal points in a multifocal lens. Finally, the metaphor of a multifocal lens also helps us interrelate multiple frameworks and practices for spiritual care.

Second, Foster's notion of diverse "streams" of Christianity provides a framework for identifying diverse streams of spiritual care. The contemplative tradition reminds us of divine care available in meditation and prayer. The pietistic-holiness tradition emphasizes that self-care through contemplation yields an honorable life which, in turn, yields ethical care of others. The charismatic tradition enlivens ethics with spirit—care can be principled and still full of vitality. The social justice tradition yields care that weds compassion and right relationship. The evangelical tradition reminds us of the importance of care in embodying good news (*evangel*, "gospel")—perhaps especially that whatever our failures, restoration is possible. The incarnational tradition recognizes the sacred in everyone and everything, and thus encourages us to expressions of care that reverence all living beings and ritualize our everyday lives.

A third framework offers paradigms or patterns for conceptualizing and expressing spiritual care.[20] Four paradigms have been identified in the evolution of care in Christian communities and are best understood by use of our multifocal lens—as different foci within care. A "spiritual" paradigm emphasizes care for spirituality, for faith traditions, and for the potential of both to offer help to believers. A "personal" paradigm emphasizes care that, through attention to the uniqueness, woundedness, and resilience of each person in the caregiving situation, yields compassionate presence and empowering response to human need. A "communal-

---

[19] Rita Hardiman and Bailey W. Jackson, "Conceptual Foundations for Social Justice Courses," in *Teaching for Diversity and Social Justice: A Sourcebook*, ed. Maurianne Adams, Lee Ann Bell, and Pat Griffin (New York: Routledge, 1997), 16–29.

[20] In Christian pastoral theology and care, two scholars have provided primary leadership for this framework. See John Patton, *Pastoral Care in Context: An Introduction to Pastoral Care* (Louisville: Westminster/John Knox, 1993) and Emmanuel Y. Lartey, *Pastoral Theology in an Intercultural World* (Cleveland: Pilgrim, 2006). To convey their meaning more broadly, what Patton calls the "classical" and "clinical-pastoral" paradigms here I call the "spiritual" and "personal" paradigms.

contextual" paradigm emphasizes the social ecology of care offered by communities, and care for communities, according to their particular contexts, especially multiple cultural particularities. An "intercultural" paradigm emphasizes care for the interaction of cultural identities, taking into account the global, historical, and current dynamics of privilege, power, and violence between (and within) persons and communities of differing cultural identities.

A fourth framework offers broad categories of the functions of spiritual care—its purposes and goals. The number of identified functions has grown in recent years. Seven are commonly agreed upon: healing, sustaining, guiding, reconciling, liberating, nurturing, and empowering.[21]

A fifth framework calls attention to the plethora of images that have arisen out of the experience of spiritual caregivers—one text,[22] which is not exhaustive, names nineteen images, such as shepherd,[23] "good" Samaritan,[24] "living human web,"[25] wise fool,[26] midwife,[27] and indigenous storyteller.[28] Images of caregiving can be found almost anywhere, but certainly in sacred texts, historical events, experience of paradox, art, and contextually-generated wisdom.

Our attention turns now to caregiving practices that, though historically developed by Christians, may also have value in interfaith spiritual care. To show how the frameworks just discussed can influence our caregiving, I use them to inform our exploration of practices. Watch for multifocal lenses, streams of living water, paradigms, functions, and images.

### Practices

Caregiving practices are not only important in moments of encounter with others, but also crucial to our preparation before and reflection after encounters. Thus, three phases of encounter structure our exploration:

---

[21] See, for example, Carroll A. Watkins Ali, *Survival and Liberation: Pastoral Theology in African American Context* (St. Louis: Chalice, 1999), 9.

[22] Robert C. Dykstra, *Images of Pastoral Care: Classic Readings* (St. Louis: Chalice, 2005).

[23] Seward Hiltner, "The Solicitous Shepherd," in Dykstra, 47–53; Alastair V. Campbell, "The Courageous Shepherd," in Dykstra, 54–61.

[24] Jeanne Stevenson-Moessner, "The Self-Differentiated Samaritan," in Dykstra, 62–68.

[25] Bonnie J. Miller-McLemore, "The Living Human Web," in Dykstra, 40–46.

[26] Alastair V. Campbell, "The Wise Fool," in Dykstra, 94–107; Donald Capps, "The Wise Fool Reframed," in Dykstra, 108–22.

[27] Karen R. Hanson, "The Midwife," in Dykstra, 200–08; Brita Gill-Austern, "The Midwife, Storyteller and Reticent Outlaw," in Dykstra, 218–27.

[28] Edward P. Wimberly, "The Indigenous Storyteller," in Dykstra, 180–87.

anticipation of encounter, encounter, and refreshment after encounter. Our multifocal lens keeps us mindful of their interrelation as mutually enriching foci in our ongoing cycle of action and reflection. Several practices recur in each grouping, with different emphases: growing in interculturality; nuancing our analysis of privilege and power; developing multiple intelligences;[29] and increasing our consciousness and self-reflexivity. The chart below provides an overview:

| Anticipation of encounter: *Emphasis on maturing our personhood* | Encounter: *Emphasis on maturing our engagement with others* | Refreshment for re-encounter: *Emphasis on maturing our learning* |
|---|---|---|
| • Communal-contextual self-care<br>• Intercultural self-care<br>• Personal self-care<br>• Spiritual self-care | • Responsive presence<br>• Emergency care<br>• Spiritual companionship<br>• Ritual | • Self-assessment<br>• Consultation<br>• Reassessing our faith stance<br>• Continuing education |

**Practices of interfaith spiritual care**

**Anticipation of encounter.** In this group of practices, whether as eager novices or experienced professionals, we ready ourselves for future spiritual care encounters through emphasis on maturing our personhood. Practices of personal maturation rightly can be considered self-care, so I will use the four paradigms of care noted above to show how they work in practice.

Anticipating the cultural complexity of interfaith care makes *communal-cultural self-care* of preeminent importance. This paradigm focuses our self-nurturing reflection on developing our social intelligence, especially the social analysis of our personhood. We seek to understand ourselves as persons-in-relation—locally, and also historically and globally. We strive to mature our consciousness of the history, multiplicity, interrelatedness, and power dynamics of our own culturally contextualized identities. Like a kaleidoscope, we are made of many variegated "parts"—internalized bits of the places, persons, and groups where we

---

[29] Howard Gardner, *Multiple Intelligences: New Horizons in Theory and Practice* (New York: Basic Books, 2006). Lists of intelligences normally include the following: bodily-kinesthetic, existential/moral/spiritual, interpersonal, intrapersonal, linguistic/literary, logical-mathematical, musical/auditory/rhythmic, naturalistic, and visual/spatial. Interpersonal and intrapersonal intelligences are detailed in Daniel Goleman, *Emotional Intelligence: Why It Can Matter More than IQ* (New York, Bantam, 1997).

have felt belonging-ness, we-ness, with the communities and contexts that have shaped us. If cultures are "patterns of experience"[30] in history and the present that shape our identities, we inherit and contribute to many such cultures—no one has just one. "Our people" are those with whom we share racial/ethnic and national cultures, yes, but we also find "our people" among those with whom we share cultures of gender, class, age, religion and spirituality, sexual and relational orientation, language, and personality. We share cultures with people who have education and do work similar to ours, enjoy the arts and sports we enjoy, or suffer tragedies similar to ours. Arguably most important, given the pervasive effects of power dynamics, we share cultures historically and in the present with people who have been targets of the same kinds of oppression we have suffered, and agents of the same kinds of oppression in which we are implicated, though this latter shared culture is more difficult to admit.

Such social intelligence and power analysis continues in *intercultural self-care*. This paradigm provides structure as we anticipate the exciting and confounding experience of our kaleidoscopic personhood interacting with the kaleidoscopic personhood of care seekers. No longer are we satisfied to know ourselves only as members of families and communities. Rather, our personhood feels incomplete until we know our families, communities, and ancestors in relationship to other families, communities, and their ancestors. Anticipating the interculturality of interfaith spiritual care requires mature affective awareness of the bewildering history of violence, current intergroup alliances and tensions, and differentials of power and privilege that trouble our human relations across cultural differences. These points of view mature our self-reflexivity—we take into account how our cultural affiliations and the history of our peoples might be affecting our relationships with care seekers and colleagues. All these differentials mean that effective interculturality requires us to mature our capacity to share power—to exert and relinquish power in relationship as appropriate to the ebb and flow of cultural identities affecting the encounter. Then again, we need to be ready to respond accordingly if all the intercultural and contextual dynamics just named are underground or in the background of the encounter.

We also carry into interfaith encounters our uniqueness as persons. As we anticipate the use of ourselves in caregiving, the paradigm of *personal self-care* focuses our attention on maturing our particular personhood. The

---

[30] David W. Augsburger, *Pastoral Counseling across Cultures* (Philadelphia: Westminster John Knox Press, 1986), 58.

image of "braided selves"[31] suggests loving care that styles the multiplicity of our personhood into coherence. Development of intrapersonal aspects of our emotional intelligence—perceiving, understanding, reasoning with, and managing our emotions—is center-stage in personal self-care. The Golden Rule is also a priority; we are compassionate with others only to the extent we have compassion for our own humanity. So, we embrace our own strangeness no less than we claim to welcome strangers. We suffer with the recognition that we are multiply paradoxical; for example, we can be imaged as wounded healers,[32] but we are also healers who wound others. Such insight into the ambiguity of our personhood continues our power analysis; tending our personal history of wounding and being wounded reduces its dominance in caregiving encounters. Similarly, personal self-care involves reflection on which of our many cultures most dominate our internal experience and self-presentation in a given encounter, and why. If we choose it, such reflection could also cultivate our consciousness of that which most of us deny—the often-subtle privileges granted to us through no effort of our own. Are we privileged because of our charisma, skin color, gender, body type, language skill, cleverness, class, religion, or something else? Only increasing consciousness of such privileges equips us to share power with others in the ebb and flow of human encounters. Personal self-care also involves exercising our bodily-kinesthetic intelligence so that we care for our bodies, through which our personhood is expressed.

Finally, anticipating interfaith spiritual care requires maturation of our personhood through *spiritual self-care*. This paradigm focuses our attention on our relationship to faith traditions—those we inherited, embrace, have renounced, and to which we are attracted. We cultivate more consciousness of the beliefs and practices most important in our lives—at this time in your life, what is your credo? Immersion in the "stream of living water" of contemplation makes space for the profound questions of spiritual self-care. What is our theology or philosophy of religious pluralism? What spiritual resources cultivate in us the authenticity, vulnerability, and mutuality that enable us to offer life-giving connection to others that does not require their acquiescence to our creed, or vice versa?[33] If spiritual caregivers are rightly imaged, at least sometimes, as

---

[31] Pamela Cooper-White, *Braided Selves: Collected Essays on Multiplicity, God, and Persons* (Eugene, OR: Cascade, 2011).

[32] Henry J. M. Nouwen, "The Wounded Healer," in Dykstra, 76–84.

[33] Judith V. Jordan, *Relational-Cultural Therapy* (Washington DC: American Psychological Association Press, 2010).

ascetic witnesses,[34] what spiritual resources enable our renunciation to be judicious and sustainable? What spiritual resources develop the depth of soul through which we can both discern and act when exerting our power or relinquishing our power is needed? What spiritual resources make it possible for us to take responsibility or take a stand? In experiences where humans disappoint us, in experiences of aloneness and despair, what sustains us?

**Encounter.** In this group of practices, we offer our care to others. Whether in brief episodes or ongoing relationships, our focus is on maturing our engagement with others, especially our capacity to engage the subjectivity of others care-fully.

All caring encounters begin with *responsive partnership*. Additional forms of care may be needed, urgently. Still, we start by addressing others from a physical and psychospiritual posture of respect, even reverence. One portion of responsive partnership is known in Christian traditions as the "ministry of presence," a compassionate companionship that is an especially precious offering when the resolution of suffering or fixing of problems are nowhere in sight. When imaged as "listening for the soul,"[35] presence is the caregiver "doing" less and "being" more—more attentive, quiet, still, patient. Presence is a quality of relationship created when our not-knowing and non-trying[36] greets a care seeker's yearning. Presence is an atmosphere of luminosity created when a caregiver's emotional intelligence shines interpersonally—the care seeker's yearnings are perceived and understood, acknowledged as reasonable and manageable. Still, presence is more than silence, space, and receptivity—it is a ministry also of response. Nonverbal recognition, validating words, and empowering actions all flow to care seekers from caregivers who have immersed themselves in the "stream of living water" that is right relationship, love, and justice intertwined. The image of an intimate stranger[37] captures the paradoxical potential of responsive partnership—closeness even without familiarity, partnership that is a combination of respectfully attentive silence and communication through words and actions that are "just right." For this to be so, we need always to be maturing an additional aspect of

---

[34] James E. Dittes, "The Ascetic Witness," in Dykstra, 137–49.

[35] Jean Stairs, *Listening for the Soul: Pastoral Care and Spiritual Direction* (Minneapolis: Fortress, 2000).

[36] Siroj Sorajjakool, *Wu Wei, Negativity and Depression: The Principle of Non-Trying in the Practice of Pastoral Care* (New York: Haworth, 2001); Siroj Sorajjakool, *Do Nothing—Peace for Everyday Living: Reflections on Chuang Tzu's Philosophy* (Philadelphia: Templeton, 2009).

[37] Robert C. Dykstra, "The Intimate Stranger," in Dykstra, 123–36.

emotional intelligence—effective relationality in situations of conflict.

Power analysis brings responsive partnership into even sharper focus. Building on our intercultural self-care, we recognize that our encounters with care seekers are always encounters-in-global-and-historical-relation. As caregivers, we know our personhood is representative not only of our individuality but also of the many communities with which we identify and are identified by others. Beyond this reflexivity, responsive presence is attentiveness to other power dynamics affecting our encounters. Much suffering is fueled by poverty and other chronic systemic injustices, which explains why the function of responsive partnership is so often sustenance and nurturance. Moreover, since the majority of persons are not privileged, responsive presence often functions as empowerment, liberation, and reconciliation. Responsive presence that serves these functions demonstrates mature interpersonal intelligence. We presume caregivers' capacities, invite their corrections, and respect their rights of refusal. We risk embracing persons and groups traditionally shunned. Wary of stereotyping, we avoid cultural caricature. Wary of universalizing, we prize difference.

A second practice in encounter is *emergency care*. In this practice, our primary concern is for safety and survival when physical and psychospiritual life is threatened or hardship cannot be immediately remedied. Offering food, clothing, shelter, visits, and other emergency care is easily seen as part of spiritual care when we acknowledge the close relationship between our bodies and our spirits. Though we can compartmentalize them conceptually, body and spirit are inseparable companions, and life and death are never far from each other. Indeed, other practices of spiritual care can be rendered meaningless in the absence of safety and survival. Emergency spiritual care is normally understood to serve the function of sustaining—providing care that sustains persons in situations that are not possible to remedy—but it could eventually function also as guidance, empowerment, and liberation. Whether emergency care is empowering or liberating, though, depends on multiple kinds of intelligence in caregivers. Does our inter- and intrapersonal intelligence keep us mindful of the risk that charity may be feeding the egos of the givers while humiliating and shaming the receivers? Does our social analysis increase our consciousness that the emergency services we offer may originate in our socio-economic privilege as much as in our care? Does our intrapersonal intelligence root out any patronization that is tainting our care? If so, we will offer concrete care only within responsive partnership, in dignified ways that are less humiliating and shaming, and, therefore, more welcome.

Included in emergency care is, first, protection of children, elders, and other dependent adults from abuse. The legal requirement that religious leaders report to authorities reasonable suspicion of abuse is best understood as a call to save the lives of the most vulnerable among us. This is better accomplished proactively, for example, through support services offered to caregivers who are frazzled, isolated, and, therefore, at risk of harming others. Another form of emergency spiritual care is disaster care—shelter, clean water, food, clothing, and services of medical, mental health, and spiritual leaders—provided to those who have experienced environmental or financial calamity. The outpouring from religious communities of supplies and work crews after tornadoes or tsunamis is an illustration. But disasters also affect lives more quietly and daily, and so emergency care needs sometimes to be regularized. Some religious communities do this, for example, through longstanding food shelters, weekly free medical clinics, and elder day care centers. A third form of emergency care is consistent visitation and services provided in times of trouble to persons and families experiencing illness, bereavement, incarceration, military service, or any such disruption or crisis. In those who excel at coordinating these forms of care we see another form of social intelligence well developed and welcome—the capacity to organize groups and negotiate details.

*Spiritual companionship* is a third caregiving practice that may serve us well in interreligious encounters. Spiritual companionship requires caregivers to know ourselves as pilgrims on our own journey and to encounter care seekers on their particular life journey, with whom we travel for a while. As travelers sharing a path, caregivers and care seekers spend time in silence, small talk, and observing the landscape. When conditions are right, there may also be meaningful conversation—reflection on the journey, considering together what values, meanings, questions, and resources might be most important in a care seeker's experience. As in spiritually integrative counseling and pastoral counseling, the emphasis in spiritual care is on care seekers' journeys and on the readiness of caregivers, having experienced maturation of the existential, spiritual, and moral dimensions of our intelligence, to aid care seekers' search. The teamwork of long-distance cycling is a fitting image. Only the cyclists themselves can run the race they have entered, but the accompaniment provided by those in the support vehicles is informed companionship that can help make the long race sustainable. Spiritual companionship, a caregiving practice at the intimate heart of human life, is guided by the ethic required in all caregiving—sobered by the vulnerability of others and the power invested in our roles, we strive above all to do no harm.

In interfaith encounters, *ritual* is a care practice that is especially important and complicated. Delicate decision-making is required when life and death circumstances evoke requests for tradition-specific ritual in interfaith caregiving encounters—when, for example, a dying Catholic soldier asks the Muslim military chaplain for last rites. More regularly, though, spiritual caregivers have opportunity to employ ritual expressions not limited to a specific tradition, and thereby access the power of symbolic actions and objects to connect and console people. On the one hand, I am drawing attention to the "stream of living water" found in the sacredness of ordinariness. When enacted ceremonially, with grace and gravitas, significant connection and meaning can be created through everyday actions—rituals of greeting, standing and sitting, looking and looking away, giving and receiving, leave-taking. On the other hand, many formal ritual actions are not tradition-specific and yet have potential to provide spiritual care. Imagine the spiritual caregiver as a contemplative artist[38]—gathering community, creating aesthetic space, providing visual images, making symbolic gestures and other symbolic movement, reading spiritually evocative texts, singing, and/or, with careful discernment of their appropriateness and form, inviting prayer or offering physical touch. Again, concern for the misuse of power must abide. Spiritual caregivers earn the right to inquire about or suggest ritual only when we relationally demonstrate respect for care seekers' spiritual locations. And, if invited to proceed, we engage the power of ritual as collaboratively as possible, with restraint, highly attuned to care seekers' response. We strive not to overrun care seekers' subjectivity but also not to neglect the power of the symbolic dimension. Our capacity for appropriate ritual action in interfaith encounter requires a certain flexibility made possible by development of multiple intelligences. For example, my tradition's ritual dependence on texts and words favors (and probably helped develop) my linguistic/literary intelligence, but for ritual leadership in interfaith settings, I have had to work on developing my kinesthetic/bodily, auditory, visual/spatial, and naturalistic intelligence.

**Refreshment for re-encounter.** Caregivers' opportunities and responsibilities do not end when caregiving encounters end. Deeply rooted motivation keeps us caring through a period of after-reflection in which

---

[38] Brita L. Gill-Austern, "Pedagogy under the Influence of Feminism and Womanism," in *Feminist and Womanist Pastoral Theology*, ed. Bonnie J. Miller-McLemore and Brita L. Gill-Austern (Nashville: Abingdon, 1999), 149–68. The reference is to 155–57.

we refresh ourselves in preparation for re-encounter. The combined effect of these practices is metaphorically comparable to the "refresh" function on our technological devices—we update our caregiving with new "data" available since we last engaged in reflection on our caregiving. What actually happens during our "refresh" is not so quick, but just as detailed, as when we refresh our tech devices. Through this group of practices, we focus on maturing our learning, and we complete one round in the action/reflection cycle by learning from our caregiving experience. For most of us, this pause is difficult—it is easier to keep moving, not resist the fast pace of most caregivers' lives. And, if reflection reveals shortcomings, this pause can be painful. However, even if we can engage in this discipline for a few minutes a day, and participate in a monthly consultation, it is a gift to ourselves and to the next care seekers we encounter.

The ground of refreshment is *self-assessment of our encounters*. Here our emphasis is on our own fair but candid appraisal of our care, and on our openness to being changed for the better. Imagine an experienced gardener, whose work over many seasons has taught her that an enchanting garden results from pruning and other hard labor, not so much from admiring her handiwork. Reasoning with emotion as well as thought, we examine our actions. We study the "text" of others' reactions to us. Did our practices of encounter seem to be well received or fall short, and why? We also study the text of our feeling-thoughts and behaviors during encounters with others. What evidence is there that we were attuned to requirements of interculturality? What do our actions reveal to us about how emotion is affecting our caregiving? Are our actions congruent with our stated values? Do our actions with care seekers demonstrate power-sharing? The practice of reflexivity is essential in this phase. In what ways has my subjectivity affected the caregiving relationship? How have I helped? How have I harmed? This practice is opportunity to join with generations of faithful people in many religious/spiritual traditions who have conscientiously tried to live an honorable life—that stream of living water surely keeps this humble practice constructive and empowering.

Refreshment is sufficient only when it includes *consultation*. The viewpoints of others who are located differently from us assure our assessment is intercultural. Consultation is good for moderating power dynamics in our caregiving. It is founded on our consciousness that our knowledge is limited and on our willingness, at any rank and age, to be learners. Consultation also lessens the risk of our self-deception and thus makes our caregiving safer for others. For full engagement in consultation, we need the emotional intelligence to manage our feelings when we make ourselves vulnerable to others, are critiqued, and receive commendation. These benefits of consultation imply that we best seek out colleagues with whom we can be honest, who are bold enough to challenge us, and who are gentle enough to encourage us. We need colleagues already standing in the stream of living water of good news where imperfection is expected and *metanoia*—radical reorientation—is always possible.

Refreshment also involves *reassessing our faith stance*. Here our learning is focused on how our caregiving is affecting, and being affected by, our personal beliefs and practices. We can think of this practice as revisiting our *credo*; encounters with the religious experiences, doctrinal struggles, and spiritual paths of others can affirm, challenge, and change our own. To continue offering spiritual care without regularly re-articulating our own spiritual and/or religious location is to lose touch with the ground on which we stand and to have less clarity about the personhood we bring to encounters with others. In the Christian tradition we speak of such times of reassessment as "going on retreat"—for caregivers, this time of reassessment is a brief retreat from caregiving in order to see how we have been or need to be changed spiritually, and to refresh ourselves. Especially when we are offering spiritual care in devastating circumstances, it is also crucial during this reassessment of our faith stance to recalibrate our hope: what "living water" will motivate and nourish our capacity to return to devastating circumstances with renewed passion, spirit, and conviction? Hope—an often-overlooked aspect of emotional intelligence—is also spiritual intelligence. In caregiving it is common to encounter the limits of religious teaching, and even harm done in the name of religion, and so this reassessment of our credo may involve some increase in our radicalism related to traditional beliefs and practices. The image of the spiritual caregiver as a reticent outlaw[39] captures our commitment to rebel against tradition, but strategically so, when our spiritual and religious power must be used to care for the souls of those who are marginalized and subjugated.

Finally, refreshment is found in *continuing education*. Whether or not it is required of us by our certifying bodies, we continuously attend to formal learning. We seek out schools, study partners, teachers, and topics that will meet us at the point of care seekers' need—more developed knowledge and skills relative to the situations we regularly encounter. Effective spiritual care depends not only on maturity in relational and emotional intelligence but also on the linguistic and logical intelligence

---

[39] Brita Gill-Austern, "The Midwife, Storyteller and Reticent Outlaw," in Dykstra, 218–27.

that is matured through formal education. Effective interfaith caregivers grow their knowledge regarding the religious and spiritual traditions embraced by the care seekers we encounter. If we are persuaded by the notion that the person who knows only one culture knows no culture, we engage in ongoing, in-depth study of a religious tradition other than our own. We need continuous education not only about religion or spirituality but also about the place of religion and spirituality in the ecology of human living, and about aspects of the human situation unfamiliar to us.

**An example**

To further illuminate how these frameworks and practices might play out in reality, we reflect briefly on a situation with which any interfaith caregiver might be confronted. Imagine: a couple active in their religious community recently became pregnant after a long period of seeming infertility, but very early in the pregnancy have suffered miscarriage.

Hopefully, we will have engaged in practices of anticipation. Since miscarriage is so common, communal-contextual practices of anticipation likely have spurred us to reflect on how this common human grief has affected us and our families. As part of our personal self-care, we have worked with the range of emotions miscarriage can evoke. During spiritual self-care, we will have considered our own religious tradition in light of miscarriage, and considered the adequacy of our credo with regard to this kind of death and grief.

On the basis of this reflection alone, we could be equipped to offer the couple responsive presence—compassion, respectful space, gentleness. We wonder silently how interculturality and power dynamics are affecting our effort to care—how are our different and shared cultures interacting? If they invite our continued accompaniment, we first address emergency care—have steps toward the medical care they need been initiated? Then, we return to responsive presence, listening as a companion on the early steps of an arduous path. We follow their lead to ascertain if religion and/or spirituality are explicitly or implicitly important at this juncture. Faced with such an irreparable sorrow, we know care can function, at best, only as sustenance, at least initially.

After an initial encounter, we have opportunity to refresh ourselves through learning. We assess the encounter and, especially, if we had not anticipated care for miscarriage, examine ourselves—how could we have been ignorant of such a commonly experienced loss? We seek consultation: from a leader in the couple's tradition if they are of a religious/spiritual tradition different from ours; with a physician, to comprehend better the physical experience of the mother; with a pastoral counselor, to comprehend better the common psychospiritual anguish of this loss. We learn that functions of care like reconciliation and healing are far in the future, if they apply at all to such a loss. We take time to reassess our beliefs and practices in light of miscarriage. To continue our education, we study the plethora of resources available on reputable websites and note for future reference the many online support groups. We revisit the practices of anticipation, self-care in anticipation of future caregiving.

If we have opportunity to be with the couple again, we are refreshed by learning and self-care. Our actions are informed by our reflection. We offer sustaining responsive presence now augmented with post-crisis nurturance. We look for ways to exercise our power on behalf of the couple and also to relinquish our power to them, thereby making space for them to influence our encounter in the direction of their needs. Our consultation and continuing education provides us a multifocal view of what the couple is enduring and thus we are more ready to respond to a range of needs. If they request it, we can identify religious texts and other resources in their spiritual tradition that honor the mourning of bereaved parents. With appreciation for the power of symbols and of the aesthetic, we might offer to help them compose a ritual that honors their loss. Respecting the power of contextualized community to offer consolation and empowerment, we could give them information about the miscarriage support group at the local hospital or offer to help them if they want to start a group for their own religious community.

**Christian wisdom for interfaith spiritual care**

This section concludes our considerations by extending them into the realm of wisdom. The ideas and actions we have been discussing are, in Christianity, rooted in a wisdom tradition beautifully explored by Daniel Schipani. He summarizes wisdom as "a holistic way of knowing, which includes discerning, making good choices, and living well in community."[40] For the difficult task of articulating wisdom I turn to a biblical text, mentioned in my credo, because it articulates what is lasting and essential: "What does YHWH require of you but to do justice, and to love kindness, and to walk humbly with YHWH?" (Mi 6:8). Wise interfaith spiritual caregivers:

---
[40] Daniel S. Schipani, *The Way of Wisdom in Pastoral Counseling* (Elkhart, IN: Institute of Mennonite Studies, 2003), 10.

**Do justice**
- We reverence all parts of the creation—no person, tradition, or other element of creation is without value. Therefore, we value right relationship with others and ourselves as an end in itself and consistently strive for justice.
- We empower and protect vulnerable persons and communities, with the goals of safety and liberation, and resist violence—our own and others'—with the goals of *metanoia* and reparation.
- We acknowledge our faith traditions as social, historical, economic, political, relational, and psychospiritual powers. We ameliorate their oppressiveness and embody their justness.

**Love kindness**
- We cultivate compassion for ourselves, so that we can treat others with compassion. Because of our compassion, we embrace multiplicity, ambiguity, and paradox in human experience.
- In every interaction we cultivate compassionate awareness of how all persons and groups, including ourselves, might be both agents and targets of oppression. In the ebb and flow of each interaction, we engage in relinquishing and exerting power accordingly.
- We expect conflicts in everyday life, and strive to work through them with grace, mercy, and mutuality. Where harm has been done and reparation is needed, we work toward justice with kindness.

**Walk humbly**
- Sensing our incompleteness, we cultivate relationship with G-d and others. Seeing in part, we seek ongoing revelation of Divine Mystery.
- Recognizing our own limits and errors, we avoid attitudes of self-righteousness and judgmentalism toward others.
- We are at ease in our humanness. Our interactions with others are characterized by authenticity, vulnerability, and mutuality.

## Conclusion

Though interfaith spiritual care is in many respects daunting and complex, we can learn its basics rather quickly through patient and deliberate engagement in ongoing cycles of reflection and action. True, the ultimate purpose of the foundations, frameworks, and practices provided in this chapter is to mature our humanness in ways that enable us to offer spiritual care others might find meaningful. And such maturation requires effort over time by us, and by our care seekers and other teachers. Always, however, when we meet in the profundity of relationship, Divine Mystery promises possibility.

# The Crescent of compassionate engagement
## Theory and practice of Islamic spiritual care

*Nazila Isgandarova*

This essay demonstrates how Muslim spiritual caregivers provide care primarily to Muslims using the *Qur'an* and the *hadith* as fundamental sources of effective care, as well as the writings of Muslim scholars, and the social sciences. It addresses the questions regarding why Islamic spiritual and religious care is rooted in the *Qur'an* and the *hadith*, what the limitations of these sources are in regard to time and space, and whether effective Muslim spiritual care can use the social sciences. A case study illustrates how to integrate social sciences in Islamic spiritual care. The final section discusses core competencies for effective caregiving from an Islamic perspective.

### An overview

"Islam" is an Arabic word which means peace, purity, submission, and obedience. In its religious context, Islam is submission to the will of God and obedience to His law. Muslims believe that divine laws administer everything on earth and in the universe, and that human beings possess intelligence and the freedom of choice, which make them different from other creatures. Muslims hold that Islam is not a new religion introduced by Prophet Muhammad but a religion that has existed since the age of the prophet Adam. The messengers after him, including Abraham, Moses, Jesus, and Muhammad (peace be upon them) conveyed the same message which is a belief in the One and Only Eternal God, Creator of the Universe, Lord of all lords, King of all kings, Most Compassionate, Most

Merciful. Muslims believe that God has no father or mother, no sons or daughters. He has not fathered anyone nor was He fathered. None are equal to Him (the Qur'an, 112:1–4).

Muslims accept all messengers and prophets of God without any discrimination. For them, all messengers were human beings endowed with divine revelations (*vahy*) (the Qur'an, 2:286). Although the Qur'an mentions that God sent prophets to all nations, only the names of twenty-five messengers and prophets are known. These include Noah, Abraham, Jacob, Ishmael, Isaac, Moses, David, Solomon, Jesus, and Muhammad. Their message was essentially the same in regard to calling people to One God and submitting themselves to His will. Among the 25 messengers, only five were given divine books, which are the divine pages to Abraham, the Torah of Moses, the Psalms of David, the Gospel of Jesus, and the Qur'an to Muhammad. Belief in angels, the life after death (including resurrection), and the divine destination are also among important tenets of Muslim faith. There are four major applications of Islam: prayer (*salat*), fasting (*sawm*), almsgiving (*zakat*), and pilgrimage (*hajj*).

Islam is not to be viewed as a segment in Muslim life but a code of life which includes spiritual, intellectual, personal, family, social, economic, political, and international dimensions and understandings. This code of life is based on the unity of God and the core values of compassion, justice, and benevolence. I will try to shed light on the spiritual life of Muslims in terms of health and well-being, although other aspects of life are also important in providing spiritual care in Islam.

The main sources of Islamic spiritual care are the Qur'an, hadith, and works of Muslim scholars. The Qur'an addresses various diseases, especially of the heart, which often lead to direct or indirect physical and mental ailments. It also mentions blindness, deafness, lameness, and leprosy; mental conditions such as sadness and anxiety; and disorders, including psychoses and neurotic diseases.[1] However, the primary focus of the Divine message is on moral and ethical diseases. It is one of the main reasons that the Qur'an itself is referred to as a book of healing (the Qur'an, 41:44) and emphasizes that there is reward from God for those who patiently persevere in suffering (the Qur'an, 39:10 and 31:17). The Qur'an emphasizes healthy spirituality because unhealthy spirituality may be directly or indirectly connected to physical and mental ailments such as depression accompanied with chronic pain, fatigue, or grief. There may

---

[1] Nazila Isgandarova, "Islamic Spiritual Care in a Health Care Setting" in *Spirituality and Health: Multidisciplinary Explorations*, ed. Augustine Meier, Thomas St. James O'Connor, and Peter Lorens VanKatwyk (Waterloo: Wilfrid Laurier University Press, 2005), 85–101.

also be a connection with certain organic and physiological conditions.[2]

The traditional Islamic texts and the life of the Prophet Muhammad are the essential foundations of Islamic spiritual and religious care; otherwise, caregiving is not truly Islamic. There are many reasons for this approach. First of all, the Qur'an and the *Sunnah* (the actions, sayings, and silent permissions or disapprovals of the Prophet) are the two fundamental sources of Islam. Muslims value the Qur'an as a source of guidance and inspiration and unchanged word of God since its revelation. Muslims also appropriate it as a source of healing and cure for illness and a source of comfort and peace. The Qur'an has always been treated with high respect among Muslims, who usually take ablution before touching and reading the Qur'an. They also expect others to follow special rules before they handle the Qur'an. Second, the Qur'anic verses and prophetic traditions emphasize more humane and scientific approaches to disease. Third, the Sunnah has always been treated as an important source for understanding the Qur'an because the Prophet was its practical demonstration. He was the living Qur'an by carrying out the ideals and values of the Qur'an. Muslims not only read the hadith, but also are eager to learn it and then follow the prophetic teachings. However, hadith should be related to the Qur'an.

**Literature review**

The literature on Islamic spiritual care emerges in broad outline, but we are handicapped because of the inadequacy of the available sources. Apart from the medical texts of the medieval and contemporary writers, references to Islamic spiritual care are difficult to locate, few in number, and often impossible to apply directly to spiritual care. However, the historical references are very significant in reviewing the potential effectiveness of Islamic spiritual care.

From the beginning of Islamic history, Muslim scholars produced literature on spiritual care. Abu Bakr Muhammad ibn Zakariya al-Razi (865–925), Abu Yusuf Ya'qub ibn Ishak al-Kindi (d. 873), Ibn Sina, or Avicenna (d. 1037), Shams al-Din al-Dhahabi (1274–1348), Ibn al-Qayyim al-Jawziyyah (d. 1351), and Jalal al-Din al-Suyuti (1445–1505) were among the first and most prominent writers on religion and health.[3]

---

[2] For a fuller discussion of this topic, see Nazila Isgandarova, "The Concept of Compassionate Engagement in Islam," *The Yale Journal for Humanities in Medicine*, March 2, 2010, http://yjhm.yale.edu/essays/nisgandarova20100302.htm.

[3] Salih Yucel, "The Effects of Prayer on Muslim Patients' Well-being" (PhD diss., Boston University School of Theology, 2008), 12.

Ibn Sina supported the view that spiritual care starts with prayer; however, he also mentioned that spiritual care should follow proper medical treatment.[4] Such a view has been supported by, among others, the modern Muslim scholar Rahman who also said that making *du`a* (prayer) without seeking medical treatment would not contribute to effectiveness of spiritual care; therefore, it is obligatory for Muslims to seek medical treatment.[5]

Al-Dhahabi, a prominent Muslim scholar and historian, defined spiritual care in the light of the benefits of Islamic ritual prayers that contribute to the spiritual, psychological, physical, and moral well-being of the client. For him, effective spiritual care with ritual prayer is a form of worship and has a psychological benefit by helping to concentrate on prayers and diverting the mind from pain. Prayer involves certain bodily movements which cause some organs, such as the muscles, to relax, and can elicit a sense of happiness and satisfaction; it can suppress anxiety and extinguish anger.[6] Adnan al-Tharshi investigated the relationship between prayer and healing. Employing empirical methods, he found out that prayer, which includes *salat*, *du`a*, recitation of Qur'an, and *dhikr*, has physical, psychological, and spiritual benefits that are important parts of effective spiritual care.[7]

Bediuzzaman Said Nursi, the famous Turkish scholar of the 20th century, stated that spiritual caregivers should know that medicine is a science and also an art; its final point and reality relies on one of the important attributes of Allah, which is Healer. For him, medicine finds its full potential through seeing God's compassionate manifestations in the vast pharmacy of the mother earth. He interpreted the verse from the Qur'an, "*I shall heal the blind and the leper and I shall quicken the dead, by God's leave*" (The Qur'an, 3:49), in this way:

> Just as the Qur'an explicitly urges man to follow Jesus's (upon whom be peace) high morals, so too it allusively encourages him towards the elevated art and Dominical medicine of which he was the master. . . . Thus, dead hearts were raised to life through the light of guidance. And sick people who were as though dead found

---

[4] Mebrure Dogan, "Duanin psikolojik ve psikoterapik etkileri [The effects of prayer on psychology and psychotherapy]" (PhD diss., Cumhuriyet University, Turkey, 1997), 7.

[5] Fazlur Rahman, *Health and Medicine in the Islamic Tradition* (New York: The Crossroad Publishing Company, 1987), 48.

[6] Shams al-Din al-Dhahabi, *Al-tibb an-Nabawi* [Medicine of the Prophet] (Riyadh: Maktabat Nizar Mustafa al-Baz, 1996), 140.

[7] Adnan al-Tharshi, *As-salaat war-riyadhiyya wal-badan* [Prayer, exercise, and the body] (Beirut: Maktabatul Islami, 1992), 6.

health through his breath and cure. You too may find the cure for every ill in the pharmacy of My wisdom. Work and find it! If you seek, you will certainly find. Thus, this verse traces the limit, which is far ahead of man's present progress in regard to medicine. And it hints at it, and urges him towards it.[8]

His student Fethullah Gulen elaborated this idea and asserted that prayer is a mysterious key to God's everlasting treasures; a point of support for the poor and hurt; and the most secure shelter for those in distress.[9]

Shahid Athar, a medical doctor, writes in his article "Health Guidelines from Qur'an and Sunnah," that spiritual care is an act of worship. Therefore, the spiritual care provider should identify the problem which is,

> not literal translation of *Iman* into belief, nor *Salaat* into prayer, nor *Wudu* into washing hands, face and feet; nor *Sawm* into fasting nor *Zakat* into charity nor *Hajj* into pilgrimage to Mecca. They are more than the translation offers.[10]

Iqbal suggests Muslim spiritual caregivers see both health and illness as coming from God; therefore, they closely link the art of healing to worship. For him, spiritual caregiving and all its practices are the art of healing which is for the sake of God's pleasure. The physician and the patient are thus united through a spiritual bond.[11]

Islamic spiritual care can be helpful as a system of thought and practices by Muslims that give the Muslim care receivers a frame of orientation and an object of devotion. Such a system of spiritual healing is viewed as related to the cosmic order in the universe through the basic doctrine of the correspondence between all levels of reality, as Seyyed Hossein Nasr has pointed out in his book *Science and Civilization in Islam*:

> There is in the Hermetico-alchemical natural philosophy which was always closely tied to medicine in Islam via basic doctrine of the correspondence between all the various orders of reality: the intelligible hierarchy, the heavenly bodies, the order of numbers,

---

[8] Bediuzzaman Said Nursi, *The Words* (Istanbul, Turkey: Sozler Publishing House, 1996), 232.

[9] Fethullah Gulen, "Time to Pray," *The Fountain*, no. 42 (2003): 13–14.

[10] Shahid Athar, "*Health Guidelines from the Qur'an and Sunnah*, Soundvision, accessed July 11, 2010, http://www.soundvision.com/Info/halalhealthy/DivineHelp.asp.

[11] Muzaffar Iqbal, "Islamic Medicine: The Tradition of Spiritual Healing," *Science & Spirit* 9, no. 4 (1998): 3–5.

the parts of the body, the letters of the alphabet which are the "elements" of the Sacred Book....[12]

Postmodern Islamic literature offers new interpretations of the prophetic practice of spiritual care and counseling and focuses on the techniques used in contemporary spiritual and religious care practice. Only the historical Muslim scholars such as al-Dhahabi and Ibn Sina, and post-modernist Muslim scholars such as Esmat Danesh,[13] Azizah Othman, Mimi Iznita Mohamed Iqbal, Hawa Rahmat,[14] Somayya Abdullah,[15] and M. B. Badri,[16] among others, strongly support the notion of the integration of theology and the social sciences in effective Islamic spiritual care. However, it is hard to generalize the results to other populations. We need larger samples from diverse religious and ethnic Muslim communities, including Shia, Ismaili, Ahmediyya, Indian, Pakistani, Arab, and other communities. The works of Ahmad and Ahmad[17] affirm not only supplying a framework for spiritual care and counseling in Islam but also providing knowledge of Islam's basic tenets. However, Muslim spiritual care providers, especially imams, who are the main spiritual caregivers for Muslims, have little formal training in care and counseling. This lack of competence undermines their effectiveness in terms of being able to respond to the emotional and relational needs of Muslims. Therefore, postmodern Muslim scholars try to integrate Western counseling techniques with the traditional Islamic spiritual and religious care tools.

Muslim scholars have made remarkable contributions to the theoretical framework of Islamic spiritual and religious care and its effectiveness. The development of science and technology, including medicine, has also challenged Muslims to update their knowledge and information

---

[12] Seyyed Hossein Nasr, *Science and Civilization in Islam*, 2nd ed. (Lahore, Pakistan: Suhail Academy, 1987), 120.

[13] Esmat Danesh, "The Efficacy of Islamic Counseling on Improving Marital Adjustment Levels of Incompatible Couples," accessed March 11, 2010, http://www.iranpa.org/pdf/054.pdf.

[14] Azizah Othman, Mimi Iznita Mohamed Iqbal, and Hawa Rahmat, "The Imam's Role in Meeting the Counseling Needs of Muslim Communities in the United States," *Psychiatric Services*, no. 56 (2005): 202–05.

[15] Somayya Abdullah, "Islamic Counseling and Psychotherapy Trends in Theory Development," in IslamiCity, June 2, 2009, http://www.islamicity.com/articles/Articles.asp?ref=CF0906-3865.

[16] M. B. Badri, "Training Psychosocial and Medical Practitioners in Fighting Substance Abuse Addiction in Muslim and Arab Cultures," *The American Journal of Islamic Social Sciences* 15, no. 4 (1998): 1–18.

[17] Mohammad Ahmad and Nikhat Ahmad, "Islam and Psychosomatic Medicine," (2001), accessed August 27, 2010, http://www.islamnet.health.medic.

and understand modern developments according to the sacred Book of Islam and narrations of the Prophet Muhammad in order to make Islamic spiritual care more effective. Muslim scholars do see effective Islamic spiritual care as a very important intervention to bring complete cure for Muslim care receivers. Western Muslims need more effective Islamic spiritual care, especially after September 11, 2001, because of increased Islamophobia and xenophobia in Western societies. Interventions used by Muslim spiritual care providers may be comparable to Western counseling methods but are mainly located in three sources of Islamic doctrine and practice: *fiqh* (Islamic jurisprudence), Islamic traditional healing based on the practice of the Prophet Muhammad, and Sufism, the mystical tradition of Islam.

## The process of therapeutic relationship

In many situations, Muslim clergy usually start their care with a recitation of certain chapters from the Qur'an, especially *suras al-Fatiha, Baqarah, Saad, Falaq, Naas*, and others, for the purpose of healing.[18] The narrations from the Prophet Muhammad demonstrate that special chapters from the Qur'an have been revealed for the purpose of healing. For instance, "*Fatihat al-Kitab* [the chapter of *al-Fatiha*] addresses healing for every disease."[19] For Muslims, the Qur'an is the first source of healing because in it there are "*such things that have healing and mercy for the believers*" (the Qur'an, 15:82). Even though there are different views about the scope of Qur'anic healing, there is no question that it addresses both physical and spiritual diseases and elicits a healing force for those who believe in and practice its message.[20] Such healing is mainly about the spiritual healing which includes removing doubts, greed, temptation, and hopelessness from the hearts of the believers and also can give believers security, confidence, and patience in the face of adversities and illnesses.[21]

Muslim spiritual caregivers also apply to the therapeutic relationship the prophetic traditions of special supplications for healing. The traditions of the Prophet Muhammad emphasize the importance of healing and sickness. He considered health to be one of the greatest blessings to have been given to human beings.[22]

---

[18] Rahman, *Health and Medicine in the Islamic Tradition*, 74–75.

[19] Sahih al-Bukhari, trans. M. Muhsin Khan (New Delhi, India: Kitab Bhaban, 1984), 2704.

[20] Nursi, 2005.

[21] Sayyid Qutb, *Fi zilal al-Qur'an* [In the shade of the Qur'an] (Cairo: Dar Us-Sharuuq Publications, 1976), 171.

[22] Sahih al-Bukhari, 1232.

This is especially well-known among Muslims: whenever the Prophet (pbuh) paid a visit to a patient, or a patient was brought to him, he used to invoke God, saying, "Take away the disease, O the Lord of the people! Cure him as You are the One Who cures. There is no cure but Yours, a cure that leaves no disease" or "O the Lord of the people! Remove the trouble, the cure is in Your Hands, and there is none except You can remove it (the disease)."[23]

There are different forms of spiritual care in Islam. *'Iyâdah* (visiting the sick) is the practice, *rifq* (exemplary kindness/care) is the approach, and *ihsân* (doing what is beautiful) is the optimal state in which spiritual care should be offered.[24] The prophetic words *"Doing what is beautiful (ihsân) means that you should worship God as you see Him, for even if you do not see Him, He sees you."* This points toward the state of vigilance and self-awareness also known as *"murâqabah"* that is essential in spiritual care work.

The Arabic *'iyâdah* comes from the root that means "to return." This kind of visit is brief in order not to put a burden on the patient.[25] The Prophet Muhammad affirmed such visits by saying, "The most rewarding visitation of the sick is the one that is appropriately brief." This kind of spiritual visit is rewarding because it takes into account the condition and state of the patient. The reward of *'iyâdah* is twofold. It is purification for the visitor and one of the important sources of hope for the sick. In the former, the Muslim spiritual caregiver may ask the patients to pray for them, since the prayers of patients can be very effective according to *hadith* literature. God is also near to those who suffer and are confronted with pain and anguish (the Qur'an, 2:153; 9:40). According to this understanding of sickness, sickness and pain are viewed not as manifestations of the wrath of God, as some suggest; rather God states that these afflictions are to test and try humans. It describes the imperfection of human life: "Verily, we have created man into a life of pain, toil and trial" (Qur'an 90:4).

Prophet Muhammad also said that when "you visit an invalid tell him to make supplication for you, for his supplication is like that of the angels" (*Sunan of Ibn Majah*). Another narration from the *Forty Qudsi Hadeeth* reminds us of the reality of God's presence in times of illness:

---

[23] Ibid., 1232.

[24] Naveed Baig, "Theology of the Heart and Spiritual Care—Reflections from an Islamic Perspective," *Spiritual Care in Islam*, September 18, 2007, http://naveedbaig.religionblog.dk/spiritual-care-in-islam--english--post413.

[25] Ibid.

God will say on the Day of Judgment: "O son of Adam, I was sick but you did not visit me." "My Lord! How could I visit you when You are the Lord of the whole world," we will reply. God will say: "Did you not know that so-and-so from among my servants (i.e., human beings) was sick, but you never visited him or her? Did you not know that if you had visited, you would have found me there?" God says: "O my servant! Health unites you with yourself but sickness unites you to me." God also visits the sick and says, "O My servant! Health unites you with yourself, but sickness unites you to Me."[26]

Therefore, visitation of the sick is a religious and social obligation in the Muslim community, and for this purpose many imams go to local hospitals to visit the sick. It is considered one of the basic forms of worship to bring one closer to God. In times of distress or illness, the Muslim finds the greatest solace and comfort in the remembrance of God. Severely ill persons who might be distracted by their pain greatly appreciate a companion who can read the Qur'an to them and remind them of God. In this way, Muslim spiritual caregivers help Muslims to have peace during illness by praying and asking for forgiveness.

The Prophet also encouraged Muslims to say good words to a patient for the sake of God; even though it may not prevent any harm, it still brings relief to the patient's heart.[27] Good words include prayer, words of hope, good news, or advice, and all these can relieve the anxiety of sick persons and bring relief to them.[28] So, good words are not limited to prayer only. The practice of prayer is designed to reconnect the person to God, but the majority of Muslim spiritual caregivers not only care for their clients in the form of supplication but also help them to understand and face different problems in their lives. They know that their interventions are not necessarily effective in the case of severe mental or physical illness. In any event, they may also integrate social science resources as long as they do not hinder or interfere with Islamic duties and obligations.[29]

---

[26] Yahya ibn Sharaf al-Nawawi, *Al-Nawawi's Forty Hadith*, trans. Ezzeddin Ibrahim (Islamic Texts Society; New edition, 1997), 15–17.

[27] E. F. Deylemi, "Dua," in *Hadis Ansiklopedesi* [Hadith Encyclopedia] 5, ed. Ibrahim Canan (Istanbul: Akcag Publishing).

[28] Ibn Al-Qayyim al-Jawziyyah, *Healing with the Medicine of the Prophet*, trans. Jalal Abu Al-Rab, ed. Abdul R. Abdullah (Riyadh: Darussalam Publications, 1999), 109.

[29] Nazila Isgandarova, "Imams and Muslim Spiritual Care Givers' Perceptions on What is Effective Spiritual Care in Islam" (DMin diss., Wilfrid Laurier University, 2011), 81.

The case study that follows describes how I, a female Muslim spiritual caregiver, am favorably inclined toward and hopeful about integrating theology with the social sciences in working with my client. I am inspired by the historical legacy of Islamic spiritual care which has been multidimensional in the past. Muslim scholars have emphasized "holistic medicine" involving the spiritual, psychological, physical, and moral aspects of being.[30] The recovery of their vision contributes to making care more holistic and person-centered. I strongly believe that both spirituality and social sciences are relevant, and therefore propose a holistic approach to health by seeing the whole person consisting of mind, body, and spirit.

## A case study

The following is an example of Islamic spiritual care designed to illustrate how to provide spiritual care integrated with a Solution Focused Brief Therapy (SFBT) approach.[31] The therapeutic conversation illustrates various possibilities in defining and addressing a caregiving situation from an Islamic perspective. It is based on a conversation between Nadir (N), a man in his mid-forties who is a husband and father of three children, and a Muslim spiritual caregiver (S).

S 1   How can I help?

N 1   Mmmm ... (Pause). I am not sure ... I think I do not need it ... I am a normal functioning man, work and care for my family, and gambling is my hobby like a normal man.

S 2   I think you are here because your wife Salma is worried about you. Right?

N 2   Yes, she always complains even when I am home in time ...

S 3   Do you want to tell me more what her major concern is?

N 3   She says that if I gamble more I will lose my job ... And gambling is not what a Muslim should do. My boss called home when I was late ... She thinks that if I lose my job, I cannot pay our $40,000 debt and we will depend on her salary ... I never had this huge a debt before ... Anyway, Canada is not so cheap a country ... We pay rent, utilities, children's expenses ... If she does not work as well, we cannot provide for our children ...

---

[30] Isgandarova, "Islamic Spiritual Care in a Health Care Setting," 93.

[31] Solution Focused Brief Therapy (SFBT) is a therapeutic approach that sees therapy as a process in which client and caregiver construct a reality of healthy behavior or abstinence from behavior. See Steve de Shazer and Ivonne Dolan et. al, *More than Miracles: The State of the Art of Solution Focused Therapy* (Birmingham, NY: Haworth Press, 2007).

S 4  So, it means that right now your wife is the main provider for the family because your salary is not even enough to pay your $40,000 debt and support your family. It is a larger debt than you've ever had before. Salma and your children are concerned about the future. You can't make your payments in time.

N 4  Yes... That is why I try to get rid of my debt... I gamble with home to win... I know how to do that... But my gambling is not contributing to my family problem... I also want to relax with my friends...

S 5  It means that you have a strong belief about gambling and winning... But you also know what Islam teaches about gambling ... I see that you feel very confident in gambling, and you think that you know skills and special techniques to win at blackjack. But at the same time, you are in debt $40,000. How do you deal with the conflict between your belief and your habit?

N 5  I try... but Salma has bad temper. She does not believe that I will pay... Of course, as a man I have to pay...

S 6  You say your wife Salma is bad-tempered, and she sounds overly tense and concerned, especially around money issues. What do you think about that?

N 6  Mmmm...

S 7  On a scale of one to ten, one is best, ten is worst; where are you when you gamble...?

N 7  Mmmm... Honestly, I am not feeling well... I am on 8. I also feel guilty before Allah.

S 8  I understand you, Nadir... What you said before tells me that you also want to lead a normal life, which may enable you to cope with stressors such as raising three children in a home of two working parents. However, financial stresses that at one time you could control have increasingly burdened you, and now you are easily stressed, especially when Salma starts demanding that you leave home. However, you still try to favor games, risk your family life. You tend to live in the present. I don't think that it enables you to make long-term plans, especially in regards to your children ... I am sure you love them a lot. Don't you think that you have a wonderful children and a supportive wife?

N 8  Yeah... I know that... Salma helps me a lot... I know that she pays the bills and shops. She does it because she knows she will be rewarded by Allah.

S 9    I am sure you also want to be rewarded by Allah. What about your children... Have you tried to talk to them about your hobby?

N 9    They question me... They want me to take them to the park or zoo... my older son wants Wii but I cannot buy right now... When I have a fight with Salma, they join her...

S 10   Can you tell me what they exactly tell you?

N 10   They tell me that they feel ashamed of having a gambling dad and put pressure on Salma to push me to stop gambling. Salma tells me what kind of Muslim I am... It hurts me... I am Muslim... but I have problems with some people now... Some people do not want to see me there because I always smell of alcohol...

S 11   I see that they love you... they want to spend time with you, but your hobby takes most of your time and they do not see you much. Have you ever tried to go to mosque with your kids?

N 11   Yes, before we often went to the mosque. We went to community parties and picnics... But...

S 12   I see that your problem prevented you from many good things... You once enjoyed prayers... You also feel guilty for not being a good Muslim... I see that you also want to spend time with your family... You hope that winning in the game will solve your problems, but it hasn't happened, plus you may lose your family... I am sure that you do not want it to happen. What do you need to do?

N 12   I do not know...

S 13   *Suppose one night a miracle happened, and your problem was solved. But, because you were sleeping, you don't know a miracle has happened, and the problem is now solved. How would you know?*[32]

N 13   I would wake up without headache... Salma does not complain that I slept with my socks on... I would not be late to work, and my financial situation would be back to how it was before I began gambling.

S 14   Thank you, Nadir, for honesty... I think we can work from here... Next time, I would like you to write down five good feelings when you are with your family, and tell me why your feel that way...

N 14   OK. I will try... Thank you. I hope you will help me...

---

[32] The "miracle question" is a classic SFBT technique.

## Strategy to provide Islamic spiritual care using Solution Focused Brief Therapy (SFBT)

### The Muslim spiritual caregiver

The Muslim spiritual caregiver started to gather information regarding why Nadir became involved in gambling and drinking, why he came to counseling, and what his views, his specific gambling behaviors, and his difficulties were. She applied Solution Focused Brief Therapy (SFBT); the Muslim spiritual caregiver tried to construct a reality of healthy abstinence from gambling from an Islamic perspective, which affirms that gambling is *haram* (forbidden). These questions and techniques are some of the practical principles of SFBT, which calls for expressing empathy, developing discrepancy, avoiding argumentation, and rolling with resistance.

The caregiver was well aware that Nadir still has ambivalence and very often expresses his uncertainty about "belonging" at this "place," which is the clinic. The spiritual caregiver tried to motivate Nadir in her initial contact with him because the initial counseling session is critically important for setting the tone, clarifying expectations, and motivating him to accept help. She tried to engage the client by asking motivational questions, because Nadir would get easily distracted due to the nature of gambling disorders.

### The care receiver

Nadir was not yet fully aware of his problem and its effect on his life. However, the question, how can I help? was effective because it evoked a greater depth of response in the client. The Muslim spiritual caregiver did not assume that Nadir came to quit gambling; instead she encouraged him to articulate why he came to therapy. This questioning is client-centered and respectful, and helps the caregiver understand how the client perceives her role. Nadir was already making an effort toward positive change by coming to see the Muslim spiritual caregiver. The session reveals that, by nature, Nadir was unpredictable and needed variable reinforcement. He had often experienced numerous cycles of positive reinforcement such as winning money, feeling "high," and a temporary relief from his problems. However, when he started to lose, extreme negative consequences followed, including major losses and difficulties in the most significant relationships in his life.

Nadir may achieve awareness that he is affected by problem gambling and now seeks help to alleviate the negative consequences of his gambling (e.g., financial problems, relationship difficulties, guilt or shame). Nadir was clear enough when he said that he is seldom heard or understood by others. Therefore, counseling may be an opportunity for him to tell his problems and find somebody who listens to him and understands his reasons for seeking treatment. Nadir was still ambivalent about changing gambling behaviors but actively willing to deal with other problems that are direct consequences of his gambling. Therefore, the session started by dealing first with what the client believed to be most important in order to keep Nadir engaged and build counselor-client rapport.

**The relationship**

The initial session helped the spiritual caregiver learn more about Nadir and his gambling. He has led a relatively normal life, coping with average stressors such as raising three children in a home of two working parents. However, financial stresses that at one time he could control have increasingly burdened him, and now Nadir is easily stressed, especially when Salma starts demanding he leave home.

The therapeutic relationship in this case might predict how motivated Nadir will be to change or what problems he will present. The spiritual caregiver avoided confronting openly because of concern that the client would disengage from seeking further help. She preferred to motivate him toward further treatment and used a simple reflective statement that let Nadir know his struggles, frustrations, and challenges had been understood, which helped to keep him engaged. The caring environment was evident in the connection between the spiritual caregiver and the client. Such an environment is very important because it is impossible to provide effective care unless the provider can enter the world of the care receiver, who is sensitive and vulnerable. Connecting starts with building trust. The spiritual caregiver offered the client compassion and love so that he did not feel he was alone in the struggle.

**The context**

The interaction between the Muslim spiritual caregiver and the client raises several contextual issues, beginning with the larger therapeutic question of what constitutes help, as a focus for theological reflection: what is spiritual care in this interaction about?; when is help unhelpful?; what is the specific therapeutic relationship in Islamic spiritual care?; what is the helping image of the Muslim spiritual caregiver?

The interaction reminds us that spirituality and psychotherapy have never been strangers to each other in the history of Islam. It is possible to appreciate a strong relationship between social science and Islamic theological sources.

The SFBT model does not necessarily focus on spirituality or spiritual issues. Therefore, it is important for the spiritual caregiver to make a care plan that includes spirituality as a major concern, such as learning more about how Islam may contribute to strengthening the positive skills to avoid gambling and improve parenting.

The case study suggests that Muslim spiritual caregivers can use SFBT as one tool of social sciences to help their clients. One of the helpful techniques developed by Insoo Kim Berg and Steve de Shazer[33] is the "miracle question," which can engage spirituality as illustrated in my S 13 response ("Suppose one night a miracle happened, and your problem was solved ... How would you know?"). In SFBT, the miracle question is an effective tool because it helps clients set goals even when they are in crisis and feel stuck.[34]

SFBT was also helpful because the spiritual caregiver tried to elicit a positive experience in the face of a negative experience and sometimes reminded the care receiver that there is always something or somebody he can rely on. The therapeutic approach thus consisted of a process in which client and therapist constructed a reality of healthy behavior, especially with better patterns of thinking and decision-making. The following chart illustrates the application of specific SFBT techniques.

| Solution-focused techniques | Application in spiritual care |
| --- | --- |
| Scaling questions | a. If we take a scale, 1 is worst and 10 is best, where were you on the scale before?<br>b. Where are you now on the scale?<br>c. If change occurs, where would you be on the scale? |
| Exception questions | a. Have you ever felt differently? I mean you did not worry about what people would tell you about your performance.<br>b. Tell me more about those times; what was different? |

---

[33] Insoo Kim Berg and Steve de Shazer were co-founders of the Brief Family Therapy Center in Milwaukee, Wisconsin. Together they developed the Solution Focused Brief Therapy (SFBT) model.

[34] Steve de Shazer and Yvonne Dolan, *More than Miracles; The State of the Art in Solution-focused Brief Therapy*, 37–60. A form of *miracle question* could be: "Suppose you woke up one morning and by some miracle everything you ever wanted, everything good you could ever imagine for yourself, had actually happened—your life had turned out exactly the way you wanted it. Think about it now. What will you notice around you that let you know the miracle has happened? What will you see? What will you hear? What will you feel inside yourself? How will you be different ... ?"

|  | c. Do you think that if you do the same, the change will happen now? |
|---|---|
| Signs or questions of difference | a. Are there any other strengths or resources you have that we have not talked about?<br>b. Let's track all the strengths and resources that you mentioned.<br>c. Let's now talk about how you can use these resources. |

Although the initial session with the client with a gambling problem did not focus primarily on spiritual issues, the context of the problem demonstrates that theological studies are not enough to provide effective spiritual care simply because the health of the whole person requires the services of adequately trained spiritual caregivers. That is why many clergy integrate psychology, family therapy, counseling, and theology in their work. Family systems strategy includes the use of (post-modern) family therapy approaches such as narrative, solution focused therapy, and feminist family therapy. The "old" school of therapy includes (modernist) approaches such as structural family therapy, contextual therapy, Bowen's ideas, Satir's ideas, and family-of-origin concepts. I also work with the grief theory of Kubler-Ross[35] and other grief theories, the Myers-Briggs approach, the contributions of Jung, and the Helping Styles Inventory of Peter VanKatwyk,[36] among other resources in my chaplaincy practice. The case study with the Muslim client shows that Muslim spiritual caregivers with special knowledge of social sciences can deal with their clients' problems beyond focusing only on religion and spirituality. Thus, the Muslim spiritual caregiver may treat anxiety differently than the psychiatrist, but the theory of anxiety can be the same. Such practices indicate that using Islamic principles actively together with the modern techniques can be very effective.

### Caring for non-Muslims

Muslim spiritual and religious caregivers realize that there is a growing need to provide spiritual care to others who do not belong to the Muslim tradition. They may feel the tension that comes from differences between their religious tradition and that of the others, but they also value

---

[35] Elisabeth Kübler-Ross and David Kessler, *On Grief and Grieving: Finding the Meaning of Grief Through the Five Stages of Loss* (Simon & Schuster Ltd, 2005).

[36] Peter VanKatwyk, *Spiritual Care and Therapy* (Waterloo: Wilfrid Laurier University Press, 2003).

establishing the kind of spiritual care relationship that is highly regarded in any religious tradition. The theological foundation for such interfaith ministry can be found in S. H. Nasr's contribution. Such a theological foundation recognizes that the contemporary world is different from the world of our ancestors. We witness the use of atomic energy and flight into space, among the wonders of our time. Our ancestors did not face the social reality that we face now, which calls for journeying from one religious universe to another.[37] In previous centuries, humans saw their religious faith as having absolute status expressed in sacred teachings and rites. The values and perspectives of that religion "reigned supreme and in absolute manner over human life."[38] We may imagine that the experience of our ancestors was relatively normal and peaceful or stable.

When we face the reality of the existence of many religions, we are struck with the beauty of their spirituality in the forms of the sacred art and commonality in doctrine. In our time, we can appreciate better than ever before the sacred art of architecture, music, and literature so that "those in the West who are really educated, have to acknowledge and be aware of the presence of sacred art as a gateway to the inner courtyard of various religious traditions of East and West."[39]

A second reality involves doctrine, or *aqidah*. As Nasr states, the western theologians of the Middle Ages read and appreciated the works of Muslim scholars, especially Avicenna and al-Ghazali. However, those theologians displayed an apologetic attitude asserting that Islam is not a true religion, although those texts have religious significance and should be studied from the point of view of religious philosophy. They in fact ignored the universality of revelation and the reality of religion in diverse forms.[40] Now we can read the sacred texts of other religions as inspirational literature, theological formulation, and metaphysical exposition.

Building on the foundation laid by S. H. Nasr, my major concerns within the context of spiritual care to Muslims and non-Muslims are about death and dying, the meaning of life, loss of self-esteem, powerlessness, emptiness, and faith in God and love. I often ask myself: How does my spiritual care help care receivers connect or reconnect with the spiritual dimension of their being? How do I nurture the spirit as the dynamic force in every aspect of their lives? When do they need spiritual care,

---

[37] Seyyed Hossain Nasr, *The Essential Seyyed Hossain Nasr* (World Wisdom, 2007), 3.

[38] Ibid.

[39] Ibid, 5.

[40] Ibid, 6.

and where do they turn? When they are sick and confined to bed, how do I care for them by focusing on their spirit?

I will never forget the incident when one dying resident asked to see a chaplain. I entered the room, and the woman, whom I had known for many years and followed to the religious services, said that she was suffering with pain which neither she nor the doctors could control. She then asked why humans should suffer and how she could make the pain go away. I realized that she did not expect me to answer but she wanted to share with me her sense of powerlessness and vulnerability. She did not expect me to neutralize her pain; rather, she wanted to talk with me as a person who was her companion. As a companion in her spiritual journey, I tried to help her by reflecting with a similar question: "You survived the Holocaust which was one of the greatest sources of pain for millions... I remember that you many times wondered, 'Why was I subjected to this kind of suffering?'" She responded: "Yes, but I never found an answer..." I affirmed her and said, "I feel powerless and vulnerable when it comes to finding an answer to the suffering of humanity... I am still vulnerable and puzzled..." These kinds of encounters turn my attention from personal suffering to global suffering. I never find an answer but more questions and the need to keep wondering whether God is just a "Watcher" over us, or a "Victim" like us.[41]

## Core competencies in Islamic spiritual care

Muslims turn to Muslim spiritual caregivers, especially imams, for help, most often for religious or spiritual guidance and because of relationship or marital concerns. Further, as indicated above, there has been an increase in the need for care and counseling since September 11, 2001. The following discussion of key competencies applies to all forms and settings of spiritual care.

Mercy, respect, forgiveness, and listening are the key characteristics of good Muslim spiritual caregivers, and both the Qur'an and hadith are replete with references to the virtues of, and guidance about, these qualities. The theology of respect and honoring is laid down in many verses of the Qur'an, and mention is made that humans are honored creatures and have an honorable status in Islam. Allah says: "And indeed We have honored the Children of Adam, and We have carried them on land and sea, and have provided them with lawful good things, and have preferred them above many of those whom We have created with

---
[41] For a fuller discussion of this topic, see Isgandarova, "Effectiveness of Islamic Spiritual Care: Foundations and Practice of Imams and Muslim Spiritual Caregivers," 4.

a marked preferment" (Al-Israa': 70); "Muhammad is the Messenger of Allah. And those who are with him are severe against disbelievers, and merciful among themselves" (Al-Fath: 29); "Then he became one of those who believed (in Islamic Monotheism) and recommended one another to perseverance and patience, and (also) recommended one another to pity and compassion. They are those on the Right Hand (the dwellers of Paradise)" (Al-Balad: 17–18).

Muslim spiritual caregivers may help care receivers decrease their symptoms by using traditional healing techniques; however, persons who are psychotic, suicidal, have addiction or substance abuse problems, or are severely depressed and confused should be referred to other professionals such as counselors, social workers, psychiatrists, or clinical psychologists for specialized help. Spiritual caregivers often serve as front-line mental health care providers and facilitators but their role depends on the presence and severity of mental-health problems.[42] However, imams have little formal training in counseling, which means that if they are asked to help congregants who come to them with mental health, family, and social-service issues, imams need more support from mental health professionals to determine the needs of their Muslim clients and fulfill a potentially vital role in improving access to services for them.[43] If the person poses a danger to others, the Muslim spiritual caregivers need to use the evaluation of diseases and referral skills as additional sources of assistance for certain types of mental health problems.

Muslim caregiving is a special ongoing practice which emphasizes profound patience, humility, and serenity of soul, and the desire to acquire beneficial knowledge. Such training should equip the Muslim spiritual caregivers with wisdom to interpret the personal and community suffering of Muslims from Anton Boisen's view of the "living human document,"[44] which requires a fresh look at the unique life story and conflict of the client. Such helping interaction is the heart of healing since the spiritual caregiver demonstrates the skill to integrate theoretical and clinical knowledge.[45] From an Islamic perspective, such practice is supportive for care receivers

---

[42] P. S. Wang, P. A. Berglund, and R. C. Kessler, "Patterns and Correlates of Contacting Clergy for Mental Disorders in the United States," *Health Services Research* 38, no. 2 (2003): 647–73.

[43] Osman M. Ali, Glen Milstein, and Peter M. Marzuk, "The Imam's Role in Meeting the Counseling Needs of Muslim Communities in the United States," *Psychiatric Services* 56, no. 2 (2005).

[44] Anton Boisen, *Out Of The Depths: An Autobiographical Study of Mental Disorder and Religious Experience* (New York: Harper & Brothers, Publishers, 1960).

[45] Ibid, 191.

in the way of liberation from evil or destructive forces or trauma, and the reestablishment of personal communication with the Creator and self. The duty of the spiritual and pastoral caregiver is to help care receivers see their problems differently and transcend them by offering a creative imagination or theological reflection using the theological and social resources. Islamic spiritual care is also "a ministry of presence, which is centered on a caring acceptance, a nonjudgmental stance, and physical and emotional availability."[46]

Fostering the development of core competencies in Islamic spiritual caregiving depends on three aspects: first, a strong belief in the Qur'an and the Sunnah, as well as taking the Prophet as a role model; second, participation in the Muslim community such as attendance at mosques and other Islamic institutions; and third, a healthy spirituality.

Other themes important to this study from the review of Islamic sources are as follows: It is *fard* (a religious obligation) for Muslim spiritual and religious caregivers to make their intervention effective. Effective Islamic spiritual care is evident when the patient or client seeks proper medical treatment besides praying, and so on. The Qur'an and the Sunnah present many tools and techniques for effective Islamic spiritual care. The most common and most used practices are to recite the Qur'an and to read the supplications of the Prophet Muhammad.

Imams and other Muslim spiritual caregivers need to learn from Western-based literature about the effectiveness of spiritual and religious care, and that there is a direct relationship between spiritual, physical, psychological, and emotional health. Further, that effective spiritual care generally gives comfort and reduces fears and anxieties. They should also recognize that there is no definite way to measure the effectiveness of Islamic spiritual care. Such a tool might be helpful to assess the effectiveness of Muslim spiritual and religious caregivers. Finally, imams and others should know that the practical human sciences, such as family therapy, couples counseling, and others, can help make the spiritual care effective.

## Conclusion

By way of summary, Islamic spiritual care is the Muslim term to describe religiously-based care offered by believers and religious leaders (e.g., imams). It is based on main sources of Islamic literature such the Qur'an and hadith. However, Islamic spiritual care is not limited to a traditional

---

[46] Christina M. Puchalski and Carlos Sandoval, "Spiritual Care," in *A Clinical Guide on Supportive and Palliative Care for People with HIV/AIDS*, ed. Joseph F. O'Neill, Peter A. Selwyn, and Helen Schietinger, 2003, http://www.thebody.com/content/art34061.html.

understanding of care. Islamic spiritual care is today a separate discipline which also employs the resources of behavioral and social sciences such as developmental theory, grief theory, and gender studies. It has many forms and goals to help the Muslim patients deepen their theological understanding and strengthen their abilities to face the personal, relational, and public challenges, including grief and loss, parenting, violence, and many more life challenges and struggles. Its main goal can be defined in terms of healing, sustaining, guiding, and reconciling. Adequately trained, Muslim spiritual caregivers can play an important role in health care, primarily on a one-on-one basis.

Imams and other Muslim spiritual care providers are professionals who offer supportive spiritual care through empathetic listening and demonstrating an understanding of people in distress. They usually make accessible information or advice to help Muslims enhance their personal development, provide emotional support and promote spiritual growth. However, Muslim caregivers are not yet being regulated by one body and may have less accountability to the public.

The description of the problem in the case study reveals that, in order to provide effective care, Muslim spiritual caregivers need to understand and apply not only Islamic theology but also pertinent cultural and psychosocial aspects of care. Therefore, Muslim spiritual caregivers should further develop clinical and professional competence. Taking the Qur'anic and prophetic tradition as primary guidelines, Muslim healers see illness as an opportunity to serve, clean, purify, and help care receivers physically, emotionally, mentally, and spiritually. They can thus apply the powerful medicine of a loving Lord, including the effective tools of human science, so that many human lives can be restored.

# *Worldviewing* competence for narrative interreligious dialogue
## A Humanist contribution to spiritual care

*Hans Alma and Christa Anbeek*

In this chapter we will introduce spiritual or existential[1] care and counseling as it is inspired by humanism. Humanism has developed as a worldview both in Western and Eastern traditions, building on experiences of what it means to be a human being living a finite life. We hold that all religions and worldviews are rooted in human experience, and this makes it possible to compare them. To really understand humanism as a worldview, we need to be able to characterize it in ways that make it comparable to religions and other worldviews. No definition can do justice to the complex phenomenon of worldview or world philosophy, but the seven dimensions Ninian Smart identifies to describe religions serve our purpose well.[2] These dimensions are:

1. Narrative and mythic dimension: every religion is characterized by important stories that are transmitted to the next generation. Some stories are historic in nature, others are parables or myths;
2. Doctrinal and philosophical dimension: the systematic formulation of religious teachings in an intellectually coherent form;
3. Ethical and legal dimension: religious values and rules about human behavior;

---

[1] In this chapter, the authors use the terms "spiritual" and "existential" (the preferred term in their Dutch context) as synonyms.

[2] Smart also describes secular worldviews like Soviet Atheism and Maoism with the help of these dimensions. Ninian Smart, *The World's Religions* (Cambridge: Cambridge University Press, 1989), 426, 510.

4. Ritual dimension: the forms and orders of ceremonies, private and/or public, that give structure to life and mark special moments;
5. Experiential and emotional dimension: the experience of, for example, hope, awe, inner peace, a sense of justice, dread, bliss, etc.;
6. Social and institutional dimension: the way in which a religion is organized, both internally and externally (i.e., in relation to the broader society);
7. Material dimension: buildings, art, and ordinary objects and places that symbolize or manifest the sacred or supernatural.

We propose that these dimensions can be used to gain a better understanding of humanism as a source for humanist care and counseling. In the next section, we will provide a general overview of humanism as a worldview, followed by an interpretation of humanism according to Smart's dimensions of religion. We will then explore the characteristics of humanist existential care by describing the experiences of a counselor working in a psychiatric institution in the Netherlands. Reflecting on these experiences, we will look for insights contributing to interfaith spiritual care. Finally, we will make a more general statement about the core competencies of existential counselors and spiritual caregivers.

## Humanism as a worldview

### Searching for a common core

Describing humanism as a worldview is not an easy task. Of course, this holds for every worldview since there is no such thing, for example, as *the* Christian worldview, or *the* Islamic worldview. However, what makes the task of describing humanism as a worldview even more difficult is the fact that it has not always defined itself as a separate worldview and still does not do so unequivocally. During the Renaissance, most European humanists were loyal Christians. Only since the Enlightenment in Western Culture can we speak of humanism as a worldview to be distinguished from other (religious) worldviews. Nevertheless, the values and thoughts characteristic of humanism can be found to overlap with those of religions. Furthermore, humanists are not always in agreement over the basic tenets of humanism. Secular humanism, which strongly holds to an atheistic worldview, distinguishes itself sharply from religious humanism, which is open to experiences of, and reflection on transcendence. Still others are looking for a secular humanist spirituality that is closely related to aesthetic experiences and the search for a humane society. Amidst this variety, what sense does it make to speak of a humanist worldview?

Humanism as a separate worldview has its roots in Western philosophy, especially in those philosophies in which the unique and intrinsic value of human beings is recognized. These philosophies are not necessarily anti-religious, but they do stress the potential intentionality, creativity, rationality, and responsibility of humans, and they search for ways to advance these human potentials. Against this background, humanism has unfolded as a stream of thought in Western culture that adapts itself to changing contexts. Philosophy, politics, literature, and the arts have always been domains in which humanist values could flourish. Today, in our globalized world, humanism finds itself in new surroundings. Secularization did not lead to the vanishing of religion. Instead, we find that new forms of spirituality continue to flourish, world religions meet one another in unexpected ways, and humanist values are now recognized in Eastern philosophies and religions. Humanism today is both enriched and unsettled.

Dutch philosopher and humanist Peter Derkx formulates two principles that can be seen as a minimal core common to humanism in all its varieties:

- A worldview is always context-bound and human-made;
- All humans are equal and are to be treated as such; the unique value and irreplaceability of every individual is essential.[3]

Derkx argues for an *inclusive* humanism that is open, dialogical, tolerant, and to be found both within and outside of religions. In order to understand this position, we need a new understanding of the very conception of *worldview*. Under this conceptualization, a worldview is not a phenomenon with strong and clear boundaries, but something in flux. It is more like a river that is recognizable from source to estuary, but that adapts to the different landscapes it runs through and can flow together with other rivers and waters it meets along the way. A worldview is a platform for the dialogical exchange of values, thoughts, and practices that are judged on their merits and that can change without losing touch with the platform that shapes them. Perhaps the term *worldviewing* is a better way to conceive of humanism.

---

[3] Peter Derkx, "Humanisme als moderne levensbeschouwing," in *Waarvoor je leeft: Studies naar humanistische bronnen van zin*, ed. Hans Alma & Adri Smaling (Amsterdam: SWP/Humanistics University Press, 2010), 43–57.

We see worldviewing as a process that includes both intrapersonal and interpersonal dialogue. From a psychological perspective, we can best understand this process by relating it to the theory of *the dialogical self* as articulated by Hubert Hermans and Harry Kempen.[4] In this view, a person's identity or self has a polyphonic character. The self is no coherent unity unequivocally guiding the person in his or her life, but is better conceived as an ongoing dialogue nourished by experiences in different life domains (e.g., work, family, religious community, sports club, etc.). The different voices taking part in this dialogue correspond with relations to significant others in these life domains. They come into existence in the social process, in which we take on and internalize the perspectives of others. In addition to the individual voices of, for example, a parent or teacher, Hermans and Kempen distinguish collective voices, which represent the perspectives of social groups or the broader culture we participate in. Worldviewing is part of this continuing dialogue that constitutes our identity. According to this dynamic conception of the self, people differ in their flexibility when taking on different perspectives and integrating them into the internal dialogue that constitutes the self. Interpersonal and interreligious dialogue is more possible with a greater flexibility in the intrapersonal dialogue. Can one's level of flexibility be influenced, and can humanist existential care and counseling increase it? This will be the leading question in the second part of this essay.

When we speak of "humanism" and "worldview" in the remainder of this essay, these concepts should be understood against the background offered by Derkx's conception of humanism and by the theory of the dialogical self. Although we wish it were possible to do justice to every school of humanism, the need for clarity requires us to make choices in a way that is less nuanced than the complexity of humanism deserves.

**Smart's seven dimensions**

The seven dimensions of religion Smart distinguishes help us better understand humanism in its present state as a worldview, and can clarify humanism's strengths as well as those dimensions which are less valued, or neglected.

*Narrative and mythic dimension*. Stories from different backgrounds—religion and/or literature—are a source of inspiration to humanism; however, humanism does not have its own canon. The humanist movement in the Netherlands has tried to develop a literary canon, but it is characterized

---

[4] Huebert J. M. Hermans and Harry J. G. Kempen, *The Dialogical Self: Meaning as Movement* (San Diego: Academic Press, 1993).

by a high degree of diversity. Most valued are those stories in which the core experiences of human existence and the way people cope with these experiences are convincingly painted. Characteristic of humanism is that these stories are never seen as revealed by a higher power but always as created by human beings. They are bound to specific times and places, and they require interpretation before they can be applied to one's own situation. In this way, humanism and hermeneutics are close friends.

With its emphasis on the unique value of each individual person, it goes without saying that humanism values personal stories just as much as literary or religious ones. In fact, telling and retelling personal stories, and integrating cultural meanings into one's own life story, is seen as the fundamental way in which humans find meaning in their lives. People weave the fragmented experiences of their life together in a personal narrative that connects past and present, which makes it possible to anticipate the future. They tend to find and express the values they live by through telling narratives—both to themselves and to others.

Yet, humanism is also interested in the larger story of human life. Since the Renaissance, humanism has turned to philosophy and science to develop this story. Especially since the Enlightenment, religious cosmologies were pushed aside by a scientific narrative. The philosopher Henk Manschot points out that by doing so, humanism contributed to a purely technological approach to the problems that face humanity, nature, and the world.[5] The human being became the centre of the universe. Values such as freedom, autonomy, and dignity were emphasized, and they continue to be an important legacy of modernity. But humanism did not develop a cosmology, because this was associated with the religious consciousness it attempted to leave behind. For this reason, humanism continues to have difficulty with valuing the non-human and can rightly be criticized for its anthropocentric bias.[6]

Manschot stresses that the evolutionary and ecological situation we find ourselves in asks for a rethinking of what it means to be a human being on a finite planet in an expanding universe no one can fully comprehend. This doesn't mean that humanism should turn away from science. "In our time, a cosmology cannot ignore the role of the scientific narrative about the position of the human being in the evolutionary process. The need to develop a contemporary cosmological worldview partly emanates

---

[5] Henk Manschot, "Leven op aarde: het verhaal van de mens," in *Waarvoor je leeft*, ed. Alma & Smaling, 59–82.

[6] See Ton Lemaire, *Met open zinnen: Natuur, landschap, aarde* (Baarn: Ambo, 2002).

from actual scientific knowledge."[7] The challenge for humanism in our time is persuading people that humanism offers a meaningful narrative that can guide them in their experiences and actions. Its emphasis on the responsibility of human beings places humanism in the crossfire of the problems we face in our time. Humanism's narrative needs a cosmology based on the value of human responsibility, without isolating humans from and elevating them above the non-human. Humanism can only meet this challenge when it enters into dialogue with other worldviews and helps to facilitate interreligious dynamics.

*Doctrinal and philosophic dimension.* It is possible to speak of the systematic formulation of humanist teachings in an intellectually coherent form. One of the founding fathers of the humanist movement in the Netherlands, Jaap van Praag (1911–1981), attempted this in a way that is still influential. He systematized his ideas in the book *Grondslagen van Humanisme* (Foundations of Humanism)[8] by distinguishing ten characteristics of the humanist worldview, five characteristic views of the human being, and five views of the larger world. Summarized, the five views of the human being are: naturalness (human beings are inexorably related to nature), social connectedness, equality, freedom, and reasonableness, especially in the distinction between good and evil. The five characteristic views of the larger world are: the world can be experienced by the human senses (this is the one source of knowledge of the world), connection between humans and the world, completeness (knowledge of the world through the human senses is complete), contingency (the world has no intrinsic purpose), and dynamism (the world and humans are part of a never-ending process of change).

Although the characteristics distinguished by van Praag are recognizable in many writings of Dutch humanists, they never achieved a real doctrinal status. In fact, such an authoritative status would be in contradiction with the view that human experience is the only source of knowledge of the world. Van Praag himself defined his postulates as provisional. Critical reflection and the impact of other worldviews or life experiences can lead to changes.[9]

*Ethical and legal dimension.* Humanism is a rich tradition when it comes to the ethical dimension, yet its focus on individual freedom

---

[7] Manschot, "Leven op aarde," trans. Hans Alma, 232.

[8] Jaap P. van Praag, *Grondslagen van Humanisme* (Amsterdam: Boom, 1978).

[9] See M. C. Otten, "Humanisme en humanistiek," 2011, accessed June 25, 2011, www.hvo.nl/HVO/vorming/onderzoek+en+literatuur/Humanisme+en+humanistiek.htm.

is in contradiction with a legalistic ethic. The endeavor is both to give shape to humanist values like freedom, autonomy, and authenticity in concrete practices, and to critically reflect upon those same values: how can they be related to other important values like social connectedness and engagement, or cultural/religious diversity? As we have seen, Derkx considers equality to belong to the core principles of humanism. Humanism not only cares about individual well-being, but also about social justice and a humane society. It stresses the importance of the Universal Declaration of Human Rights, even as it acknowledges the problem of the declaration's interpretation in different cultural contexts. Once again, humanism argues in favor of intercultural and interreligious dialogue to flesh out human rights in its practical consequences.

Of critical concern to humanism is reflection upon sources of the "good life" or the art of living. Such sources are typically found not only in philosophical texts or in world literature but also in the life stories of individuals.[10] The values people live by come to expression in the activities they engage in, the role models they choose, the goals they strive for, and the ideals they are committed to. By doing justice to these personal moral expressions, humanism compensates for the universalist claims it sometimes makes concerning human nature and human development.

*Ritual dimension.* We need not say much concerning the ritual dimension: humanism does not abound in rituals. Of course, humanist organizations have their rituals of gathering in meetings, conferences, and festivals, and ritualistically award prizes to outstanding figures in the humanist movement. Some groups meet on Sunday mornings for reflection and contemplation, and there are even humanist weddings and funeral ceremonies. Humanism, however, does not have a longstanding tradition with ritual characteristics and depends heavily on other traditions like Christianity and Buddhism for its rituals.

*Experiential and emotional dimension.* In a way, the experiential dimension of humanism is strong, for it holds that all knowledge is based on experience, and worldviews are context-bound and human-made. What is accepted as a reliable experience to provide knowledge about the world depends on the school of humanism one adheres to. Some humanists

---

[10] See the following texts: Joep Dohmen, "Filosofische bronnen van zelfzorg en zin," in *Waarvoor je leeft*, ed. Alma & Smaling, 181–96; Michel Foucault, *Histoire de la sexualité III: Le souci de soi* (Paris: Èditions Gallimard, 1984); Pierre Hadot, *Philosophy as a Way of Life: Spiritual Exercises from Socrates to Foucault* (Malden, MA: Blackwell Publishing, 1995); Wilhelm Schmid, *Philosophie der Lebenskunst: Eine Grundlegung* (Frankfurt/M.: Suhrkamp Taschenbuch Wissenschaft, Nr. 1385, 1998).

only accept sense perception and subsequent rational reflection on such perception as a reliable source of knowledge. Other humanists recognize broader possibilities of human experience, such as spiritual or religious experiences, as reliable sources of knowledge.

An informative humanist view on religious experience can be found in the philosophy of John Dewey.[11] Dewey ascribes religious quality to an experience when it has transformative power to the extent that it significantly changes a person or their way of living. For Dewey, describing an experience as religious does not imply that it refers to a transcendent reality in a metaphysical sense. In Dewey's view, *religious* refers to an attitude that can be taken in regard to any object, ideal, or purpose. The term indicates a quality of experience that can come with, for example, friendship. An experience becomes religious when it brings about a feeling of harmony within the person and his or her relation to the external world. A religious experience causes a better, deeper, and enduring adjustment to life involving "our being in its entirety."[12] It provides a person with "the sense of values which carry one through periods of darkness and despair."[13] The religious experience arouses an ideal that gives focus to one's self-image and relation to the world, and thus unites the fragmentary elements of daily life. Once again, we find a humanist perspective in which the day-to-day practices and their consequences for people's lives are of overriding importance in worldviewing.

*Social and institutional dimension.* In many countries, humanists have organized themselves in local or national leagues or associations. They are also internationally organized as, for example, in the International Humanist and Ethical Union (IHEU). Yet, these are small groups when compared to the impact values like autonomy and authenticity have made in Western culture. Humanist values are also adhered to by people who do not consider themselves to be humanists.

Humanist worldviewing does not transfer very well into institutional form. As we have seen, it does not have its own canon or set of doctrines, and it does not have a strong legal and ritual dimension. It is attractive to people who want to share their commitment to humanist values with others but who are critical about rules and organizational structures they see as standing in the way of their own freedom and responsibility.

*Material dimension.* Humanism doesn't have buildings, art, and ordinary

---

[11] See John Dewey, *Art as Experience* (New York: Perigee Books, 1980, orig. 1934); John Dewey, *A Common Faith* (New Haven: Yale University Press, 1934).

[12] Dewey, *A Common Faith*, 16.

[13] Ibid., 14.

objects and places that symbolize or manifest the sacred or supernatural. Even religious humanists tend to be very cautious when it comes to material symbols of their faith or spirituality. With its strong emphasis on human experience and responsibility, humanism is not inclined to endow objects or places with transcendent power. On the other hand, this emphasis on experience does make humanists sensitive to art (for Dewey, aesthetic and religious experiences are closely related to one another) and to historical sites or objects that preserve the memory of important humanists. Yet worship associated with those sites or objects would contradict the value placed on independence and autonomy.

Interpreting humanism with the aid of Smart's dimensions of religion clarifies that within humanism's narrative, philosophical, ethical, and experiential dimensions, a strong emphasis lies on human experience, creativity, diversity, and responsibility. Worldviewing from a humanist perspective is always context-bound and depends on interpretative or hermeneutic activity in which critical reflection and the possibility of change are highly valued. It is a process that depends in large measure on personal moral expressions and day-to-day practices. We now come to the question of how humanist existential care and counseling can contribute to this process of worldviewing and to the flexibility that is needed for intercultural and interreligious dialogue and caregiving.

## Humanist existential care and counseling
### Existential caregivers

In health care institutions in the Netherlands, existential or spiritual counselors are part of the caregiving staff. Their task is to help patients cope with the impact of their illness on their lives. Although this impact is different in each situation and for each individual, in many cases dealing with a serious physical or mental disorder has an effect on the patient's experience of the meaning of his or her life. In his study of religion and coping, Kenneth Pargament shows that people tend to attempt to retain the meaning they used to give to their lives. Even in the most threatening of circumstances, people try to protect their values and stay within the world they know. It is only when this no longer succeeds and their meaningful world collapses that people are willing to let go of former values. At this point, they are in need of adopting new values and transforming the character of significance itself. Those individuals have to attempt to relinquish their old values, discover new ones, and build a life around this new center. They must look for a framework they can use to orientate themselves in an unknown world.[14]

Existential despair is a very threatening and painful experience accompanied by feelings of emptiness, insecurity, isolation, and alienation. It is important for people not to become trapped in this situation but to move forward in the direction of reorienting themselves toward new meaning. Existential counselors support those who are in this difficult process by inviting people to articulate the (broken) stories of their lives. By listening carefully, they help their clients gather the fragments of what was once important to them. A vital first step for the counselor is to show respect for the often immense pain of loss their client is experiencing.[15]

Researchers have found that a crucial element in finding new meaning is an emotional experience.[16] This can be an experience of connectedness, wonder at one's existence, feeling a part of nature, or feeling oneself to be an element of an encompassing unity, which can be an experience of deep contact with oneself or with another person. In principle this emotional experience is more important than the intellectual or cognitive search for new meaning. Intellectual arguments do not help in a situation of shattered meaning. The emotion of wonder, or profound connection, can open up a new way. This new opening should be followed by further cognitive exploration of the content of the experience and the values inherent in the experience.[17]

With regard to the seven dimensions of worldview, existential counselors must be familiar with the experiential and emotional dimension of their clients. Caregivers should have an open and respectful attitude toward experiences of meaning as well as toward experiences of loss of meaning. Only in this way are they able to come close to their client's experience of brokenness.

**Experiences of a humanist existential counselor**

For ten years, a humanist existential counselor served in a psychiatric institution where she worked in a team of counselors with different

---

[14] Kenneth I. Pargament, *The Psychology of Religion and Coping: Theory, Research, Practice* (New York: Guilford Press, 1997), 110–27.

[15] Susanne Rütter, "'Von deinen Sinnen hinausgesandt, geh bis an deiner Sehnsucht Rand:' Zur Philosophischen Tiefe der Ärtzlichen Seelsorge," in *Sinn und Person: Beitragezur Logotherapie und Existenzanalyse von Viktor E. Frankl*, hrsg. Otmar Wiesmeyr and Alexander Batthyány (Weinheim: Beltz Verlag, 2006), 53–64.

[16] Ibid.; Merteen B. ter Borg, *Waarom geestelijke verzorging?: Zingeving en geestelijke verzorging in de moderne maatschappij* (Nijmegen: KSGV, 2000); William Yang and Tom Staps, *Kanker: eindigheid, zin en spiritualiteit. Bevindingen van eenonderzoek* (Groesbeek: Taborhuis, 2007), electronic version.

[17] See Rütter and also Irvin D. Yalom and Molyn Leszcz, *The Theory and Practice of Group Psychotherapy* (New York: Basic Books, 2005).

religious backgrounds. Some were Protestants, one was Catholic, and the Humanist counselor herself was familiar with a Buddhist perspective. The work among the counselors was organized and divided according to the departments of the hospital and not according to the religious backgrounds of the patients. Thus, each caregiver worked with clients of different religious perspectives.

Toward the beginning of her career, this existential counselor often felt disconcerted. She worked in a wide range of departments in the hospital such as a geriatrics department, a department for adolescents, and three different departments for those struggling to overcome addictions. She was often shocked by the terrible life stories her patients told her. Their stories of darkness and despair made her restless and angry, and in spite of the fact that her doctoral studies focused on Buddhist and Christian meanings of death and suffering, she often had the feeling that she could do nothing.

At a certain point, she decided to start group work. During visits with her patients individually, she noticed how important it was for people to be able to talk about their lives. By telling their stories, they were able to weave the fragmented experiences of their lives into a personal narrative. The idea behind the group work project was that by broadening the range of participants, more recognition of the variety of life experiences would become possible. The groups were restricted to their respective departments, so, for example, there was a group of adolescents, a group of elderly patients, and several groups of those struggling to overcome addictions. But within these groups, the participants were from completely different religious backgrounds. This psychiatric institution was in a region of the Netherlands called the *Bible Belt*, which naturally brought some Reformed participants into the groups. But there were also Catholics, people interested in Buddhism, occasionally a Muslim, and people with no religious background and/or interest at all. Besides the differences in religious backgrounds, the participants were diverse in that each was coping with a different form of illness, had a different educational level, a particular social background, and unique family history. Yet they all had one thing in common. They all shared the experience that life at times stagnates, and that unexpected problems in one's life can arise, bringing one into a different perspective.

To prepare for the group work, this counselor wrote curriculum addressing existential topics tailored to the needs of the target group, such as "Who am I?"; "What does friendship mean to me?"; "Values given to me in childhood and my own values in adulthood"; "Dealing with adversity, illness, aging, and death"; "Faith, art, literature, and film"; and "A bridge to the future."

She also formulated objectives for the groups. For example, the objectives for the elderly group were:

- By dwelling on different life stages, tell and reconstruct your own life story;
- Identify values and norms that were important to you in previous life stages;
- Investigate to what extent former values and norms could be integrated into your current life;
- Identify strengths in yourself and mobilize these strengths;[18]
- Find new meaning for your present life and for the future by examining and sharing your own life story and the life story of others.

These objectives refer to the narrative and experiential dimension of humanism. The starting point is the emphasis on the unique value of each individual and the principle that unveiling values hidden within life stories can be transformative. The discussions within each group revealed that people tend to enjoy talking about their own lives, not only about current difficulties, but also about their past, their work, their education, what they consider to be highly important and valuable, and problems they encountered and how they resolved them. They also shared about their futures, such as what they would like to take up again and new ventures they hoped for, despite everything that had changed in their lives. Telling stories about their lives helped these individuals discover meaning in their own pasts as well as find new meaning for the future.

The group work project also demonstrated that people enjoy listening to the stories of others. It is inspiring to discover that everyone's life story has highs and lows, and particularly inspiring to learn how others have moved on despite the difficulties they faced. The sharing of joy and sorrow can create bonds despite differences in personal histories.

**Reflection on interfaith spiritual care**

As one educated in the philosophy of religion, this humanist counselor found it striking that when people were asked about important events in their lives, they seldom talked about their religion. Instead they talked about their childhoods, a sick mother, meeting the ideal partner even though it failed to work out, their children, and the work that gave their

---

[18] Christopher Peterson and Martin E. Seligman, *Character Strengths and Virtues: A Handbook and Classification* (Oxford: Oxford University Press, 2004).

lives meaning. Some only mentioned religion when asked about their support systems, but when someone would speak about their history with religion, everyone in the group—religious or not—understood what they were talking about. The reason for this was that participants tended not to mention dogmas or rituals which others might have failed to understand, but rather they focused on the way their faith had developed in their lives. They spoke of the comfort religion had given them, their doubts, their questions, and sometimes their resignation to the fact that faith and life itself remained ultimately incomprehensible.

These insights have led to the awareness of what we refer to as *narrative interreligious dialogue*.[19] Narrative interreligious dialogue is an important approach to interfaith spiritual care. When a counselor or spiritual caregiver is leading group work with participants of different religious backgrounds, it is important not to focus on these different religious backgrounds. This will create confusing discussions about the philosophical, ritual, and practical dimensions of the different worldviews. Discussions of these dimensions tend to focus on the differences between the worldviews of the participants, and as a result, they often grow apart from each other.[20]

Narrative interreligious dialogue is not directed at inter-religiousness at all, but rather deals with ordinary contact between human beings. Primary questions here are: "Who are you?"; "What have you been through?"; "How have you coped with all that crossed your path?"; and finally, "What has been your source of strength?" The diverse answers to the last question can only be understood in relation to one's answers to the previous questions. Insight into a person's religious history and worldview can only be attained by understanding his or her life story.[21]

This inter-human approach to interfaith spiritual care shows that the wide range of answers to the question, "What has supported you?" is not to be lamented but valued. It reveals great diversity of creativity and inspiration of equal value. Behind religious and spiritual differences is the shared adventure of being human, in which sooner or later everyone is confronted with joy and sorrow, health and illness, birth and

---

[19] Christa W. Anbeek, "Christian and Buddhist Spiritualities: Their Differences and Complementarities," in *Crossroad Discourses Between Christianity and Culture*, ed. Jerald D. Gort, Henry Jansen, and Wessel Stoker (Amsterdam: Rodopi, 2010), 413–30.

[20] Christa W. Anbeek, "The Beauty of Ten Thousand Blooming Flowers," *Journal of the European Society of Women in Theological Research* 17 (2009): 59–68.

[21] Manuela Kalsky, Ida Overdijk. en *Moderne devoties.Vrouwen over geloven*, ed. Inez van der Spek (Amsterdam/Antwerpen: Uitgeverij de Prom, 2005).

death—together with the challenge of coping strategies.[22]

This inter-human approach to interfaith spiritual care also opens the way to an ecosophical interfaith dialogue. Ecosophy stresses the diversity and richness of cultures and life forms. Additionally, it encourages people to open their eyes to the fact that in spite of this diversity, we form one global community that is extremely vulnerable. Dialogue from an ecosophical perspective seeks unity amidst diversity and finds this in our common responsibility for a viable global society that is based on respect for nature, universal human rights, economic justice, and a culture of peace.

## Core competencies for existential counselors and spiritual caregivers

In order to be able to support people in their search for meaning, the existential counselor should possess certain competencies. In the Netherlands, the competence of primary importance for a spiritual counselor is called "religious competence." Earlier we introduced the term *worldviewing*, and, in the same line of thought, we would like to also introduce the term *worldviewing competence*. Since we defined the term "worldviewing" with the help of Smart's seven dimensions of religion, we need to consider that the basic worldviewing competence should also cover all seven dimensions. The basic worldviewing competence for humanist existential counseling could be formulated as follows: it is the ability to understand the life story of a client with regard to its religious or existential meaning, and the capability to relate this story and its religious and/or existential background to the resources of the counselor. In this basic overarching competence, we distinguish three core competencies that strongly cohere with each other: hermeneutic, self-reflective, and heuristic.

### The hermeneutic competence

Earlier in our discussion of the narrative dimension of religion we saw that humanism and hermeneutics are closely related to each other. The hermeneutic competence of the counselor consists of the capability to read the stories and experiences of individuals with regard to their existential meaning and the capability to engage in dialogue about this meaning. In order to be able to do this, existential counselors need knowledge first

---

[22] Taking life stories as a starting point provides a view of the diversity of people. There is significant variation in what human beings experience and how they give meaning to their experiences. In the midst of this variety unexpected similarities can appear despite cultural differences. See Halleh Ghorashi and Christien Brinkgreve, *Licht en schaduw: Vijftien vrouwen over leven en overleven* (Amsterdam: VU Uitgeverij, 2010), 17.

of all. They need to be able to understand the different religious backgrounds of the clients, yet also should have a deep awareness of their own humanist background. This knowledge should cover all of the dimensions of worldviews: narratives, philosophical insights, social organizations, material expressions, experiential givens, rituals, and ethics.

This hermeneutic competence not only asks for knowledge but also for a process of application. In this process, the strengths and weaknesses of other worldviewing traditions should be translated into the particular situation of the client and the counselor. An ongoing exchange of resources occurs between worldviewing traditions as well as the here and now of the client and counselor. In order to facilitate this exchange, one not only needs knowledge of traditions but also dialogical skills. Dialogical expertise is needed to transfer the richness of the tradition to the here and now of the client and counselor, and to be able to answer current questions about the meaning of one's life with regard to these traditions. Counselors who work with clients from different religious backgrounds, or with no religious background at all, need to have high competency in dialogical expertise in order to support this exchange of resources between traditions and the actual context and experiences of their clients.

**The self-reflective competence**

The self-reflective competence concerns the inner dialogue of the counselor. In order to be able to support individuals in their search for meaning, the counselor should develop his or her own spiritual or existential identity. Counselors should be competent in expressing what elements and values are important for their own experienced meaning in life. This enables them to be open and committed to their clients, and to support them in their own search for meaning.

As we have seen, the development of this identity is an ongoing process of intrapersonal and interpersonal dialogue.[23] Often, the stories of other people will initiate a new step in one's own self-reflection in light of the differences, similarities, ambiguities, and common themes across different cultures and worldviews. Identities, even spiritual identities, are dynamic. They are not static, are never complete, but are always changing and often indefinable. New experiences and new contexts invite self-reflection on what this means for one's own identity. This is the case not only for the client but also for the counselor as well. An ongoing commitment to self-reflection is needed to stay open and sensitive to the other.

---

[23] See Hermans and Kempen, *The Dialogical Self*.

### The heuristic competence

The heuristic competence refers to the attitude of the counselor in relation to the client. The counselor's attitude and methodological approach should not begin from the unilateral position of an expert working *for* an unknowing client. The relation should be seen as a bilateral and common quest. An attitude of "not-knowing" (or, existential counselor's suspension of "knowing") and openness is needed for this. This approach can be very difficult for the professional, but it is related to the second competence of self-reflection. It asks for a letting go of one's own interpretation of life's significance and of the handholds of an expert concerning the "meaning of life" questions. No one has definitive answers to the significance of life, death, illness, and loss. In order to be able to help people in their search for provisional answers (that will do for some time), the counselor should be willing to undertake a collaborative quest. In this quest, the starting point is the situation, experiences, and questions of the client. The answers and views of the counselor are not of primary importance; they are tentative options that could be of help in an unknown journey. This heuristic competence is of special importance for the concept of worldviewing as a flux or a river. Worldviewing is always fluid. In every situation, in every new experience, the stream finds its way through new and different landscapes. The work of the counselor is not so much to reorient the river to the way it used to run, but to support the development of new streams that are fruitful to the landscape of the client.

### Concluding remarks

In this chapter we have applied Ninian Smart's seven dimensions of religion in order to gain a better understanding of humanism as a source for spiritual or existential care and counseling. Stressing the open and dialogical nature of humanism, we have argued that it can best be characterized by the more active term *worldviewing*. By humanist worldviewing, we mean a process of giving existential meaning to life by intrapersonal and interpersonal dialogue, in which the humanist tradition participates as a "collective voice" representing a stream of thought in both Western and Eastern cultures.

Interpreting humanism from this perspective, and with the help of Smart's dimensions of religion, we find that it manifests itself particularly in the narrative, philosophical, ethical, and experiential dimensions. In these dimensions, humanism is characterized by a strong emphasis on human experience, creativity, diversity, and responsibility. We have seen that worldviewing from a humanist perspective is always context-bound and depends on interpretative or hermeneutic activity, and makes use of personal moral expressions and day-to-day practices.

This hermeneutic activity plays a central role in humanist existential counseling, in which clients are supported in coping with existential despair and in moving forward in the direction of orienting themselves toward new meaning and hope. Existential counselors invite their clients to articulate the (broken) stories of their lives. We have seen how this plays out in practice through the case study of a humanist existential counselor working in a psychiatric institution.

The case study made it clear that people like to listen to the stories of others, and that sharing joy and sorrow with others can create bonds despite differences in personal or religious backgrounds. This is an important insight when it comes to the question of how humanist existential counseling can contribute to the process of worldviewing and provide the flexibility that is needed for intercultural and interreligious dialogue.

As a contribution to the issue of intercultural and interreligious dialogue, we have introduced the concept of "narrative interreligious dialogue" as an important approach to interfaith spiritual care. Narrative interreligious dialogue does not begin with the philosophical, ritual, or practical dimensions of different worldviews, but instead begins with the ordinary interactions of human beings in their attempts to cope with the existential challenges of life. There are many different answers to the question, "What has been your source of strength?" and a wide range of creative and inspiring narratives of equal value can be revealed through existential counseling.

We have argued that in order to initiate and support narrative interreligious dialogue, the existential counselor needs a basic worldviewing competence; namely, the ability to understand the life story of a client with regard to its religious or existential implications and the capability to relate this story and its religious and/or existential background to the resources of the counselor. In this basic competence we distinguished three core competencies that strongly cohere with each other: hermeneutic, self-reflective, and heuristic. They are clearly related to the characteristics of humanism as we interpreted it in light of Smart's seven dimensions of religion. We propose that by inspiring and strengthening this basic competence in existential caregivers, humanism can contribute significantly to spiritual care in multifaith contexts.

# The heart of the matter
Engaging the *spirit* in spiritual care

*Daniel S. Schipani*

The authors of the previous chapters illumine the field of spiritual care from the unique vantage point of seven different traditions. All of them offer valuable insights and practical guidelines for excellent spiritual care in multifaith contexts. Their material also includes diverse foundational understandings and highlights ways of caring well that can be appreciated as complementary and mutually enriching.

The considerable common ground revealed thus far is not due merely to some common (minimum) denominator shared by these seven traditions; in fact, their distinctness and differences must be duly recognized. Further, it should not be superficially dismissed as the source of "generic" or unspecified care, pejoratively speaking. Finally, common ground should not be explained only in terms of the similar clinical training or professional formation of caregivers represented in each case. Rather, common ground can be perceived as actually reflecting the reality of the holy ground of human encounter created in spiritual caregiving situations. Indeed, as so clearly illustrated by the authors, those encounters deal with fundamental needs and questions, potential and resourcefulness that point to existential issues of meaning, connectedness, vocation, and destiny; in short, the very concerns of the human spirit through the ages.

The purpose of this final chapter, simply stated, is to offer a systematic response to the question, what is meant by *spiritual* in "spiritual care"?[1]

---

[1] I practice, teach, supervise, and reflect on spiritual care as a Christian man born and raised in a Latin American socio-cultural context. Nevertheless, I offer this chapter with the convictions articulated in the previous paragraph. Therefore, I assume that colleagues who represent other traditions and points of view will be able to make helpful connections with their own frameworks and perspectives; and I am confident that they will be willing to offer in turn meaningful criticism and suggestions as well, which I welcome in advance.

Following my own story as a care receiver in the hospital, I discuss several theoretical issues to take into account when relating mental health and spiritual health. A case study then introduces a number of guidelines for further reflection and practical integration. These guidelines arise out of my understanding of the self and intra-self dynamics and my view of the unique contribution of spiritual care professionals—pastoral counselors and psychotherapists, chaplains and spiritual care specialists, and others—to health, healing, and wholeness.

**My story as a care receiver**

*Early morning on Tuesday, May 20, 1997, I was taken to the emergency department of the local hospital with excruciating abdominal pain. Soon after arriving, I underwent surgery for a ruptured appendix. Only two days before, I had begun to feel some discomfort similar to the signs of a mild stomach flu. The discomfort had continued and become more intense as the hours progressed. (I have never been good at experiencing pain, so perhaps, in retrospect, my low level threshold for physical pain contributed to saving my life.)*

*This was my first experience as a patient in the hospital, and when I woke up from surgery, I naively assumed that my life was already almost back to "normal." Still under the effects of anesthesia, I began making work-related phone calls. It did not take long, however, for reality to set in. I realized I would need to adjust to the utterly disempowering effects of the hospital setting, and I also would have to face two difficult weeks of a painful and (at one point) uncertain recovery process.*

*Initially I was overwhelmed by the constant care I received on the part of several nurses who dutifully and repeatedly checked my temperature and performed a number of "procedures" on me (including a well-intentioned yet unnecessary and hurtful catheter on the second night). I also was at first uncomfortable, to say the least, when needing to be helped or washed by a soft-spoken, deeply caring African American aid, though she eventually became a trusted companion. Obviously I had not been prepared to experience such dislocation, vulnerability, and loss of privacy and sense of agency. To make matters worse, a trip to the Caribbean with my family, which included lecturing at a theological school, had to be cancelled. And I knew I would also miss the commissioning and commencement celebrations at the end of the academic year in my seminary. In other words, my situation was a textbook illustration of a critical incident (unexpected surgery) triggering a multidimensional crisis.*

*The most critical point came ten days after surgery. A scan prescribed in the face of a stubborn infection and unresponsive digestive system (despite my long walks on the hospital's sixth floor) was inconclusive. My doctor told my wife and me that another surgery was a possibility. In an effort to avoid that option, he decided to fight the infection more aggressively, significantly increase I.V. nourishment, and lessen my pain by inserting a naso-gastric tube (quite another "procedure"!) to release a huge amount of accumulated liquid.* Fortunately, my condition soon began steadily improving, and I was released fifteen days after entering the emergency room.

It is well known that crises are potentially occasions for transformation; what is less well known is the connection between transformation and spiritual care. My own hospital experience became a major transforming event for me, not only through the medical care I received, but also in direct connection to competent and timely spiritual care. That spiritual care was offered in short visits by my pastor and a trusted colleague and included listening and encouraging words, scripture reading, prayer and blessing, and anointment with oil. I also knew that many people were praying from me—family members, friends, and others—in near and far away places. In other words, I received the spiritual care and support I needed for the mental, emotional, and spiritual realities which accompanied my medical condition. Although the spiritual care I received represented primarily one faith tradition, I am confident that skilled caregivers representing different faith traditions also would have been able to care for me in transformative ways or would have sought to supplement their care with other (Christian faith) appropriate interventions and resources.[2]

A miracle-like change happened in that I became a model patient in the course of the healing process. It was a change that surprised me and those who know me well as a too-active, eager, impatient, and sometimes restless person. I learned to cooperate with the care team of nurses, aides, technicians, and physicians and even relaxed enough to serve others; two of them shared their own personal life challenges and struggles with me, and, in one occasion toward the end of my stay at the hospital, I was drawn to mediate in a conflict between a nurse and a technician.

My hospital room and the sixth floor where it was located became a truly familiar, almost homey place, and, in spite of the frequent interruptions mandated by current standards of hospital health care, the nights became an

---

[2] Dagmar Grefe helpfully discusses the spiritual caregiver's function of connecting persons in crisis to their spiritual resources and community. His model of three concentric circles of interreligious spiritual care includes the following three categories of situations that can be addressed: (1) "common (universal) human experience," in which the caregiver functions primarily as *companion*; (2) "interconnected spiritual practice," in which the caregiver functions as *representative of the sacred*; and (3) "particular religious spiritual practice," in which the caregiver functions primarily as *resource agent* who connects care receivers and their families to their spiritual communities and resources. See Dagmar Grefe, *Encounters for Change: Interreligious Cooperation in the Care of Individuals and Communities* (Eugene: Wipf & Stock, 2011), 138–45.

*anticipated time for restful meditation and prayer. Surprisingly, the expression "for a speedy recovery" printed on some of the many get-well cards I received, somehow did not feel fitting. I realized that the necessary healing process under way would take time. I further realized that such a process would involve my whole being—body, soul, and spirit.*

*Under the circumstances, I managed to accommodate to the situation remarkably well; inner and outer resources undoubtedly helped me to adapt to the realities of the hospital setting in psychologically healthy ways. But something deeper was also going on, which I later recognized as manifestations of my spiritual self. I was experiencing a new sense of existential meaning and truth; a transcendent sense of love and communion with God and others near and far; and a sense of purposeful re-orientation and destiny. I believe that a process of spiritual transformation undergirded and strengthened my mental and emotional health and very likely contributed to the healing of my body as well. Anxiety and fear of death in the face of the unknown gave way to peace and joy truly beyond understanding. I left the hospital with a profound sense of grace and gratitude.*

One way to address the question, what is meant by *spiritual* in "spiritual care"?, is found in relating mental (including "emotional") health and spiritual health. As indicated below, such theoretical exercise must include a number of interrelated considerations.

### Connecting mental health[3] and spiritual health: Understandings and guidelines for spiritual health care practitioners[4]

The purpose of the following sections is twofold; namely, to highlight issues encountered when relating current notions of mental health and spiritual health, and to suggest guidelines for further theoretical reflection and practical integration. The case study located between the sections addressing key theoretical and practical considerations illustrates the kind of opportunity and responsibility that spiritual caregivers assume as they seek to care well in a holistic manner.

---

[3] I will use "mental health" and "mental and emotional health" interchangeably in the remainder of this chapter.

[4] The group of "spiritual health care practitioners" includes pastoral counselors, chaplains (a term increasingly reserved for caregivers who represent a certain faith tradition and/or who work in a faith-based health care institution) and "spiritual care and counseling specialists" as defined, for example, by the Canadian Association for Spiritual Care ("clinical practitioners who help people draw upon their own spiritual, religious, and cultural resources for direction, strength, wisdom, and healing as they journey through life's stages"; from the CASC/ACSS document, "Competencies for Spiritual Care and Counselling Specialist," May 2011, 1).

## Theoretical issues for reflection
### What is in a label?: *Semantic* considerations

We can start by recalling that the word *health* is related etymologically to the Anglo-Saxon word from which *healing*, *holiness*, and *wholeness* are derived.[5] This is something to keep in mind as we consider theoretical issues when relating the three main senses of "mental health" and "spiritual health."[6] Those notions of "health" carry diverse meanings and connotations, as indicated briefly below.

Mental and *emotional* health and illness or "disorder" are often used as synonyms both colloquially and in academic or professional speech. Mental health can be characterized simply as the capacity to think, feel, and behave in ways that enhance our ability to enjoy life and deal with the challenges and struggles we face. Healthy and "mature" spirituality is harder to define. It can be assumed by assessing enduring and life-giving manifestations of meaning, purpose, peace, joy, love of self and others, connectedness with a transcendent source of light and grace, and with the non-human environment, and so on.[7] Further, concepts of mental (or emotional) maturity as well as "spiritual maturity" are often closely associated with mental and spiritual health (or "healthy spirituality") respectively, especially in the case of adult men and women. It is helpful, therefore, to agree on some definitions or commonly held understandings for each of those concepts.

Another point of semantics is that there is confusion or, at least, inconsistency, regarding the use of terms such as *soul* (Greek, ψυχή = *psyche*) and *spirit* (Greek, πνεῦμα = *pneuma*). Such inconsistency is detectable both in everyday speech and in fields such as literature, philosophy, religious studies, and theology. I hold that it is helpful to assume a conceptual distinction between "soul" and "spirit" while

---

[5] The World Health Organization defines health in simple terms as "a state of complete physical, mental and social well-being and not merely the absence of disease or infirmity."

[6] "Mental health" denotes not only a human condition that can be described and assessed somehow, but also a special kind of science or discipline and a profession as well. The same can be said regarding "spiritual health." Our discussion of the relationship between mental and spiritual health can be enhanced by keeping in mind those three different kinds of meanings and connotations—a human condition, a science, and a profession—and their inter-relationships.

[7] From a Christian perspective, "spiritual health" can be considered, for example, by focusing on someone's relationship with God, others, oneself, systems and structures, and creation (see Dan Schrock, *A Spiritual Health Inventory* (2008), htpp://www.danschrock.org/inventory.aspx). It is, of course, possible to identify a plurality of "healthy" spiritualities with distinct features, such as contemplative, prophetic, charismatic, etc. And it is also possible to assess unhealthy or "toxic" spiritualities, Christian or otherwise.

maintaining their integration and inseparability within the larger notion of the embodied human self, as depicted in the section on the tripartite nature of the self.

**What is behind the label?:** *Philosophical-sociocultural-theological* **issues to ponder**

Our agenda for reflection and discussion must include a second set of issues that are not inherently "scientific," strictly speaking; they point to the metaphysical and ethical non-neutrality of theoreticians and practitioners in both the "mental" and "spiritual" health fields. "Mental health" and "spiritual health" are, in the language of philosophy of science, *practical human sciences*; in other words, not unlike education, those sciences deal with guidance, support, and transformation of human behavior and life. Therefore, they must develop goals and methodologies consistent with fundamental questions and norms of humanness, healing, and wholeness that stem in part from philosophical, theological, and other sources outside their respective scientific fields narrowly viewed.

The very notions of mental and spiritual "health" (and "maturity") rest on value-laden defining criteria. Those criteria are always articulated within specific socio-cultural contexts (not normally recognized as such) and do change over time. For example, changing definitions and (psychopathological) criteria are easily documentable in the case of mental health,[8] as registered, for instance, in the history of the American Psychiatric Association's widely used *Diagnostic and Statistical Manual of Mental Disorders* (DSM).[9] Further, in the case of both psychiatry and clinical psychology (including disciplines such as personality theory, psychopathology, and psychotherapy theory) there exists a variety of views and approaches not necessarily compatible among themselves.[10]

---

[8] There is a reason for this significant difference between the histories of "mental health" and "spiritual health," including the fact that changing definitions and criteria are not easy to document in the case of the latter. In any case, the discipline of spiritual health has always dealt with perennial questions concerning human life and the spirit, meaning and love, vocation and destiny, health, suffering, sickness and death, the Divine, and so on. That is why we still benefit from appropriating the wisdom of ancient texts, for example! The field of mental health is much younger as a branch of modern medicine.

[9] American Psychiatric Association, *Diagnostic and Statistical Manual of Mental Disorders*, 4th ed. Text Revision (Washington, DC: American Psychiatric Association, [1994] 2000). The 5th edition of the *DSM* is scheduled to be released in 2013.

[10] There are hundreds of clinical psychotherapeutic strategies roughly identifiable in terms of "families" of psychodynamic, behavioral, humanistic-existential, and systemic views and approaches. Spiritual caregivers can benefit greatly from their contributions, especially when their implicit metaphysical and ethical assumptions are duly unveiled and taken into consideration.

Our reflection must always include explicit consideration of multicultural and multifaith factors which condition the very notions of "good" mental and spiritual health. Those factors also determine the approaches, methods, and treatments employed to support, enhance, or restore "health," or foster the process and the experience of suffering and dying well from the perspective of the care receivers and their communities.

**Who has the authority and power to label?:** *Ideological and professional-political* **considerations**

Related questions of ideology and power must also be part of our conversation. It matters greatly who has the authority and power to define "health" and to label "disorder" or "sickness" and "cure." It matters also what kinds of assumptions and understandings determine the form and content of the definitions and labels, and the implications regarding care deemed appropriate in light of such categorizations. The following sets of issues immediately come to mind.

The challenge to consider ideological and professional-political factors obviously pertains to the field of mental health in light of the major role of powerful organizations such as the American Psychiatric Association.[11] It also relates to government and institutional entities which decide, for example, who qualifies to receive certain kinds of medical or psychological assistance, for how long, and under what conditions. Economic and financial considerations are, therefore, a major factor to take into account whether or not we are dealing with public or private health care programs and centers, insurance policies, and related matters.

We must also ponder ideological, legal, and other issues in the science and the practice of spiritual health. Spiritual care providers must work with normative understandings of "healthy" and "unhealthy" or "toxic" spirituality, which are heavily conditioned by their ideological frameworks (whether philosophical, ethical, political, or theological), and their preferred approaches to care. This is an area where the Positive Psychology movement and Gestalt Pastoral Care can be particularly helpful.[12]

---

[11] Psychiatrists, clinical psychologists, clinical social workers, and pastoral psychotherapists, all routinely use psychiatric labeling (or "diagnoses"). Potential conflict emerges to the extent that ethical and legal questions are raised (e.g., whether making diagnoses of mental illness constitutes a "medical" act requiring medical supervision, or whether [in the United States, for sure] insurance policies will pay for certain counseling or psychotherapeutic treatments, etc.).

[12] Positive Psychology presents a convincing critique of the dominant "pathogenic" and symptom reduction model of mental illness. It offers a new "salutogenic" paradigm which, in addition to symptom reduction, points to optimal functioning, wholeness, and "flourishing." Together with the contributions of Humanist-Existential Psychology (e.g., Viktor Frankl), Positive Psychology provides a helpful new framework and language for spiritual caregivers. See the following

In order to illumine this discussion further, let us consider now the situation of someone needing holistic care. It is an abbreviated and simplified case study based on a real-life situation I encountered.

### Caring for Arthur

*Arthur*[13] *was a 78-year-old man born and raised on a Caribbean island. He had been in the United States for about thirty years. His wife had died three years earlier, after a painful dying process; his daughter and her family lived not far from him in the same town; and his son lived in another state. At the time I met Arthur he had a growing, inoperable tumor increasingly compromising his digestive system, and hospice care was soon to be arranged for him. Arthur was referred to me by his family physician because he frequently experienced anxiety and depression. The diagnosis registered in Arthur's clinical chart was "Adjustment disorder with mixed anxiety and depressed mood (309.28)."*[14] *He would continue using prescribed medication to lessen both his anxiety and depression and to manage pain.*

*Arthur and I established good rapport. He was eager to receive help, especially from someone whom he thought might consider addressing his spiritual anguish, so he readily welcomed my therapeutic companionship. Arthur's personal and family story was seemingly unremarkable at first. However, as our relationship unfolded, he shared the secret of living with the burden of, in his words, unforgivable sin. He was struggling with guilt and the sense of having lost forever the opportunity to communicate regret to his wife and to receive forgiveness for not being more fully present with her during the last months of her life. He didn't feel free to talk with his children about the situation, and prayers of confession had not been helpful. The diagnosis and treatment of his terminal illness compounded Arthur's sense of being in a truly limit situation and facing condemnation.*

---

works: Mihaly Csikszentmihaly and Isabella Selega Csikszentmihaly, eds., *A Life Worth Living: Contributions to Positive Psychology* (New York: Oxford University Press, 2006); Corey L. M. Keyes and Jonathan Haidt, eds., *Flourishing: Positive Psychology and the Life Well-Lived* (Washington, DC: American Psychological Association, 2003); and C. R. Snyder and Shane J. López, eds., *Handbook of Positive Psychology* (New York: Oxford University Press, 2005). For its part, Gestalt Pastoral Care integrates the contributions of Gestalt "growth work" with the riches of (Christian) spirituality, as presented in Tilda Norberg's *Consenting to Grace: An Introduction to Gestalt Pastoral Care* (Staten Island: Penn House Press, 2006).

[13] "Arthur" is the fictional name of a real care receiver for whom I changed several pieces of information concerning this experience of care in order to preserve confidentiality. I am grateful to him and hundreds of other care receivers like him with whom I have explored the inseparable and complex connection between mental and spiritual health.

[14] This psychiatric label appears within the category of "Adjustment Disorders" in the American Psychiatric Association, *Diagnostic and Statistical Manual of Mental Disorders*, 680, 683.

*These are goals and commitments that I set for myself in that situation as a spiritual caregiver:*[15] *to accept Arthur's welcoming me and, in turn, to welcome him in a safe and caring space where he could express himself freely; to represent and mediate Grace and Wisdom and a healing community as Arthur needed to move away from the severe disorientation linked to both unresolved guilt and grief, and terminal illness; to become, for a short while, a companion in Arthur's journey toward reorientation and, hopefully, healing even without physical cure (by being a witness who listens well, comforts, helps him to embrace new life, guides him in a discernment process leading to wise decisions, and gently holds him accountable); and to offer care and counseling competently (e.g., by deliberately employing a narrative approach as well as cognitive restructuring*[16] *to help Arthur re-story his life and to perceive his world more realistically, changing misconceptions and expectations directly connected with his anxiety and depression).*

*Arthur and I agreed that our relationship would be oriented toward the following interrelated objectives: understanding what was actually going on in his life; revisiting his life story and spiritual journey with an eye to rekindling hope; finding specific, practical ways for him to transform the struggle with guilt and sense of sinfulness while experiencing a closer communion with God; and making key decisions about next steps, especially regarding the transition to hospice care and the relationship with his family. In short, we were aiming at moving from barely coping to an experience of healing and wholeness.*

I sought to bring a holistic approach to the medical care Arthur was receiving by caring for him in a manner that would engage both his psychological and his spiritual self. The following sections present several key principles that undergirded the therapeutic relationship with him and continue to orient my practice of spiritual care; they also include a few illustrative references to my caring for Arthur.

## Guidelines for further reflection and practical integration

### What is our view of the self?: *A tripartite anthropology*

I respond to this question from the perspective of a theological

---

[15] It is essential for caregivers to have clarity regarding certain key goals and commitments that we must in principle set for ourselves and for which we are primarily responsible even as we remain open to including appropriate expectations on the part of those with and for whom we care.

[16] As a therapeutic intervention, cognitive restructuring is a broadly used method associated with cognitive psychotherapies. It is employed to help people change their learned negative cognitions and to teach them more realistic sets of beliefs, including the practice of reformulating irrational thoughts in light of a new vision of reality.

anthropology which has biblical and, especially, Christian (Pauline) grounding. Even though one does not find a systematic anthropology in the writings of Paul the Apostle, his understanding of human nature can be drawn from his pastoral and theological reflections, which appear contextually articulated in different New Testament epistles. I find it useful to critically re-appropriate that Pauline legacy as a way to address anthropological concerns raised in pastoral theology and spiritual health as a discipline and in spiritual care as a profession.[17] I hope that spiritual care theorists and practitioners representing other traditions might find the following claims and observations meaningful in some ways. I am open to continue learning from their views as well.

Viewed from that perspective, human beings have an embodied, animated, spiritual self. A tripartite anthropology of body, psyche, and spirit can thus be pictured structurally, as in the diagram that follows. The external full line symbolizes the self's bodily separateness; the other two lines represent the close connection of body-psyche (as appreciated from long ago, for instance, in so-called psycho-somatic pathology and medicine), and the inseparable relationship of psyche-spirit.

**A tripartite view of the self**
(within family, social, global, cosmic contexts)

---

[17] The following observations are supported by Pauline scholarship (see, for example, James D. G. Dunn, *The Theology of Paul the Apostle* [Grand Rapids: William B. Eerdmans Publishing Co., 1998], 51–78):

- "Body" (*soma*) includes but is larger than physical body; it is a relational concept denoting the person embodied in a particular environment. "Body" for Paul expresses the character of created humankind—embodied existence—that makes possible a social dimension to life, that is, participation in human community. The concept is, for the most part, morally neutral. (In contrast, the notion of "flesh" [*sarx*] in the epistles, which is never equated with "body" [*soma*], is for the most part morally negative; it connotes human finitude, vulnerability, and proclivity to sinful behavior.)

- "Soul" (*psyche*) denotes the person and the focus of human vitality. It includes the dimensions of "heart" (*kardia*, the seat of affection and will) and "mind" (*nous*, reason or

The *psychological* (dimension of) self and the *spiritual* (dimension of) self are integrated and inseparable, yet they are also distinct and distinguishable. At least since Aristotle, the three main, interrelated expressions of the psychological self have been viewed in terms of thinking and knowing (cognition), feeling and relating (affection), and choosing and acting (volition). Contemporary psychology refers to those closely interrelated expressions of the psychological self as cognitive, affective, and volitional *registers of behavior*. All key psychological constructs—e.g., *intelligence* (whether traditionally viewed or as emotional, social, or moral intelligence) and *personality*—are usually reflected and studied in terms of cognitive, affective, and volitional behaviors. Analogously in the case of pathologies, mental and emotional disorders can be broadly defined as health conditions characterized by alterations of thinking, mood, or behavior, or some combination among those expressions of the psychological self, associated with distress and/or impaired functioning.

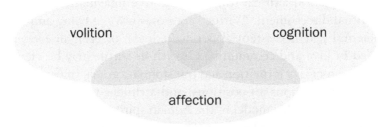

**Threefold expression of the psychological self**

I propose that the *spiritual* self can be visualized analogously as having three interrelated expressions which I have chosen to name "Vision," "Virtue," and "Vocation." Thus, the following drawing may be viewed as a functional model of the wholesome human spirit.

---

rationality). By integrating Hebrew and Greek anthropological views, "Paul . . . sought . . . to maintain a balance between the rational, the emotional, and the volitional" (Dunn, *The Theology of Paul the Apostle*, 75).

- "Spirit" (*pneuma*) is that dimension of the human being by means of which the person can relate most directly to (the Spirit of) God. It is the deeper, transcendence-oriented or "God-ward" dimension of the human self. In fact, for Paul it is by opening the human spirit to the Holy Spirit that human beings can become truly whole and experience newness of life expressed interpersonally and communally with "spirit-fruit"—love, joy, peace, patience, kindness, generosity, faithfulness, gentleness, self-control . . . etc. Hence, the holistic blessing: "May the God of peace [Godself] sanctify you entirely; and may your spirit and soul and body be kept sound and blameless . . ." (I Thessalonians 5:23).

160 | Multifaith Views in Spiritual Care

>
> Purpose/Destiny
> Vocation
> Hope
>
> Perception/Meaning
> Vision
> Faith
>
> Being/Communion
> Virtue
> Love

**Threefold expression of the (wholesome) spiritual self**

"Vision" connotes ways of seeing and knowing reality, both self and world. Fundamentally, it names the need and potential for *deep perception* and *meaning*. Growth in Vision necessitates deepening dispositions and behaviors such as heightened awareness; attentiveness; admiration and contemplation; critical thinking; creative imagination; and moral and spiritual discernment. "Virtue" connotes ways of being and loving; fundamentally, it is existential connectedness, or *being in communion* grounded in love and community. Growth in Virtue may be viewed as requiring a process of formation and transformation shaping one's inmost affections and passions, dispositions, and attitudes (i.e., "habits of the heart"). Finally, in this model of the human spirit, "Vocation" connotes a sense of life's *purpose* and existential orientation and *destiny*. It is about investing one's life, energies, time, and human potential in creative, life-giving, and community-building ways.[18] From a theological perspective, we can also posit a direct connection between these faces of the spiritual self and the gifts of Faith, Love, and Hope.[19]

Consequently, existential threats to the human spirit and spiritual health may include, respectively but not exclusively, manifestations such as the following: meaninglessness, emptiness, illusion, deceit; alienation, isolation, condemnation, annihilation; and aimlessness, disorientation (lostness), fate, and despair. These and related existential threats can be

---

[18] In the case of Christian theology this model can be understood in light of Trinitarian anthropological conceptions of the human self developed through the history of Christian thought from, say, Augustine (*Treatise on the Holy Trinity*) to Catherine Mowry LaCugna (*God for Us: The Trinity and Christian Life* [San Francisco: Harper, 1991]).

[19] I believe that caregivers from other traditions, including Humanism, also can broadly consider the categories of (religious and nonreligious) faith, love, and hope, as potentially helpful to name three main sets of existential experiences or conditions concerning spirituality and the spiritual self as such.

considered as faces of the "Void" and expression of a "languishing life" (as opposed to "flourishing life") as presented at the end of this chapter in reference to the four-dimensional view of reality spiritual caregivers must hold. It is also possible to find helpful correlations between normal and pathological anxieties on the one hand and existential (or spiritual) anxieties on the other hand, as insightfully proposed by Paul Tillich in his classic work, *The Courage to Be*.[20]

*With such a view of the spiritual self, I sought to assist Arthur in a process of gaining wisdom in the sense of* spiritual (including moral) intelligence, *that is,* wisdom *demonstrated in improving discernment, making life-giving choices, and dying well. From this perspective, the overarching purpose of spiritual care included helping Arthur find new and better ways of seeing and understanding reality and, especially, himself and others. (Theologically viewed, he would see better, as with the eyes of God, metaphorically speaking: "Vision.") This would allow Arthur to find and create meaning in transforming ways. Second, our brief relationship would encourage Arthur to re-appropriate the experience of personal integrity and having been loved and having loved deeply. (Theologically viewed, this would amount to Arthur's heart being restored according to the heart of Christ: "Virtue.") Third, spiritual healing also would entail a retrospective vocational reappraisal together with a fresh sense of ultimate purpose and destiny. (Theologically viewed, Arthur would experience a new realization of participating in the life of the Spirit in the world now and somehow beyond this life: "Vocation.")*

**How do mental and spiritual health "connect"?:** *Intra-self dynamics*

As asserted above, the psychological and spiritual dimensions of the self can be viewed as integrated and inseparable, but they are also

---

[20] Paul Tillich, *The Courage to Be* (New Haven: Yale University Press, 1953), 32–77. This well-known theologian interested in psychology and health (see, for instance, *The Meaning of Health: The Relation of Religion and Health* [Richmond: North Atlantic Books, 1981]), writes in this book as an existentialist philosopher of being. He reframes standard views on normal and pathological anxiety in terms of *existential* and *neurotic* anxiety in the face of the threefold threat of nonbeing (emptiness, condemnation, and annihilation). Further, he asserts that it is the responsibility of pastoral counselors and chaplains to focus on the challenges posed by the expressions of "existential anxiety"; psychotherapists will concentrate on the manifestations of "pathological anxiety" reflected in diverse syndromes of mental disorders.

For another classic contribution to our discussion from a therapist's perspective, see Viktor E. Frankl, *Man's Search for Meaning: An Introduction to Logotherapy* (New York: Washington Square Press, 1963); *The Unheard Cry for Meaning: Psychotherapy & Humanism* (New York: Simon & Schuster, 1978); and, *The Will to Meaning: Foundations and Applications of Logotherapy*, expanded ed. (New York: New American Library, 1988). Frankl's focus on the human quest for meaning, however, must be understood holistically, that is, as inseparable from the quests for connectedness (communion) and purpose (orientation); in other words, we must avoid reductionistic notions of spirituality and the spiritual self.

distinguishable. The following claims are therefore in order.

In principle, the condition of mental health, emotional maturity, and wellness makes it possible to experience spirituality more freely (for example, less fearfully, compulsively, or obsessively) and to express it verbally and otherwise more authentically than in the case of mental illness. Mental disorders and emotional immaturity always affect the subjective experience as well as the visible expressions of spirituality and spiritual health in some way and degree.[21] We must add, however, that mental health and emotional maturity are necessary but not sufficient conditions for spiritual health and maturity. Progress in treatment, or the restoration of mental health, does not automatically enhance people's spirituality and spiritual health; the spiritual self must be engaged intentionally.[22]

Toxic spirituality, in the form and content of sternly judgmental religiosity, for instance, can seriously undermine mental health. And the healing of the spiritual self—also known as *inner healing*—by the experience of grace and forgiveness, for example, always positively affects the psychological self. Therefore, even though spiritual caregivers are not mental health professionals strictly speaking, their work always engages the psychological self in ways that can contribute significantly to improved mental health and emotional maturity.

*Intra-self dynamics were clearly apparent in caring for Arthur. His mental and emotional distress, expressed with high levels of anxiety and depression, was directly related to unresolved grief and guilt, a weakened spirituality, and the hurtful realities of terminal physical illness. Arthur's psychological distress significantly affected his spiritual self; in turn, spiritual and moral anguish exacerbated Arthur's mental and emotional distress and, very likely, also made his struggle with cancer more difficult and painful. Arthur and I*

---

[21] For a popular language discussion of the relationship between emotional maturity and (Christian) spirituality, see Peter Scazzero, *Emotionally Healthy Spirituality* (Nashville: Thomas Nelson, 2006).

[22] This claim is analogous to the one applicable to the possible connection between "natural" psycho-social development and spiritual (including moral) development in the course of our life cycle. The fact that psychological development occurs in the natural flow of our life does not ensure that spiritual (and moral) growth will take place as well. Nevertheless, such psychological development has the effect of opening broader and more complicated worlds to us, thus increasing the range and complexity of our spiritual self. Hence, the range and complexity of our spirituality (e.g., in terms of deeper awareness of one's existential situation, sense of life orientation, connectedness with others, transcendence, etc.) and ways to nurture it (e.g., contemplation, meditation, prayer, compassionate service, etc.) tend to increase as well. Development can thus bring with it enhanced intentionality in, and responsibility for, both the personal ("inner") experience of spirituality and its visible expressions or manifestations.

*both hoped that spiritual care would help not only to restore spiritual health but also to alleviate psychological distress, while also bringing a measure of relief for his failing body.*

## What is unique about spiritual caregivers' contribution?: Two *key core competencies*

Recent work on core competencies in spiritual care has produced a number of valuable guidelines.[23] It is clear that we must keep in mind the whole competency profile whenever we focus on practical and theoretical issues of mental and spiritual health.[24] Two special core competencies—bilingual proficiency and a four-dimensional view—can be highlighted, as briefly discussed and illustrated below.

The unique contribution of spiritual caregivers within any health care team is that they need to view and work with the care receivers holistically while primarily engaging them psychologically as well as spiritually.[25] Therefore spiritual caregivers must develop the core competency of "bilingual proficiency" in terms of understanding the languages and resources of psychology and spirituality/theology and employing such understanding and resources in spiritual assessment and all other verbal and nonverbal (e.g., rituals) caregiving practices.[26]

---

[23] Canadian colleagues have recently done significant work on core competencies for spiritual care. See, for example, Canadian Association of Spiritual Care, "Competencies for Spiritual Care and Counselling Specialist"; and Manitoba Health, "Core Competencies for Spiritual Health Care Practitioners" (2011). In the Epilogue I include a comprehensive discussion of core competencies for wise interfaith spiritual care.

[24] For a good illustration of competent spiritual care in the face of mental illness, see Sherry Sawatzky-Dyck, "Caring for People with Mental Illness," in Leah Dawn Bueckert and Daniel S. Schipani, eds. *Spiritual Caregiving in the Hospital: Windows to Chaplaincy Ministry*, rev. ed. (Kitchener: Pandora Press, 2011), 209–20.

[25] This assertion does not imply that concern for and engagement with the care receiver's body is absent. That is not the case at all, even when the body as such is not the primary focus of spiritual caregiving practice. Competent spiritual caregivers are always sensitive to body language and nonverbal communication; further, they also know when and how to suggest, for example, specific bodily activity such as certain ways of breathing, body posture and relaxation, healing massage, etc. Gestalt Pastoral Care presents a holistic approach to care and healing in particular, which offers valuable resources to counseling as well. See Norberg, *Consenting to Grace*.

[26] For a systematic discussion of the questions of becoming bilingual with regard to the perspectives, languages, and understandings of psychology and theology, see Deborah van Deusen Hunsinger, *Theology and Pastoral Counseling: A New Interdisciplinary Approach* (Grand Rapids: Eerdmans, 1995). For a detailed case illustration of how to identify psychological as well as spiritual counseling agenda and objectives, see Daniel S. Schipani, "A Wisdom Model for Pastoral Counseling," in Kathleen J. Greider, Deborah van Deusen Hunsinger, and Felicity Brock Kelcourse, eds., *Healing Wisdom: Depth Psychology and the Pastoral Ministry* (Grand Rapids: Eerdmans, 2010), 94–108.

**Spiritual care as holistic care**
(within family, social, global, cosmic contexts)

Spiritual care that is intentionally and consistently offered and reflected upon as a spiritual health discipline also calls for a four-dimensional view of reality. Psychotherapeutic and psychiatric approaches normally, however, assume a two-dimensional view involving the self (or selves, in the case of couples, family, or group therapy) and the lived world. The recent and ongoing "recovery" of spirituality in health care and, especially, counseling and psychotherapy, includes emphasis on spiritual assessment,[27] engaging clients' spirituality (e.g., beliefs, sources of meaning, and hope, etc.) during therapy,[28] and integration of spirituality into the therapeutic process[29] including issues and practices (e.g., meditation, prayer, sacred readings).[30] This is a welcome development. However, much is still missing in terms of clinical research and theoretical reflection, to

---

[27] P. Scott Richards and Allen E. Bergin, *A Spiritual Strategy for Counseling and Psychotherapy*, 2nd ed. (Washington, DC: American Psychological Association, 2005), 219–49. This text, originally published in 1997, is the first on an expanding list of significant contributions related to counseling/psychotherapy and spirituality and published under the sponsorship of the American Psychological Association. All the texts identified in the following footnotes include chapters on assessment of clients' spirituality and religion.

[28] William R. Miller, ed., *Integrating Spirituality into Treatment: Resources for Practitioners* (Washington, DC: American Psychological Association, 1999); Kenneth I. Pargament, *Spiritually Integrated Psychotherapy: Understanding and Addressing the Sacred* (New York: Guilford, 2007).

[29] See works such as these: Jamie D. Alten and Mark M. Leach, eds., *Spirituality and the Therapeutic Process: A Comprehensive Resource from Intake to Termination* (Washington, DC: American Psychological Association, 2009); James L. Griffin and Melissa Elliott Griffith, *Encountering the Sacred in Psychotherapy: How to Talk with People about their Spiritual Lives* (New York: The Gilford Press, 2002); Gary W. Hartz, *Spirituality and Mental Health: Clinical Applications* (New York: Routledge, 2005); Philippe Huguelet and Harold G. Koenig, *Religion and Spirituality in Psychiatry* (Cambridge: Cambridge University Press, 2009).

[30] Thomas G. Plante, *Spiritual Practice in Psychotherapy: Thirteen Tools for Enhancing Psychological Health* (Washington, DC: American Psychological Association, 2009).

say nothing of the arena of caregiving practice as such. A large majority of clinicians and theorists simply collapse the spiritual into the psychological and do not recognize the distinct place and function of the spiritual self and its inseparable connection to the psychological self. In any event, the relationship between the psychological and the spiritual self can be further understood in light of James E. Loder's contribution. In his words: "being human entails environment, selfhood, the possibility of nonbeing, and the possibility of new being. All four dimensions are essential, and none of them can be ignored without decisive loss to our understanding of what is essentially human."[31]

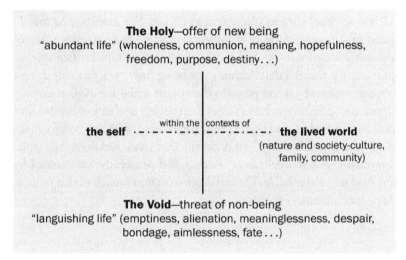

The four-dimensional framework of spiritual care

*Arthur was entering the final phase of his life journey. His three-year widowhood experience had been extremely challenging and much more so since the diagnosis and treatment of cancer. He was a resourceful person who was able to take care of himself, but he had chosen to carry the burden of grief and guilt alone as a kind of shameful, self-inflicted punishment. Good relationships with children and grandchildren, a few friends, and occasional participation*

---

[31] James E. Loder, *The Transforming Moment*, 2nd ed. (Colorado Springs: Helmers & Howard, 1989), 69. For Loder, the four dimensions of human existence are the self, the lived world, the Void, and the Holy. The "Void" is the third of the fundamental four dimensions of human existence: human existence is destined to annihilation and the ultimate absence of being. The many faces of the Void include existential loneliness, despair, and death. The "Holy" constitutes the fourth dimension of human existence which has, by the power of the Spirit of God, the capacity to transform the other three dimensions (80–91). Illustrations of how to apply this guideline in actual counseling practice and reflection can be found in Daniel S. Schipani, *The Way of Wisdom in Pastoral Counseling* (Elkhart: Institute of Mennonite Studies, 2003), 11–36.

*in worship services were necessary but insufficient resources at his disposal. At that particular juncture, spiritual health care became available for Arthur through the caregiving relationship with me, and he welcomed it.*

*Our caregiving relationship identified a number of issues to consider on a psychosocial level: a review of decisions that remained to be made regarding finances and personal belongings; anticipated personal and interpersonal adjustments connected with hospice care; and expectations and fears related to declining energy and the process of dying. On the spiritual level, we needed to deal with the fundamental questions of guilt, sin and sinfulness, images of God, fate and the faces of evil, and forgiveness and grace, to name a few.*

*I needed to assist Arthur by integrating the kinds of knowledge and skills that define spiritual care as characterized above. For example, he and I collaborated in devising a form of therapeutic imaging and role-play whereby he could experience confession and receive forgiveness from his late spouse. In this process, we realized that Arthur's not being fully present to his dying wife (he actually missed by a few minutes the instant when she died) was a sign of emotional and spiritual weakness rather than neglect and lack of compassion. In due time, when Arthur could appropriate forgiveness, including self-forgiveness, I performed a ritual "priestly" act declaring that grace had overcome guilt and condemnation. A few weeks later, Arthur died peacefully, surrounded by his family. And we celebrated his life and death with the conviction that faith, love, and hope had ultimately prevailed.*

# Epilogue
## Competencies for wise interfaith spiritual care

*Daniel S. Schipani*

The following paragraphs present a picture of excellence, or *professional wisdom*.[1] Wisdom in interfaith care involves not only what we know but also who we are and what we do. In other words, professional wisdom for quality interfaith care may be viewed as the integration of three interconnected domains: *knowing, being,* and *doing* as represented in the diagram below.[2] This is the case concerning both the clinical (i.e., attitudes, knowledge, and skills that define expertise) and ministerial (i.e., vocational identity, philosophy of care, and consistent practice) dimensions connoted in the adjective "professional."

We can draw a portrait by focusing on a number of core competencies within each of these domains. The resulting profile of wise spiritual care consists of three sets of core *competencies* which we can identify in the course of our spiritual care practice, in teaching and supervision, in specialized research, and in extensive consultations and collaboration.

**Three domains of core competencies**

---

[1] An earlier version of this model of professional excellence is found in Leah Dawn Bueckert & Daniel S. Schipani, "New Directions in Interfaith Spiritual Care," in *Religion, Diversity and Conflict*, ed. Edward Foley, International Practical Theology Volume 15 (Berlin: LIT Verlag, 2011), 152–60.

[2] This way of characterizing professional wisdom in spiritual care in terms of knowing, being, and doing, is partially indebted to John Patton's notion of "pastoral wisdom," as presented in his book,

Competencies are dispositions and capacities necessary to care well in interfaith situations. Core competencies correlate with professional standards normally articulated by organizations such as the Association for Clinical Pastoral Education, the Canadian Association for Spiritual Care, and the Association of Professional Chaplains. Governmental and faith-based organizations such as the National Association of Catholic Chaplains and the National Association of Jewish Chaplains, also identify normative professional standards of certification and practice for their members.

Standards embody key values and vocational commitments; they also prescribe certain legally binding professional and ethical requirements for effective caregiving. In sum, competencies are personal and professional qualities or assets with which caregivers meet the standards of practice in a wide variety of caregiving settings. Before proceeding with a characterization of core competencies, it will be useful to keep in mind some normative guidelines that support the view of necessary competencies for wise spiritual care.

## Normative guidelines

The following normative guidelines serve as a rationale for the way we identify, seek to embody, discuss, teach, and assess core competencies in spiritual care. Focusing on core competencies is not only a matter of *how* (i.e., functionality, how they "work" in actual caregiving practice) and *for what* (purpose, outcomes envisioned) but also a question of *why* (foundation, their reason for being). A threefold response to the *why* question follows.

First, core competencies are not only desirable *clinical-professional* features of excellence in spiritual care but also indicators of *personal, interpersonal, and institutional integrity*. Spiritual care is inherently partial (i.e., non-neutral) *in favor of* wellness; quality of life; meaningful suffering, healing, and dying; and compassion and justice, among other fundamental values. Spiritual care rightly viewed is also *against* meaningless and unnecessary suffering and dying, hopelessness, neglect, discrimination, and injustice. To be consistent with that realization calls for grounding core competencies explicitly in an *ethic*

---

*Pastoral Care: An Essential Guide* (Nashville: Abingdon Press, 2006), chapters 1, 2, 3. In presenting this model, I also intend to show that it is analogous to the model of the spiritual self offered in the last chapter of this book. A kind of correlation is actually suggested between core competencies that professionally define wise spiritual caregiving in terms of *knowing, being,* and *doing,* and the dimensions of *virtue, vision,* and *vocation,* respectively, as expressions of the spiritual self.

*of care.*[3] Therefore, becoming holistically competent is a moral imperative, first and foremost. In fact, it can be persuasively argued that the absence of such explicit ethical grounding and vocational commitment fosters a view of competence and competencies as merely a question of appropriate technique.

Second, *spiritual* care focuses primarily, although by no means exclusively, on *spirituality* and *spiritual experience*. In the last chapter, I propose that it is necessary to work with an inclusive understanding of the *human spirit* that is not collapsed into either our psychological views of "mind" or our theologically specific conceptualizations about "spirit." Ironically, in spite of so much discussion about replacing "pastoral" with "spiritual," a systematic reflection on the human spirit is hard to find in the spiritual care literature! I have proposed that one way to conceptualize *human spirit* inclusively (that is, with language not primarily reflective of a given religious tradition or theological orientation) is to view it functionally as interrelated dimensions—*Vision*, *Virtue*, and *Vocation*—within a web or system. The practice of spiritual care always includes the possibility of visualizing how the relationship of caregiver-care receiver might contribute to the latter's ongoing process of human emergence, that is, personal growth understood as life-long "humanization," or becoming "more human," viewed contextually in the care receiver's terms. It follows that desired outcomes of a counseling session or a spiritual caregiver's visit, for instance, will not only include objectives such as neutralizing anxiety and evoking hope but also supporting and resourcing the larger process of formation and transformation of the care receiver's *person as embodied psychological and spiritual self*. And that must be the case whether the care receiver contemplates emotional or physical recovery, or faces sickness and an uncertain diagnosis or treatment, or even death.

Third, as implied in the two previous paragraphs, core competencies should reflect the inherent normativeness of spiritual care and the need to focus on spirituality and the human spirit. Accordingly, we can then articulate guidelines that call for *good*, *true*, and *right* qualities that define wise or competent spiritual care. By using the Greek prefix "ortho," we might say that competencies must be identified in terms of the following: (a) *orthopathy* or *orthokardia* ("good heart": attitudes toward self and others, character strengths, etc., that make being genuinely present to care receivers and others possible); (b) *orthodoxy* (true beliefs and knowledge,

---

[3] See Leah Dawn Bueckert and Daniel S Schipani, "The Ethic of Care in Spritual Caregiving," in *Spiritual Caregiving in the Hospital: Windows to Chaplaincy Ministry*, ed. Leah Dawn Bueckert and Daniel S. Schipani, rev. ed. (Kitchener: Pandora Press, 2011), 273–86.

duly contextualized, that foster understanding); and *orthopraxis* (right action for effective strategy, performance, and assessment of spiritual care as the art of companioning). This is precisely the reason for adopting the categories of *knowing*, *being*, and *doing*, in our work and reflection on core competencies in spiritual care.[4]

Finally, even if the focus on competencies is more comprehensive than the primary spiritual care workers such as chaplains, counselors, and volunteers, the relationship of care receiver-caregiver always supplies the fundamental normative clues for any discussion of core competencies in spiritual care on any level—departmental, institutional, or other—within a health care system.

## A profile of core competencies for wise spiritual care

A number of practitioners and researchers in the wider field of care and counseling have also presented three sets of core competencies. This is the case, for example, with the well-known contribution of Derald Wing Sue and David Sue concerning multicultural competence in counseling practice. These authors discuss fourteen competencies under the three categories of *awareness* (e.g., being aware of and sensitive to one's own cultural heritage, and to valuing and respecting differences); *knowledge* (e.g., becoming knowledgeable and informed on a number of culturally diverse groups, especially groups with which therapists work); and *skills* (e.g., being able to generate a wide variety of verbal and nonverbal helping responses).[5] Other writers have integrated the contribution of Sue and Sue and others in their own threefold characterization in terms of (a) caregivers' awareness of their own values and biases, (b) understanding of the clients' worldviews, and (c) developing culturally appropriate intervention strategies and techniques.[6] Government organizations also usually present a tripartite view of core competencies as, for example, "the essential knowledge, skills, and attitudes necessary for the practice of public health."[7]

Those considerations are very useful and, in principle, transferable with regard to interfaith caregiving. At the same time, we can see that the larger

---

[4] The earliest version of this model appears in Daniel S. Schipani & Leah Dawn Bueckert, *Interfaith Spiritual Care: Understandings and Practices* (Kitchener: Pandora Press, 2009), 315–19.

[5] Derald Wing Sue and David Sue, *Counseling the Culturally Diverse: Theory and Practice* (Hoboken: John Wiley & Sons, 2008), 42–52.

[6] Gerald Corey, Marianne Schneider Corey, Patrick Callanan, *Issues and Ethics in the Helping Professions*, 8th ed. (Belmont: Brooks/Cole, 2011), 141–48.

[7] Public Health Agency of Canada, *Core Competencies for Public Health Service in Canada* (Ottawa: Ministry of Health, 2008), 1.

categories of *knowing, being,* and *doing* help us to present a more complete view of professional wisdom. That is especially the case regarding the "being" dimension, because in it we can include competencies definable in terms of virtues (viewed as values embodied in the moral character of the caregiver)[8] and faith development broadly viewed, which are not usually explicitly considered in current discussions and writings in the field. The following profile, which includes competencies highlighted by the contributors to this book, is comprehensive but certainly not assumed to be complete; it is meant as an ongoing collaborative work of reflection.[9]

## Competencies of *knowing (understanding)*

In order to grow in pastoral wisdom, spiritual caregivers participate in what we might call "circles of learning" that include four dimensions: (1) actual experience of being cared for and caring for others (learning by "feeling"); (2) observation and reflection on care provided by others (learning by actively "seeing" and "hearing"); (3) systematic analysis of those practices of care (learning by "thinking"); and (4) active experimentation with new ways of caring well for others (learning by "doing"). The more intentionally and consistently we participate in the four dimensions of the "circle," the more likely that our knowledge about interfaith care will increase. Supervision, seminars, and consultation groups can be fertile settings for developing knowledge and understanding related to spiritual care in interfaith situations. A sample of indicators of professional wisdom directly connected with this domain (knowing) includes:

- A philosophy of spiritual care, including a view of human wholeness, truth, the good life, and excellence in professional work

---

[8] A helpful conceptualization of "character strengths"—the psychological ingredients and processes which define the "virtues"—has been provided by Positive Psychology. See Christopher Peterson and Martin E. P. Seligman, *Character Strengths and Virtues: A Handbook and Classification* (New York and Oxford: American Psychological Association and Oxford University Press, 2004).

[9] One way to enhance reflection on competencies is by relating them to *capabilities* as articulated, for example, in the United Kingdom: "A Capability describes the extent to which an individual can apply, adapt and synthesise new knowledge from experience and continue to improve his or her performance, and within that context a Competence describes what individuals know or are able to do in terms of knowledge, skills and attitudes": Janet Foggie, Chris Levison, Iain Macritchie, and David Mitchell, "Spiritual and Religious Care Capabilities and Competencies for Healthcare Chaplains," *Scottish Journal of Healthcare Chaplaincy* 11, no. 2 (2008): 3. The article then identifies ten "essential capabilities" that inform the standards of professional practice as follows: working in partnership, respecting diversity, practicing ethically, challenging inequality, identifying the needs of people using chaplaincy services, providing safe and responsive patient-centred care, promoting best practice, promoting rehabilitation approaches, promoting self-care and empowerment, and pursuing personal development and learning.

(as seen especially in an ethic of care), grounded in one's faith tradition.
- Optimal theoretical integration of spirituality, behavioral, and social science, and philosophical and theological perspectives that include a four-dimensional view of reality and knowing.
- Understanding of the complexities, dynamics, and richness of interfaith situations, with appreciation for human and spiritual commonalities and due consideration to gender, culture, religious, family, and social and political contexts; *worldviewing* competence (with its hermeneutic, heuristic, and self-reflective dimensions).
- Philosophical and theological assessment that includes revisiting the validity of certain absolute, normative doctrinal claims; selective re-appropriation of theological and religious convictions; rediscovery of the simplicity and beauty of core spiritual clues for interfaith care, etc.
- Linguistic-conceptual and "multilingual" competency (knowing a variety of psychological, theological, and spiritual languages) born out of theological and human science perspectives and resources.
- Clinical ways of knowing, such as interpretive frameworks (psychodynamic, systemic, etc.), that enhance understanding, communication, and ministerial practice of spiritual care.

Such comprehensive ways of *knowing* must always be closely related to the *being* and *doing* dimensions of professional wisdom, as briefly considered below.

### Competencies of *being (presence)*

Professional wisdom is also a matter of "being" as well as "being with" that defines *presence*. Caregiving in interfaith situations involves special sensitivity and self-awareness regarding what one feels and experiences in the relationship. It also involves the sense that one represents not only a religious tradition and community but also, somehow, healing Grace. We deem such embodiment essential to remind care receivers that a caring Presence is available. Therefore, a sense of personal and professional (ministerial) identity is an essential component of being and presence. It is indispensable to engage the care receiver in a relationship characterized first of all by respectful attending and listening. Such relationship allows the spiritual caregiver to be a witness, not primarily to "tell" care receivers how to cope with or fix their situation, but rather to "admire," to behold with love and hope, the mystery that is the stranger. Among the traits related to the *being* dimension of professional wisdom, we find the following to be essential:

- Self-awareness, and other indicators of emotional and social intelligence, including acknowledgment of strengths and limitations; movement beyond preoccupation with one's "ministerial-therapeutic" self (while maintaining clarity regarding identity as spiritual caregiver); and recognition of ways in which that ministerial self influences the interfaith encounter; *quietude*.
- Moral character that integrates a plurality of attitudes and virtues, such as a capacity for wonder and respect in the face of the stranger; sensitivity and receptivity; courage to risk and to be surprised; freedom to be vulnerable and open to learning and growth; a disposition to recognize, accept, and honor those deemed to be different; hospitality grounded in compassion, humility, patience, and generosity; passion to care and creative energy to transform the inherent violence of separation, prejudice, and alienation into a way of being with (empathy) and for (sympathy) the other as neighbor and partner in care and healing; living out the "seven Sacred Teachings" (love, respect, courage, humility, truth, honesty, wisdom).
- Spirituality defined in part in terms of a mature or "conjunctive faith" which informs ministry style[10] and denotes a desirable level of faith development: an ability to embrace ambiguity and paradox; a sense of truth that is multiform and complex; post-critical receptivity ("second naiveté") and readiness to participate in the reality expressed in symbols, myths, and rituals of one's own tradition; genuine and disciplined openness to the truths of communities and traditions other than one's own (not to be equated with relativism); movement from the prevalence of certainty to the centrality of trust.
- A sense of personal and spiritual well-being, integrity, and growth. (While being aware of their own woundedness, wise spiritual caregivers normally experience holistic wellness of body, soul, and spirit and an existentially fruitful and fulfilling life journey).

---

[10] The concept of "conjunctive faith" is taken from the work of James W. Fowler on faith development. See James W. Fowler, *Stages of Faith: The Psychology of Human Development and the Quest for Meaning* (San Francisco: Harper & Row, 1981), 184–98; and *Faith Development and Pastoral Care* (Philadelphia: Fortress Press, 1987) 71–74, 92–98.

- A connection or sense of partnership with a transcendent Source of wisdom and grace; dedication to one's own awakening; appropriate devotion to one's mentors, or guru.

**Competencies of *doing (companioning)***

*Accompaniment* and *guidance* are words that name well what we actually do in spiritual care. On the one hand, spiritual caregivers are responsible for attending to and guiding the actual caregiving process as such. Guidance is a form of leading which includes, for example, setting appropriate boundaries of time, space, and contact, and remaining fully aware of what is going on in the caregiving process. Guidance may include gently probing questions, encouragement and support, instructing, confronting, and mediating. On the other hand, except in emergency or crisis situations, spiritual caregivers will not be directive and try to resolve the problems and struggles faced by care receivers. Rather, especially in interfaith situations, wise caregivers will help patients and others use the specific spiritual resources that have been part of their lives or that may now be available for them. In short, accompaniment and guidance will optimally be a practice of wisdom—knowing how to relate and act in order to care well in interfaith situations. There is actually an interesting etymological connection between *wisdom* and *guidance*. In English, the words *wisdom* and *wise* derive from the Indo-European root *weid-*, which means *to see* or *to know*. They are related to the Greek *eidos* (idea, form, seeing), to the Latin *videre* (to see), and to the modern German *wissen* (to know). The word *guide* comes from an ancient Romanic word, *widare*, which means to know. The words *wise, wisdom, wit,* and *guide* all share the same origin. Therefore, among other competencies and skills, effective caregivers will be able to:

- Relate to care seekers, their relatives, and colleagues in ways that engage their spirituality and facilitate spiritual assessment, including the skill to articulate desired outcomes of spiritual care.
- Internally monitor ongoing caregiving practice so as to remain care receiver-centered, avoiding cultural and spiritual invasion or intrusiveness, and open to receiving manifold gifts from care receivers even while caring well for them.
- Actively listen and discern the appropriateness and timeliness of specific caregiving gestures, use of language, and action. Fittingly provide opportune responses in a variety of caregiving modes (e.g., probing, supporting, encouraging, comforting, guiding, con-

fronting, mediating, reconciling, evoking, advocating; praying, blessing, anointing, and others).
- Reflect pastorally-theologically on ministerial practice on an ongoing basis and continually develop a practical theology of interfaith care, including assessment, consultation, and collaboration.
- Actively emulate or partner with a transcendent Source of wisdom and grace or the Spirit of God while anticipating and participating in caregiving ministry (e.g., by privately praying for oneself and for care seekers, engaging in contemplation and meditation, and other spiritual disciplines).
- Maintain patterned practices of self-care with adequate attention to physical, emotional, and relational needs, and to spiritual nourishment; consistently participate in a community that offers psycho-social and spiritual nurture, support, and accountability.

Finally, we must also keep in mind two additional key guidelines regarding core competencies. They have to do with timing and level of proficiency. First, concerning timing, some competencies pertain especially, although not exclusively, before, during, or after actual spiritual caregiving practice. This guideline is clearly illustrated by Kathleen Greider in this book where she discusses necessary spiritual care dispositions and skills in terms of "anticipation of encounter," "encounter," and "refreshment for encounter."[11] Second, in order to teach, practice, and assess core competencies, it is possible and, indeed, necessary, to identify increasing levels of proficiency and, therefore, guideposts to mark professional growth.

## Holistic professional formation

It has become more and more apparent that the education of interfaith spiritual caregivers in professional wisdom requires that theological education and clinical and ministerial formation be holistic and comprehensive. For example, as articulated in the standards of the Association of Theological Schools in the United States and Canada, such formation must include three equally important and interrelated aspects: academic, personal-spiritual, and professional. Further, such education must include specific pedagogies of interpretation and contextualization, formation, and performance.

---

[11] See chapter 6, "Do Justice, Love Kindness, Walk Humbly: A Christian Perspective on Spiritual Care," 95–106.

The *academic* formation of interfaith caregivers is indispensable because, among other things, it includes learning about one's own (religious or nonreligious) faith tradition or heritage, and as much as possible about other traditions. Philosophies, theoretical frameworks, and other resources stemming from the human sciences are also indispensable. Academic formation further includes learning about the social, cultural, and institutional contexts of caregiving work. Therefore, this dimension of education and ministerial formation must focus primarily, although by no means exclusively, on learning and developing competencies of *knowing* for wise caregiving as highlighted above.

*Personal-spiritual* formation focuses on the identity and integrity of interfaith spiritual caregivers, especially but not exclusively, as representatives of a given tradition. Personal-spiritual formation primarily involves attending to oneself as a human and spiritual being, nurturing one's moral character and particularly one's vocation. Hence, this dimension of education and ministerial formation is concerned primarily with fostering and nurturing the competencies of *being* for wise ministry practice. Indeed, those competencies will directly inform the content of specific curricular learning goals toward personal-spiritual formation.

The *vocational-professional* formation of wise spiritual caregivers centers on the development of clinical and other habits, skills, methods, and approaches necessary for caring effectively and faithfully. Therefore, the third aspect of theological education and ministerial formation of interfaith spiritual caregivers must focus primarily on the development and practice of competencies of performance—i.e., the *doing* dimension of the profile—as the main curricular goal.

## Complementary pedagogies

These three resulting sets of goals of theological education and ministerial formation must be duly integrated and approached through appropriate, mutually complementary pedagogies. Recent reflection on pedagogies for educating clergy can be helpfully applied to the formation of wise spiritual caregivers as described below.[12]

*Pedagogies of interpretation* focus the attention of caregivers as interpreters on their interaction with their tradition and with other sources of knowledge, particularly their relationship with care seekers. These pedagogies cultivate the abilities to adequately "read" and analyze

---

[12] See Charles Foster, Lisa E. Dahill, Lawrence A. Golemon, and Barbara Wang Tolentino, *Educating Clergy: Teaching Practices and Pastoral Imagination* (San Francisco: Jossey-Bass, 2006), 67–186.

human situations, and to think and reflect critically and creatively. They are aimed at expanding and deepening *understanding* through interpretive practice. Pedagogies of contextualization are closely related, as they seek to develop the spiritual caregivers' consciousness of context, the ability to participate constructively in the encounter of diverse contexts, and the ability to engage in the transformation of contexts. From the students' perspective, academic formation that is primarily fostered by pedagogies of interpretation and contextualization—including supervision in clinical education and advanced training in spiritual care—constitutes the curricular realm of "theory"[13] and theoretical learning and knowing.

*Pedagogies of formation* aim at fostering personal integrity and professional identity. Specific strategies that contribute to the formation of ministering caregivers, especially those representing certain religious traditions, may include: awakening students to the presence of God; practicing holiness; i.e., nurturing dispositions and habits that embody religious commitments integral to the identity of ministering persons; and practicing spiritual leadership whose very *presence* communicates Grace and Wisdom. Therefore, students' personal-spiritual formation will be supported primarily with pedagogies of formation within the curricular realm of "experience" and experiential learning and knowing in particular.

Finally, *pedagogies of performance* focus on the interaction of academic and religious expectations for effective leadership in ministerial practice. They seek to prepare caregivers to be proficient in meeting a wide variety of expectations for excellence in interfaith care in multifaith settings. In sum, they are learning strategies aimed at equipping caregivers for the ministerial art of *companioning*. Vocational-professional formation sustained with pedagogies of performance will therefore pertain in the curricular realm of "practice" and practical learning and knowing.

---

[13] I am intentionally using three categories—theory, experience, and practice—as fittingly holding the kinds of theoretical, experiential, and practical wisdom normally described as complementary ways of learning and knowing in educational theory.

# Spiritual Caregiving in the Hospital
## Windows to Chaplaincy Ministry
*Revised edition*

**Leah Dawn Bueckert and Daniel S. Schipani, editors**

www.pandorapress.com

Even as hospitals increasingly recognize spiritual care as an essential component of holistic care, chaplains are still in the process of defining their role. This book acknowledges and celebrates the unique contribution of hospital chaplains, fosters understanding and support for their work, and seeks to elicit interest in their ministry of spiritual caregiving. The writers bring together a wealth of conceptual and practical information for those engaged in the challenging ministry of caring for persons in crisis. Required reading for any chaplain or spiritual care provider, this book is also an excellent resource for those training professional caregivers.
  *Teresa E. Snorton,*
  *Executive Director, Association*
  *for Clinical Pastoral Education*

# Interfaith Spiritual Care
Understandings and practices

Daniel S. Schipani, and Leah Dawn Bueckert, editors

www.pandorapress.com

The twofold overarching concern of the project leading to this publication is to foster reflection and enhance the practice of interfaith spiritual care in health care institutions and beyond. Endorsed by the Society for Intercultural Pastoral Care and Counseling, the book meets the following goals:

- to explore the dynamics of interfaith spiritual care as a work of practical and pastoral theology;
- to identify reliable guidelines for competent practice and duly contextualized interfaith spiritual care;
- to invite further conversation and collaboration among practitioners and scholars.

This book is intended for chaplains, pastors, Clinical Pastoral Education students, and other caregivers such as counselors and psychotherapists, both in training and already in practice.

Made in the USA
Middletown, DE
10 January 2024

47578200R00116